Nathaniel Hawthorne

Passages from the English note-books of Nathaniel Hawthorne

Nathaniel Hawthorne

Passages from the English note-books of Nathaniel Hawthorne

ISBN/EAN: 9783742817334

Manufactured in Europe, USA, Canada, Australia, Japa

Cover: Foto ©Thomas Meinert / pixelio.de

Manufactured and distributed by brebook publishing software (www.brebook.com)

Nathaniel Hawthorne

Passages from the English note-books of Nathaniel Hawthorne

COLLECTION
OF
BRITISH AUTHORS

TAUCHNITZ EDITION.

VOL. 1139.

PASSAGES FROM THE ENGLISH
NOTE-BOOKS OF NATHANIEL HAWTHORNE.

IN TWO VOLUMES.

VOL. I.

PASSAGES FROM

THE ENGLISH NOTE-BOOKS OF
NATHANIEL HAWTHORNE

COPYRIGHT EDITION.

IN TWO VOLUMES.
VOL. I.

LEIPZIG
BERNHARD TAUCHNITZ
1871.

The Right of Translation is reserved.

TO

FRANCIS BENNOCH, ESQ.

THE DEAR AND VALUED FRIEND

WHO, BY HIS GENEROUS AND GENIAL HOSPITALITY, AND

UNFAILING SYMPATHY, CONTRIBUTED SO MUCH

TO RENDER MR. HAWTHORNE'S RESIDENCE IN ENGLAND

AGREEABLE AND HOMELIKE

THESE ENGLISH NOTES ARE DEDICATED WITH SINCERE RESPECT

AND REGARD BY

THE EDITOR.

PREFACE.

It seems justly due to Mr. Hawthorne that the occasion of any portion of his private journals being brought before the public should be made known, since they were originally designed for his own reference only.

There had been a constant and an urgent demand for a life or memoir of Mr. Hawthorne; yet, from the extreme delicacy and difficulty of the subject, the Editor felt obliged to refuse compliance with this demand. Moreover, Mr. Hawthorne had frequently and emphatically expressed the hope that no one would attempt to write his Biography; and the Editor perceived that it would be impossible for any person, outside his own domestic circle, to succeed in doing it, on account of his extreme reserve. But it was ungracious to do nothing, and therefore the Editor, believing that Mr. Hawthorne himself was alone capable of satisfactorily answering the affectionate call for some sketch of his life, concluded to publish as much as possible of his private records, and even extracts from his private letters, in order to gratify the desire of his friends, and of literary artists, to become more intimately acquainted with him. The Editor has been severely blamed and wondered at, in some instances, for allowing many things now published to see the light; but it has been a matter both of conscience and courtesy to withhold nothing that could be given up. Many of the journals were doubtless destroyed; for the earliest date found in his American papers was that of 1835.

The Editor has transcribed the manuscripts just as they were left, without making any new arrangement or altering any sequence—merely omitting some passages, and being especially careful to preserve whatever could throw any light upon his character. To persons on a quest for characteristics, however, each of his books reveals a great many, and it is believed that with the aid of the Notes (both American and English) the Tales and Romances will make out a very complete and true picture of his individuality; and the Notes are often an open sesame to the artistic works.

Several thickly written pages of observations—fine and accurate etchings—have been omitted, sometimes because too personal with regard to himself or others, and sometimes because they were afterwards absorbed into one or another of the Romances or papers in "Our Old Home." It seemed a pity not to give these original cartoons fresh from his mind, because they are so carefully finished at the first stroke. Yet, as Mr. Hawthorne chose his own way of presenting them to the public, it was thought better not to exhibit what he himself withheld. Besides, to any other than a fellow-artist, they might seem mere repetitions.

It is very earnestly hoped that these volumes of Notes—American, English, and by-and-by Italian—will dispel an often expressed opinion that Mr. Hawthorne was gloomy and morbid. He had the inevitable pensiveness and gravity of a person who possessed what a friend of his called "the awful power of insight;" but his mood was always cheerful and equal, and his mind peculiarly healthful, and the airy splendour of his wit and humour was the light of his home. He saw too far to be despondent, though his vivid sympathies and shaping imagination often made him sad in behalf of others. He also perceived morbidness, wherever it existed, instantly, as if by the illumination of his own steady cheer; and he had the plastic power of putting himself into each person's situation, and of looking from every point of view, which made his charity most comprehensive. From this cause he necessarily attracted confidences, and became confessor to very many sinning and suffering souls, to whom he gave tender sympathy and help, while resigning judgment to the Omniscient and Allwise.

Throughout his journals it will be seen that Mr. Hawthorne is *entertaining*, and not *asserting*, opinions and ideas. He questions, doubts, and reflects with his pen, and, as it were, instructs himself. So that these Note-books should be read, not as definite conclusions of his mind, but often merely as passing impressions. Whatever *conclusions* he arrived at are condensed in the works given to the world by his own hand, in which will never be found a careless word. He was so extremely scrupulous about the value and effect of every expression that the Editor has felt great compunction in allowing a single sentence to be printed unrevised by himself; but, with the consideration of the above remarks always kept in mind, these volumes are intrusted to the generous interpretation of the reader.

When a friend unexpectedly calls upon an artist in his morning hours, and finds him not in full dress, apologies are unnecessary, and might be thought unbecoming on either side.

The Editor is very glad to be in England while the English edition of this work is going through the press.

THE KNOLL, BLACKHEATH,
May, 1870.

PASSAGES FROM HAWTHORNE'S ENGLISH NOTE-BOOKS.

LIVERPOOL, *August 4th*, 1853.—A month lacking two days since we left America,—a fortnight and some odd days since we arrived in England. I began my services, such as they are, on Monday last, August 1st, and here I sit in my private room at the Consulate, while the Vice-Consul and clerk are carrying on affairs in the outer office.

. . . . .

The pleasantest incident of the morning is when Mr. Pearce (the Vice-Consul) makes his appearance with the account-books, containing the receipts and expenditures of the preceding day, and deposits on my desk a little rouleau of the Queen's coin, wrapped up in a piece of paper. This morning there were eight sovereigns, four half-crowns, and a shilling,—a pretty fair day's work, though not more than the average ought to be. This forenoon, thus far, I have had two calls, not of business,—one from an American captain and his son, another from Mr. H. B., whom I met in America, and who has shown us great attention here. He has arranged for us to go to the theatre with some of his family this evening.

. . .

Since I have been in Liverpool we have hardly had a day, until yesterday, without more or less of rain, and so cold and shivery that life was miserable. I am not warm enough even now, but am gradually getting acclimated in that respect.

Just now I have been fooled out of half-a-crown by a young woman who represents herself as an American and destitute, having come over to see an uncle whom she found dead, and she has no means of getting back again. Her accent is not that of an American, and her appearance is not particularly prepossessing, though not decidedly otherwise. She is decently dressed and modest in deportment, but I do not quite trust her face. She has been separated from her husband, as I understand her, by course of law, has had two children, both now dead. What she wants is to get back to America, and perhaps arrangements may be made with some shipmaster to take her as stewardess or in some subordinate capacity. My judgment, on the whole, is that she is an Englishwoman, married to and separated from an American husband,—of no very decided virtue. I might as well have kept my half-crown, and yet I might have bestowed it worse. She is very decent in manner, cheerful, at least not despondent.

At two o'clock I went over to the Royal Rock Hotel, about fifteen or twenty minutes' steaming from this side of the river. We are going there on Saturday to reside for a while. Returning, I found that Mr. B., from the American Chamber of Commerce, had called to arrange the time and place of a visit to the Consul from a delegation of that body. Settled for to-morrow at quarter past one at Mr. Blodgett's.

August 5th.—An invitation this morning from the Mayor to dine at the Town Hall on Friday next. Heaven knows I had rather dine at the humblest inn in the city, inasmuch as a speech will doubtless be expected from me. However, things must be as they may.

At quarter past one I was duly on hand at Mr. Blodgett's to receive the deputation from the Chamber of Commerce. They arrived pretty seasonably, in two or three carriages, and were ushered into the drawing-room,—seven or eight gentlemen, some of whom I had met before. Hereupon ensued a speech from Mr. B., the Chairman of the delegation, short and sweet, alluding to my literary reputation and other laudatory matters, and occupying only a minute or two. The speaker was rather embarrassed, which encouraged me a little, and yet I felt more diffidence on this occasion than in my effort at Mr. Crittenden's lunch, where, indeed, I was perfectly self-possessed. But here, there being less formality, and more of a conversational character in what was said, my usual diffidence could not so well be kept in abeyance. However, I did not break down to an intolerable extent, and, winding up my eloquence as briefly as possible, we had a social talk. Their whole stay could not have been much more than a quarter of an hour.

. . . . .

A call, this morning, at the Consulate, from Dr. Bowring, who is British minister, or something of the kind, in China, and now absent on a twelvemonths' leave. The Doctor is a brisk person, with the address of a man of the world,—free, quick to smile, and of agreeable manners. He has a good face, rather Ame-

rican than English in aspect, and does not look much
above fifty, though he says he is between sixty and
seventy. I should take him rather for an active lawyer
or a man of business than for a scholar and a literary
man. He talked in a lively way for ten or fifteen
minutes, and then took his leave, offering me any
service in his power in London, as, for instance, to introduce me to the Athenæum Club.

August 8th.—Day before yesterday I escorted my
family to Rock Ferry, two miles either up or down
the Mersey (and I really don't know which) by steamer,
which runs every half-hour. There are steamers going
continually to Birkenhead and other landings, and almost always a great many passengers on the transit.
At this time the boat was crowded so as to afford
scanty standing-room; it being Saturday, and therefore
a kind of gala-day. I think I have never seen a
populace before coming to England; but this crowd afforded a specimen of one, both male and female. The
women were the most remarkable; though they seemed
not disreputable, there was in them a coarseness, a
freedom, and—I don't know what, that was purely
English. In fact, men and women here do things that
would at least make them ridiculous in America. They
are not afraid to enjoy themselves in their own way,
and have no pseudo-gentility to support. Some girls
danced upon the crowded deck, to the miserable music
of a little fragment of a band which goes up and down
the river on each trip of the boat. Just before the
termination of the voyage a man goes round with a
bugle turned upwards to receive the eleemosynary pence
and halfpence of the passengers. I gave one of them,

the other day, a silver fourpence, which fell into the vitals of the instrument, and compelled the man to take it to pieces.

At Rock Ferry there was a great throng, forming a scene not unlike one of our muster-days or a Fourth of July, and there were bands of music and banners, and small processions after them, and a school of charity children, I believe enjoying a festival. And there was a club of respectable persons, playing at bowls on the bowling-green of the hotel, and there were children, infants, riding on donkeys at a penny a ride, while their mothers walked alongside to prevent a fall. Yesterday, while we were at dinner, Mr. B. came in his carriage to take us to his residence, Poulton Hall. He had invited us to dine; but I misunderstood him, and thought he only intended to give us a drive. Poulton Hall is about three miles from Rock Ferry, the road passing through some pleasant rural scenery, and one or two villages, with houses standing close together, and old stone or brick cottages, with thatched roofs, and now and then a better mansion, apart among trees. We passed an old church with a tower and spire, and, half-way up, a patch of ivy, dark-green, and some yellow wall-flowers, in full bloom, growing out of the crevices of the stone. Mr. B. told us that the tower was formerly quite clothed with ivy from bottom to top, but that it had fallen away for lack of the nourishment that it used to find in the lime between the stones. This old church answered to my transatlantic fancies of England better than anything I have yet seen. Not far from it was the Rectory, behind a deep grove of ancient trees; and there lives the Rector, enjoying a thousand pounds a year and his nothing-to-do, while a curate performs the real duty on a stipend of eighty pounds.

We passed through a considerable extent of private road, and finally drove over a lawn, studded with trees and closely shaven, till we reached the door of Poulton Hall. Part of the mansion is three or four hundred years old; another portion is about a hundred and fifty, and still another has been built during the present generation. The house is two stories high, with a sort of beetle-browed roof in front. It is not very striking, and does not look older than many wooden houses which I have seen in America. There is a curious stately staircase, with a twisted balustrade much like that of the old Province House in Boston. The drawing-room is a handsome modern apartment, being beautifully painted and gilded and paper-hung, with a white marble fireplace and rich furniture, so that the impression is that of newness, not of age. It is the same with the dining-room, and all the rest of the interior so far as I saw it.

Mr. B. did not inherit this old hall, nor, indeed, is he the owner, but only the tenant of it. He is a merchant of Liverpool, a bachelor, with two sisters residing with him. In the entrance-hall there was a stuffed fox with glass eyes, which I never should have doubted to be an actual live fox except for his keeping so quiet; also some grouse and other game. Mr. B. seems to be a sportsman, and is setting out this week on an excursion to Scotland, moor-fowl shooting.

While the family and two or three guests went to dinner, we walked out to see the place. The gardener, an Irishman, showed us through the garden, which is large and well cared for. They certainly get every-

hing from nature which she can possibly be persuaded
to give them, here in England. There were peaches
and pears growing against the high brick southern
walls,—the trunk and branches of the trees being
spread out perfectly flat against the wall, very much
like the skin of a dead animal nailed up to dry, and
not a single branch protruding. Figs were growing in
the same way. The brick wall, very probably, was
heated within, by means of pipes, in order to re-enforce
the insufficient heat of the sun. It seems as if there
must be something unreal and unsatisfactory in fruit
that owes its existence to such artificial methods.
Squashes were growing under glass, poor things! There
were immensely large gooseberries in the garden; and
in this particular berry, the English, I believe, have
decidedly the advantage over ourselves. The raspberries, too, were large and good. I espied one gigantic
hogweed in the garden; and, really, my heart warmed
to it, being strongly reminded of the principal product
of my own garden at Concord. After viewing the
garden sufficiently, the gardener led us to other parts
of the estate, and we had glimpses of a delightful valley, its sides shady with beautiful trees, and a rich,
grassy meadow at the bottom. By means of a steam-engine and subterranean pipes and hydrants, the liquid
manure from the barn-yard is distributed wherever it
is wanted over the estate, being spouted in rich showers
from the hydrants. Under this influence, the meadow
at the bottom of the valley had already been made to
produce three crops of grass during the present season,
and would produce another.

The lawn around Poulton Hall, like thousands of

other lawns in England, is very beautiful, but requires
great care to keep it so, being shorn every three or
four days. No other country will ever have this charm,
nor the charm of lovely verdure, which almost makes
up for the absence of sunshine. Without the constant
rain and shadow which strikes us as so dismal, these
lawns would be as brown as an autumn leaf. I have
not, thus far, found any such magnificent trees as I
expected. Mr. B. told me that three oaks, standing in
a row on his lawn, were the largest in the county.
They were very good trees, to be sure, and perhaps
four feet in diameter near the ground, but with no
very noble spread of foliage. In Concord there are,
if not oaks, yet certainly elms, a great deal more
stately and beautiful. But, on the whole, this lawn,
and the old Hall in the midst of it, went a good way
towards realising some of my fancies of English life.

By-and-by a footman, looking very quaint and
queer in his livery coat, drab breeches, and white
stockings, came to invite me to the table, where I
found Mr. B. and his sisters and guests, sitting at the
fruit and wine. There were port, sherry, madeira, and
one bottle of claret, all very good; but they take here
much heavier wines than we drink now in America.
After a tolerably long session we went to the tea-room,
where I drank some coffee, and at about the edge of
dusk the carriage drew up to the door to take us home.
Mr. B. and his sisters have shown us genuine kindness,
and they gave us a hearty invitation to come and
ramble over the house whenever we pleased, during
their absence in Scotland. They say that there are
many legends and ghost-stories connected with the
house; and there is an attic chamber, with a skylight,

which is called the Martyr's chamber, from the fact of
its having, in old times, been tenanted by a lady, who
was imprisoned there, and persecuted to death for her
religion. There is an old black-letter library, but the
room containing it is shut, barred, and padlocked,—
the owner of the house refusing to let it be opened,
lest some of the books should be stolen. Meanwhile
the rats are devouring them, and the damps destroying
them.

August 9th.—A pretty comfortable day, as to warmth,
and I believe there is sunshine overhead; but a sea-
cloud, composed of fog and coal-smoke, envelops Liverpool. At Rock Ferry, when I left it at half-past nine,
there was promise of a cheerful day. A good many
gentlemen (or, rather, respectable business people) came
in the boat, and it is not unpleasant, on these fine
mornings, to take the breezy atmosphere of the river.
The huge steamer *Great Britain*, bound for Australia,
lies right off the Rock Ferry landing; and at a little
distance are two old hulks of ships of war, dismantled,
roofed over, and anchored in the river, formerly for
quarantine purposes, but now used chiefly or solely as
homes for old seamen, whose light labour it is to take
care of these condemned ships. There are a great
many steamers plying up and down the river to various
landings in the vicinity; and a good many steam-tugs;
also many boats, most of which have dark-red or tan-
coloured sails, being oiled to resist the wet; also, here
and there, a yacht or pleasure-boat, and a few ships
lying stately at their anchors, probably on the point
of sailing. The river, however, is by no means crowded;
because the immense multitude of ships are ensconced

in the docks, where their masts make an intricate forest for miles up and down the Liverpool shore. The small black steamers, whizzing industriously along, many of them crowded with passengers, make up the chief life of the scene. The Mersey has the colour of a mud-puddle, and no atmospheric effect, as far as I have seen, ever gives it a more agreeable tinge.

Visitors to-day, thus far, have been H. A. B., with whom I have arranged to dine with us at Rock Ferry, and then he is to take us on board the *Great Britain*, of which his father is owner (in great part). Secondly, Monsieur H., the French Consul, who can speak hardly any English, and who was more powerfully scented with cigar-smoke than any man I ever encountered; a polite, grey-haired, red-nosed gentleman, very courteous and formal. Heaven keep him from me!

At one o'clock, or thereabouts, I walked into the city, down through Lord Street, Church Street, and back to the Consulate through various untraceable crookednesses. Coming to Chapel Street, I crossed the graveyard of the old church of St. Nicholas. This is, I suppose, the oldest sacred site in Liverpool, a church having stood here ever since the Conquest, though, probably, there is little or nothing of the old edifice in the present one, either the whole of the edifice or else the steeple, being thereto shaken by a chime of bells —or perhaps both, at different times—has tumbled down; but the present church is what we Americans should call venerable. When the first church was built, and long afterwards, it must have stood on the grassy verge of the Mersey; but now there are pavements and warehouses, and the thronged Prince's and George's Docks, between it and the river; and all round it is the very busiest bustle of commerce, rumbling wheels, hurrying men, porter-shops, everything that pertains to the grossest and most practical life. And, notwithstanding, there is the broad churchyard extending on three sides of it, just as it used to be a thousand years ago. It is absolutely paved from border to border with flat tombstones, on a level with the soil and with each other, so that it is one floor of stone over the whole space, with grass here and there sprouting between the crevices. All these stones, no doubt, formerly had inscriptions; but as many people continually pass, in various directions, across the churchyard, and as the tombstones are not of a very hard material, the records on many of them are effaced. I saw none very old. A quarter of a century is sufficient to obliterate the letters, and make all smooth, where the direct pathway from gate to gate lies over the stones. The climate and casual footsteps rub out any inscription in less than a hundred years. Some of the monuments are cracked. On many is merely put "The burial place" of so and so; on others there is a long list of half-readable names; on some few a laudatory epitaph, out of which, however, it were far too tedious to pick the meaning. But it really is interesting and suggestive to think of this old church, first built when Liverpool was a small village, and remaining, with its successive dead of ten centuries round it, now that the greatest commercial city in the world has its busiest centre there. I suppose people will continue to be buried in the cemetery. The greatest upholders of burials in cities are those whose progenitors have been deposited around or within the city churches. If this spacious churchyard stood in a similar position in one of our American cities, I rather suspect that long ere now it would have run the risk of being laid out in building lots, and covered with warehouses; even if the church itself escaped—but it would not escape longer than till its disrepair afforded excuse for tearing it down. And why should it, when its purposes might be better served in another spot?

* * * * *

We went on board the *Great Britain* before dinner, between five and six o'clock—a great structure, as to convenient arrangement and adaptation, but giving me a strong impression of the tedium and misery of the long voyage to Australia. By way of amusement, she takes over fifty pounds' worth of playing-cards, at two shillings per pack, for the use of passengers; also, a small, well-selected library. After a considerable time spent on board, we returned to the hotel and dined, and Mr. B. took his leave at nine o'clock.

August 10*th*.—I left Rock Ferry for the city at half-past nine. In the boat which arrived thence, there were several men and women with baskets on their heads, for this is a favourite way of carrying burdens; and they trudge onward beneath them, without any apparent fear of an overturn, and seldom putting up a hand to steady them. One woman, this morning, had a heavy load of crockery; another, an immense basket of turnips, freshly gathered, that seemed to me as much as a man could well carry on his back. These must be a stiff-necked people. The women step sturdily and freely, and with not ungraceful strength. The trip over to town was pleasant, it being a fair morning, only with a low-hanging fog. Had it been in

America, I should have anticipated a day of burning heat.

Visitors this morning. Mr. Ogden of Chicago, or somewhere in the Western States, who arrived in England a fortnight ago, and who called on me at that time. He has since been in Scotland, and is now going to London and the Continent; secondly, the Captain of the Collins's steamer *Pacific*, which sails to-day; thirdly, an American shipmaster, who complained that he had never, in his heretofore voyages, been able to get sight of the American Consul.

Mr. Pearce's customary matutinal visit was unusually agreeable to-day, inasmuch as he laid on my desk nineteen golden sovereigns and thirteen shillings. It being the day of the steamer's departure, an unusual number of invoice certificates had been required,—my signature to each of which brings me two dollars.

The autograph of a living author has seldom been so much in request at so respectable a price. Colonel Crittenden told me that he had received as much as fifty pounds on a single day. Heaven prosper the trade between America and Liverpool!

August 15*th*.—Many scenes which I should have liked to record have occurred; but the pressure of business has prevented me from recording them from day to day.

On Thursday I went, on invitation from Mr. B., to the prodigious steamer *Great Britain*, down the harbour, and some miles into the sea, to escort her off a little way on her voyage to Australia. There is an immense enthusiasm among the English people about this ship, on account of its being the largest in the world. The shores were lined with people to see her sail, and there were innumerable small steamers, crowded with men, all the way out into the ocean. Nothing seems to touch the English nearer than this question of nautical superiority; and if we wish to hit them to the quick, we must hit them there.

On Friday, at 7 P.M., I went to dine with the Mayor. It was a dinner given to the Judges and the Grand Jury. The Judges of England, during the time of holding an Assize, are the persons first in rank in the kingdom. They take precedence of everybody else,—of the highest military officers, of the Lord-Lieutenants, of the Archbishops,—of the Prince of Wales,—of all except the Sovereign, whose authority and dignity they represent. In case of a royal dinner, the Judge would lead the Queen to the table.

The dinner was at the Town Hall, and the rooms and the whole affair were all in the most splendid style. Nothing struck me more than the footmen in the city livery. They really looked more magnificent in their gold lace and breeches and white silk stockings than any officers of state. The rooms were beautiful; gorgeously painted and gilded, gorgeously lighted, gorgeously hung with paintings,—the plate was gorgeous, and the dinner gorgeous in the English fashion.

After the removal of the cloth the Mayor gave various toasts, prefacing each with some remarks,— first, of course, the Sovereign, after which "GOD save the Queen" was sung, the company standing up and joining in the chorus, their ample faces glowing with wine, enthusiasm, and loyalty. Afterwards the Bar, and various other dignities and institutions, were toasted; and by-and-by came the toast to the United States, and to me, as their Representative. Hereupon either "Hail, Columbia" or "Yankee Doodle," or some other of our national tunes (but Heaven knows which), was played, and at the conclusion, being at bay, and with no alternative, I got upon my legs, and made a response. They received me and listened to my nonsense with a good deal of rapping, and my speech seemed to give great satisfaction; my chief difficulty being in not knowing how to pitch my voice to the size of the room. As for the matter, it is not of the slightest consequence. Anybody may make an after-dinner speech who will be content to talk onward without saying anything. My speech was not more than two or three inches long; and, considering that I did not know a soul there, except the Mayor himself, and that I am wholly unpractised in all sorts of oratory, and that I had nothing to say, it was quite successful. I hardly thought it was in me, but, being once started, I felt no embarrassment, and went through it as coolly as if I were going to be hanged.

Yesterday, after dinner, I took a walk with my family. We went through by-ways and private roads, and saw more of rural England, with its hedgerows, its grassy fields, and its whitewashed old stone cottages, than we have before seen since our arrival.

August 20*th*.—This being Saturday, there early commenced a throng of visitants to Rock Ferry. The boat in which I came over brought from the city a multitude of factory-people. They had bands of music, and banners inscribed with the names of the mills they belong to, and other devices; pale-looking people, but not looking exactly as if they were underfed. They are brought on reduced terms by the railways and steamers, and come from great distances in the interior. These, I believe, were from Preston. I have not yet had an opportunity of observing how they amuse themselves during these excursions.

At the dock, the other day, the steamer arrived from Rock Ferry with a countless multitude of little girls, in coarse blue gowns, who, as they landed, formed in procession, and walked up the dock. These girls had been taken from the workhouses and educated at a charity school, and would by-and-by be apprenticed as servants. I should not have conceived it possible that so many children could have been collected together, without a single trace of beauty or scarcely of intelligence in so much as one individual; such mean, coarse, vulgar features and figures betraying unmistakably a low origin, and ignorant and brutal parents. They did not appear wicked, but only stupid, animal, and soulless. It must require many generations of better life to wake the soul in them. All America could not show the like.

August 22nd.—A Captain Auld, an American, having died here yesterday, I went with my clerk and an American shipmaster to take the inventory of his effects. His boarding-house was in a mean street, an old, dingy house, with narrow entrance—the class of boarding-house frequented by mates of vessels, and inferior to those generally patronised by masters. A fat elderly landlady, of respectable and honest aspect, and her daughter, a pleasing young woman enough, received us, and ushered us into the deceased's bedchamber. It was a dusky back room, plastered and painted yellow; its one window looking into the very narrowest of back yards or courts, and out on a confused multitude of back buildings, appertaining to other houses, most of them old, with rude chimneys of washrooms and kitchens, the bricks of which seemed half loose.

The chattels of the dead man were contained in two trunks, a chest, a sail-cloth bag, and a barrel, and consisted of clothing, suggesting a thickset, middle-sized man; papers relative to ships and business, a spy-glass, a loaded iron pistol, some books of navigation, some charts, several great pieces of tobacco, and a few cigars; some little plaster images, that he had probably bought for his children, a cotton umbrella, and other trumpery of no great value. In one of the trunks we found about twenty pounds' worth of English and American gold and silver, and some notes of hand, due in America. Of all these things the clerk made an inventory; after which we took possession of the money and affixed the consular seal to the trunks, bag, and chest.

While this was going on, we heard a great noise of men quarrelling in an adjoining court; and, altogether, it seemed a squalid and ugly place to live in, and a most undesirable one to die in. At the conclusion of our labours, the young woman asked us if we would not go into another chamber, and look at the corpse, and appeared to think that we should be rather glad than otherwise of the privilege. But, never having seen the man during his lifetime, I declined to commence his acquaintance now.

His bills for board and nursing amount to about the sum which we found in his trunk; his funeral expenses will be ten pounds more; the surgeon has sent in a bill of eight pounds, odd shillings; and the account of another medical man is still to be rendered. As his executor, I shall pay his landlady and nurse; and for the rest of the expenses, a subscription must be made (according to the custom in such cases) among the shipmasters, headed by myself. The funeral pomp will consist of a hearse, one coach, four men, with crape hat-bands, and a few other items, together with a grave at five pounds, over which his friends will be entitled to place a stone, if they choose to do so within twelve months.

As we left the house, we looked into the dark and squalid dining-room, where a lunch of cold meat was set out; but having no associations with the house except through this one dead man, it seemed as if his presence and attributes pervaded it wholly. He appears to have been a man of reprehensible habits, though well advanced in years. I ought not to forget a brandy-flask (empty) among his other effects. The landlady and daughter made a good impression on me, as honest and respectable persons.

August 24*th.*—Yesterday, in the forenoon, I received a note, and shortly afterwards a call at the Consulate from Miss H., whom I apprehend to be a lady of literary tendencies. She said that Miss L. had promised her an introduction, but that, happening to pass through Liverpool, she had snatched the opportunity to make my acquaintance. She seems to be a mature lady, rather plain, but with an honest and intelligent face. It was rather a singular freedom, methinks, to come down upon a perfect stranger in his way,—to sit with him in his private office an hour or two, and then walk about the streets with him, as she did; for I did the honours of Liverpool, and showed her the public buildings. Her talk was sensible, but not particularly brilliant nor interesting; a good, solid personage, physically and intellectually. She is an Englishwoman.

In the afternoon, at three o'clock, I attended the funeral of Captain Auld. Being ushered into the dining-room of his boarding-house, I found brandy, gin, and wine set out on a tray, together with some little spice-cakes. By-and-by came in a woman, who asked if I were going to the funeral; and then proceeded to put a mourning band on my hat,—a black silk band, covering the whole hat, and streaming nearly a yard behind. After waiting the better part of an hour, nobody else appeared, although several shipmasters had promised to attend. Hereupon the undertaker was anxious to set forth; but the landlady, who was arrayed in shining black silk, thought it a shame that the poor man should be buried with such small attendance. So we waited a little longer, during which interval I heard the landlady's daughter sobbing and wailing in the entry; and but for this tender-heartedness there would have been no tears at all. Finally we set forth,—the undertaker, a friend of his, and a young man, perhaps the landlady's son, and myself, in the black-plumed coach, and the landlady, her daughter, and a female friend, in the coach behind. Previous to this, however, everybody had taken some wine or spirits; for it seemed to be considered disrespectful not to do so.

Before us went the plumed hearse, a stately affair, with a bas-relief of funereal figures upon its sides. We proceeded quite across the city to the Necropolis, where the coffin was carried into a chapel, in which we found already another coffin, and another set of mourners, awaiting the clergyman. Anon he appeared, —a stern, broad-framed, large, and bald-headed man, in a black-silk gown. He mounted his desk, and read the service in quite a feeble and unimpressive way, though with no lack of solemnity. This done, our four bearers took up the coffin, and carried it out of the chapel; but descending the steps, and, perhaps, having taken a little too much brandy, one of them stumbled, and down came the coffin—not quite to the ground, however; for they grappled with it, and contrived, with a great struggle, to prevent the misadventure. But I really expected to see poor Captain Auld burst forth among us in his grave-clothes.

The Necropolis is quite a handsome burial-place, shut in by high walls, so overrun with shrubbery that no part of the brick or stone is visible. Part of the space within is an ornamental garden, with flowers and green turf; the rest is strewn with flat gravestones, and a few raised monuments; and straight avenues run to and fro between. Captain Auld's grave was dug nine feet deep. It is his own for twelve months; but, if his friends do not choose to give him a stone, it will become a common grave at the end of that time; and four or five more bodies may then be piled upon his. Every one seemed greatly to admire the grave; the undertaker praised it, and also the dryness of its site, which he took credit to himself for having chosen. The grave-digger, too, was very proud of its depth, and the neatness of his handiwork. The clergyman, who had marched in advance of us from the chapel, now took his stand at the head of the grave, and, putting his hat, proceeded with what remained of the service, while we stood bareheaded around. When he came to a particular part, "ashes to ashes, dust to dust," the undertaker lifted a handful of earth, and threw it rattling on the coffin,—so did the landlady's son, and so did I. After the funeral, the undertaker's friend, an elderly, coarse-looking man, looked round him, and remarked that "the grass had never grown for the parties who died in the cholera year;" but at this the undertaker laughed in scorn.

As we returned to the gate of the cemetery, the sexton met us, and pointed to a small office, on entering which we found the clergyman, who was waiting for his burial-fees. There was now a dispute between the clergyman and the undertaker; the former wishing to receive the whole amount for the gravestone, which the undertaker, of course, refused to pay. I explained how the matter stood; on which the clergyman acquiesced, civilly enough; but it was very strange to see the worldly, business-like way in which he entered into this squabble, so soon after burying poor Captain ——.

During our drive back in the mourning-coach, the undertaker, his friend, and the landlady's son still kept descanting on the excellence of the grave,—"Such a nice grave,"—"Such a nice grave,"—"Such a splendid grave,"—and, really, they seemed almost to think it worth while to die, for the sake of being buried there.

They deemed it an especial pity that such a grave should ever become a common grave. "Why," said they to me, "by paying the extra price you may have it for your own grave, or for your family!" meaning that we should have a right to pile ourselves over the defunct Captain. I wonder how the English ever attain to any conception of a future existence, since they so overburden themselves with earth and mortality in their ideas of funerals. A drive with an undertaker, in a sable-plumed coach!—talking about graves! —and yet he was a jolly old fellow, wonderfully corpulent, with a smile breaking out easily all over his face,—although, once in a while, he looked professionally lugubrious.

All the time the scent of that horrible mourning-coach is in my nostrils, and I breathe nothing but a funeral atmosphere.

Saturday, August 27th.—This being the gala-day of the manufacturing people about Liverpool, the steamboats to Rock Ferry were seasonably crowded with large parties of both sexes. They were accompanied with two bands of music, in uniform; and these bands, before I left the hotel, were playing, in competition and rivalry with each other in the coachyard, loud martial strains from shining brass instruments. A prize is to be assigned to one or to the other of these bands, and I suppose this was a part of the competition. Meanwhile the merry-making people who thronged the court-yard were quaffing coffee from blue earthen mugs, which they brought with them,—as likewise they brought the coffee, and had it made in the hotel.

It had poured with rain about the time of their

rrival, notwithstanding which they did not seem disheartened; for, of course, in this climate, it enters into all their calculations to be drenched through and through. By-and-by the sun shone out, and it has continued to shine and shade every ten minutes ever since. All these people were decently dressed; the men generally in dark clothes, not so smartly as Americans on a festal day, but so as not to be greatly different as regards dress. They were paler, smaller, less wholesome-looking, and less intelligent, and, I think, less noisy, than so many Yankees would have been. The women and girls differed much more from what American girls and women would be on a pleasure-excursion, being so shabbily dressed, with no kind of smartness, no silks, nothing but cotton gowns, I believe, and ill-looking bonnets,—which, however, was the only part of their attire that they seemed to care about guarding from the rain. As to their persons, they generally looked better developed and healthier than the men; but there was a woful lack of beauty and grace, not a pretty girl among them, all coarse and vulgar. Their bodies, it seems to me, are apt to be very long in proportion to their limbs,—in truth, this kind of make is rather characteristic of both sexes in England. The speech of these folks, in some instances, was so broad Lancashire that I could not well understand it.

A WALK TO BEBBINGTON.

Rock Ferry, August 29th.—Yesterday we all took a walk into the country. It was a fine afternoon, with clouds, of course, in different parts of the sky, but a clear atmosphere, bright sunshine, and altogether a Septembrish feeling. The ramble was very pleasant along the hedge-lined roads, in which there were flowers blooming, and the varnished holly, certainly one of the most beautiful shrubs in the world, so far as foliage goes. We saw one cottage which I suppose was several hundred years old. It was of stone, filled into a wooden frame, the black oak of which was visible like an external skeleton; it had a thatched roof, and was whitewashed. We passed through a village,—Higher Bebbington, I believe,—with narrow streets and mean houses, all of brick or stone, and not standing wide apart from each other, as in American country villages, but conjoined. There was an immense almshouse in the midst; at least, I took it to be so. In the centre of the village, too, we saw a moderate-sized brick house, built in imitation of a castle with a tower and turret, in which an upper and an under row of small cannon were mounted, —now green with moss. There were also battlements along the roof of the house, which looked as if it might have been built eighty or a hundred years ago. In the centre of it there was the dial of a clock, but the inner machinery had been removed, and the hands, hanging listlessly, moved to and fro in the wind. It was quite a novel symbol of decay and neglect. On the wall, close to the street, there were certain eccentric inscriptions cut into slabs of stone, but I could make no sense of them. At the end of the house opposite the turret, we peeped through the bars of an iron gate and beheld a little paved court-yard, and at the further side of it a small piazza, beneath which seemed to stand the figure of a man. He appeared well advanced in years, and was dressed in a blue coat and buff breeches, with a white or straw hat on his head. Behold, too, in a kennel beside the porch, a large dog sitting on his hind legs, chained! Also, close beside the gateway, another man, seated in a kind of arbour! All these were wooden images; and the whole castellated, small, village dwelling, with the inscriptions and the queer statuary, was probably the whim of some half-crazy person, who has now, no doubt, been long asleep in Bebbington churchyard.

The bell of the old church was ringing as we went along, and many respectable-looking people and cleanly dressed children were moving towards the sound. Soon we reached the church, and I have seen nothing yet in England that so completely answered my idea of what such a thing was, as this old village church of Bebington.

It is quite a large edifice, built in the form of a cross, a low peaked porch in the side, over which, rudely cut in stone, is the date 1300 and something. The steeple has ivy on it, and looks old, old, old; so does the whole church, though portions of it have been renewed, but not so as to impair the aspect of heavy, substantial endurance, and long, long decay, which may go on hundreds of years longer before the church is a ruin. There it stands, among the surrounding graves, looking just the same as it did in Bloody Mary's days; just as it did in Cromwell's time. A bird (and perhaps many birds) had its nest in the steeple, and flew in and out of the loop-holes that were opened into it. The stone framework of the windows looked particularly old.

There were monuments about the church, some lying flat on the ground, others elevated on low pillars, or on cross slabs of stone, and almost all looking dark, moss-

grown, and very antique. But on reading some of the
inscriptions, I was surprised to find them very recent;
for, in fact, twenty years of this climate suffices to give
as much or more antiquity of aspect, whether to gravestone or edifice, than a hundred years of our own,—
so soon do lichens creep over the surface, so soon does
it blacken, so soon do the edges lose their sharpness,
so soon does Time gnaw away the records. The only
really old monuments (and those not very old) were
two, standing close together, and raised on low rude
arches, the dates on which were 1684 and 1686. On
one a cross was rudely cut into the stone. But there
may have been hundreds older than this, the records
on which had been quite obliterated, and the stones removed, and the graves dug over anew. None of the
monuments commemorate people of rank; on only one
the buried person was recorded as "Gent."

While we sat on the flat slabs resting ourselves,
several little girls, healthy-looking and prettily dressed
enough, came into the churchyard, and began to talk
and laugh, and to skip merrily from one tombstone to
another. They stared very broadly at us, and one of
them, by-and-by, ran up to U. and J., and gave each
of them a green apple, then they skipped upon the
tombstones again, while, within the church, we heard
the singing,—sounding pretty much as I have heard
it in our pine-built New England meeting-houses. Meantime the rector had detected the voices of these naughty
little girls, and perhaps had caught glimpses of them
through the windows; for, anon, out came the sexton,
and, addressing himself to us, asked whether there had
been any noise or disturbance in the churchyard. I
should not have borne testimony against these little

llagers, but S. was so anxious to exonerate our own
ildren that she pointed out these poor little sinners
the sexton, who forthwith turned them out. He would
.ve done the same to us, no doubt, had my coat been
orse than it was; but, as the matter stood, his de-
eanour was rather apologetic than menacing, when he
formed us that the rector had sent him.

We stayed a little longer, looking at the graves,
me of which were between the buttresses of the
urch and quite close to the wall, as if the sleepers
ticipated greater comfort and security the nearer they
uld get to the sacred edifice.

. . . .

As he went out of the churchyard, we passed the
oresaid little girls, who were sitting behind the mound
a tomb, and busily babbling together. They called
ter us, expressing their discontent that we had be-
yed them to the sexton, and saying that it was not
cy who made the noise. Going homeward, we went
tray in a green lane, that terminated in the midst of
field, without outlet, so that we had to retrace a good
any of our footsteps.

Close to the wall of the church, beside the door,
ere was an ancient baptismal font of stone. In fact,
was a pile of roughly-hewn stone steps, five or six
t high, with a block of stone at the summit, in which
s a hollow about as big as a wash-bowl. It was full
rain-water.

The church seems to be St. Andrew's church, Lower
bbington, built in 1100.

September 1*st.*—To-day we leave the Rock Ferry
otel, where we have spent nearly four weeks. It is

a comfortable place, and we have had a good table and have been kindly treated. We occupied a large parlour, extending through the whole breadth of the house, with a bow-window, looking towards Liverpool, and adown the intervening river, and to Birkenhead, on the hither side. The river would be a pleasanter object, if it were blue and transparent, instead of such a mud-puddly hue; also, if it were always full to its brim; whereas it generally presents a margin, and sometimes a very broad one, of glistening mud, with here and there a small vessel aground on it.

Nevertheless, the parlour window has given us a pretty good idea of the nautical business of Liverpool; the constant objects being the little black steamers puffing unquietly along, sometimes to our own ferry sometimes beyond it to Eastham, and sometimes towing a long string of boats from Runcorn or otherwhere up the river, laden with goods, and sometimes gallanting a tall ship in or out. Some of these ships lie for days together in the river, very majestic and stately objects, often with the flag of the stars and stripes waving over them. Now and then, after a gale at sea, a vessel comes in with her masts broken short off in the midst, and with marks of rough handling about the hull. Once a week comes a Cunard steamer, with its red funnel pipe whitened by the salt spray; and, firing off cannon to announce her arrival, she moors to a large iron buoy in the middle of the river, and a few hundred yards from the stone pier of our ferry. Immediately comes puffing towards her a little mail steamer, to take away her mail bags and such of the passengers as choose to land; and for several hours afterwards the Cunard lies with the smoke and steam coming out of

er, as if she were smoking her pipe after her toilsome
passage across the Atlantic. Once a fortnight comes
an American steamer of the Collins line; and then the
Cunard salutes her with cannon, to which the Collins
responds, and moors herself to another iron buoy, not
far from the Cunard. When they go to sea, it is with
similar salutes: the two vessels paying each other the
more ceremonious respect, because they are inimical
and jealous of each other.

Besides these, there are other steamers of all sorts
and sizes, for pleasure-excursions, for regular trips to
Dublin, the Isle of Man, and elsewhither; and vessels
which are stationary, as floating lights, but which seem
to relieve one another at intervals; and small vessels,
with sails looking as if made of tanned leather; and
schooners, and yachts, and all manner of odd-looking
craft, but none so odd as the Chinese junk. This
junk lies by our own pier, and looks as if it were
copied from some picture on an old teacup. Beyond
all these objects we see the other side of the Mersey,
with the delectably green fields opposite to us, while
the shore becomes more and more thickly populated,
until about two miles off we see the dense centre of
the city, with the dome of the Custom-House, and
steeples and towers; and, close to the water, the spire
of St. Nicholas; and above, and intermingled with the
whole city scene, the duskiness of the coal-smoke
gushing upward. Along the bank we perceive the
warehouses of the Albert dock, and the Queen's tobacco
warehouses, and other docks, and, nigher to us, a ship-
yard or two. In the evening all this sombre picture
gradually darkens out of sight, and in its place appear
only the lights of the city, kindling into a galaxy of

earthly stars, for a long distance, up and down the
shore; and, in one or two spots, the bright red gleam
of a furnace, like the "red planet Mars;" and once in
a while a wandering beam gliding along the river, as
a steamer comes or goes between us and Liverpool.

ROCK PARK.

September 2nd.—We got into our new house in
Rock Park yesterday. It is quite a good house, with
three apartments, beside kitchen and pantry, on the
lower floor; and it is three stories high, with four good
chambers in each story. It is a stone edifice, like
almost all the English houses, and handsome in its
design. The rent, without furniture, would probably
have been one hundred pounds; furnished, it is one
hundred and sixty pounds. Rock Park, as the locality
is called, is private property, and is now nearly covered
with residences for professional people, merchants, and
others of the upper middling class; the houses being
mostly built, I suppose, on speculation, and let to
those who occupy them. It is the quietest place
imaginable, there being a police station at the entrance,
and the officer on duty allows no ragged or ill-looking
person to pass. There being a toll, it precludes all
unnecessary passage of carriages; and never were
there more noiseless streets than those that give access
to these pretty residences. On either side there is a
thick shrubbery, with glimpses through it of the
ornamented portals, or into the trim gardens with
smooth-shaven lawns, of no large extent, but still
affording reasonable breathing-space. They are really
an improvement on anything, save what the very rich

can enjoy, in America. The former occupants of our house (Mrs. Campbell and family) having been fond of flowers, there are many rare varieties in the garden, and we are told that there is scarcely a month in the year when a flower will not be found there.

The house is respectably, though not very elegantly, furnished. It was a dismal, rainy day yesterday, and we had a coal fire in the sitting-room, beside which I sat last evening as twilight came on, and thought, rather sadly, how many times we have changed our home since we were married. In the first place, our three years at the old Manse; then a brief residence at Salem, then at Boston, then two or three years at Salem again; then at Lennox, then at West Newton, and then again at Concord, where we imagined that we were fixed for life, but spent only a year. Then this farther flight to England, where we expect to spend four years, and afterwards another year or two in Italy, during all which time we shall have no real home. For, as I sat in this English house, with the chill, rainy English twilight brooding over the lawn, and a coal fire to keep me comfortable on the first evening of September, and the picture of a stranger —the dead husband of Mrs. Campbell—gazing down at me from above the mantelpiece,—I felt that I never could be quite at home here. Nevertheless, the fire was very comfortable to look at, and the shape of the fire-place—an arch, with a deep cavity—was an improvement on the square, shallow opening of an American coal-grate.

September 7th.—It appears by the annals of Liverpool, contained in Gore's Directory, that in 1076 there was a baronial castle built by Roger de Poictiers on the site of the present St. George's church. It was taken down in 1721. The church now stands at one of the busiest points of the principal street of the city. The old church of St. Nicholas, founded about the time of the Conquest, and more recently rebuilt, stood within a quarter of a mile of the castle.

In 1150, Birkenhead Priory was founded on the Cheshire side of the Mersey. The monks used to ferry passengers across to Liverpool until 1282, when Woodside Ferry was established,—twopence for a horseman, and a farthing for a foot-passenger. Steam ferry-boats now cross to Birkenhead, Monk's Ferry, and Woodside every ten minutes; and I believe there are large hotels at all these places, and many of the business men of Liverpool have residences in them.

In 1252 a tower was built by Sir John Stanley, which continued to be a castle of defence to the Stanley family for many hundred years, and was not finally taken down till 1820, when its site had become the present Water Street, in the densest commercial centre of the city.

There appear to have been other baronial castles and residences in different parts of the city, as a hall in old Hall Street, built by Sir John de la More, on the site of which a counting-house now stands. This knightly family of De la More sometimes supplied mayors to the city, as did the family of the Earls of Derby.

About 1582, Edward, Earl of Derby, maintained two hundred and fifty citizens of Liverpool, fed sixty aged persons twice a day, and provided twenty-seven hundred persons with meat, drink, and money every Good Friday.

In 1644, Prince Rupert besieged the town for [t]wenty-four days, and finally took it by storm. This [w]as June 26th, and the Parliamentarians, under Sir [J]ohn Meldrum, repossessed it the following October.

In 1669 the Mayor of Liverpool kept an inn.

In 1730 there was only one carriage in town, and [n]o stage-coach came nearer than Warrington, the roads [b]eing impassable.

In 1734 the Earl of Derby gave a great entertain[m]ent in the tower.

In 1737, the Mayor was George Norton, a saddler, [w]ho frequently took the chair with his leather apron [o]n. His immediate predecessor seems to have been [t]he Earl of Derby, who gave the above-mentioned [e]ntertainment during his mayoralty. Where George's [D]ock now is, there used to be a battery of fourteen [e]ighteen-pounders for the defence of the town; and the [o]ld sport of bull-baiting was carried on in that vicinity, [c]lose to the church of St. Nicholas.

September 12*th.*—On Saturday a young man was [fo]und wandering about in West Derby, a suburb of [L]iverpool, in a state of insanity, and, being taken [b]efore a magistrate, he proved to be an American. As [h]e seemed to be in a respectable station of life, the [m]agistrate sent the master of the workhouse to me, in [o]rder to find out whether I would take the respon[si]bility of his expenses, rather than have him put [in] the workhouse. My clerk went to investigate [th]e matter, and brought me his papers. His name [p]roves to be —— ——, belonging to ——, twenty-[fi]ve years of age. One of the papers was a passport [fr]om our legation in Naples; likewise there was a power of attorney from his mother (who seems to have been married a second time) to dispose of some property of hers abroad; a hotel bill, also, of some length, in which were various charges for wine; and, among other evidences of low funds, a pawn-broker's receipt for a watch, which he had pledged at five pounds. There was also a ticket for his passage to America, by the screw steamer *Andes*, which sailed on Wednesday last. The clerk found him to the last degree incommunicative; and nothing could be discovered from him but what the papers disclosed. There were about a dozen utterly unintelligible notes among the papers, written by himself since his derangement.

I decided to put him into the insane hospital, where he now accordingly is, and to-morrow (by which time he may be in a more conversable mood) I mean to pay him a visit.

The clerk tells me that there is now, and has been for three years, an American lady in the Liverpool almshouse, in a state of insanity. She is very accomplished, especially in music; but in all this time it has been impossible to find out who she is, or anything about her connections or previous life. She calls herself Jenny Lind, and as for any other name or identity she keeps her own secret.

September 14*th*.—It appears that Mr. —— (the insane young gentleman) being unable to pay his bill at the inn where he was latterly staying, the landlord had taken possession of his luggage, and satisfied himself in that way. My clerk, at my request, has taken his watch out of pawn. It proves to be not a very good one, though doubtless worth more than five pounds, for which it was pledged. The governor of the Lunatic Asylum wrote me yesterday, stating that the patient was in want of a change of clothes, and that, according to his own account, he had left his luggage at the American Hotel. After office-hours, I took a cab, and set out, with my clerk, to pay a visit to the Asylum, taking the American Hotel in our way.

The American Hotel is a small house, not at all such a one as American travellers of any pretension would think of stopping at, but still very respectable, cleanly, and with a neat sitting-room, where the guests might assemble, after the American fashion. We asked for the landlady, and anon down she came, a round, rosy, comfortable-looking English dame of fifty or thereabouts. On being asked whether she knew a Mr. ——, she readily responded that he had been there, but had left no luggage, having taken it away before paying his bill; and that she had suspected him of meaning to take his departure without paying her at all. Hereupon she had traced him to the hotel before mentioned, where she had found that he had stayed two nights,— but was then, I think, gone from thence. Afterwards she encountered him again, and, demanding her due, went with him to a pawnbroker's, where he pledged his watch and paid her. This was about the extent of the landlady's knowledge of the matter. I liked the woman very well, with her shrewd, good-humoured, worldly, kindly disposition.

Then we proceeded to the Lunatic Asylum, to which we were admitted by a porter at the gate. Within door we found some neat and comely servant-women, one of whom showed us into a handsome parlour, and took my card to the governor. There was a large bookcase, with a glass front, containing handsomely bound books, many of which, I observed, were of a religious character. In a few minutes the governor came in, a middle-aged man, tall, and thin for an Englishman, kindly and agreeable enough in aspect, but not with the marked look of a man of force and ability. I should not judge from his conversation that he was an educated man, or that he had any scientific acquaintance with the subject of insanity.

He said that Mr. —— was still quite incommunicative, and not in a very promising state; that I had perhaps better defer seeing him for a few days; that it would not be safe, at present, to send him home to America without an attendant, and this was about all. But on returning home I learned from my wife, who had had a call from Mrs. Blodgett, that Mrs. Blodgett knew Mr. —— and his mother, who has recently been remarried to a young husband, and is now somewhere in Italy. They seemed to have boarded at Mrs. Blodgett's house on their way to the Continent, and within a week or two, an acquaintance and pastor of Mr. ——, the Rev. Dr. ——, has sailed for America. If I could only have caught him, I could have transferred the care, expense, and responsibility of the patient to him. The governor of the asylum mentioned, by the way, that Mr. —— describes himself as having been formerly a midshipman in the navy.

. . . .

I walked through the St. James's cemetery yesterday. It is a very pretty place, dug out of the rock, having formerly, I believe, been a stone quarry. It is now a deep and spacious valley, with graves and monuments on its level and grassy floor, through which run gravel

paths, and where grows luxuriant shrubbery. On one
of the steep sides of the valley, hewn out of the rock,
are tombs, rising in tiers, to the height of fifty feet or
more; some of them cut directly into the rock with
arched portals, and others built with stone. On the
other side the bank is of earth, and rises abruptly,
quite covered with trees, and looking very pleasant
with their green shades. It was a warm and sunny day,
and the cemetery really had a most agreeable aspect. I
saw several gravestones of Americans; but what struck
me most was one line of an epitaph on an Englishwoman, "Here rests in *pease* a virtuous wife." The
statue of Huskisson stands in the midst of the valley,
in a kind of mausoleum, with a door of plate glass,
through which you look at the dead statesman's effigy.

September 22nd.— .... Some days ago an American
captain came to the office, and said he had shot one
of his men, shortly after sailing from New Orleans, and
while the ship was still in the river. As he described
the event, he was in peril of his life from this man who
was an Irishman; and he fired his pistol only when
the man was coming upon him, with a knife in one
hand, and some other weapon of offence in the other,
while he himself was struggling with one or two more
of the crew. He was weak at the time, having just
recovered from the yellow fever. The shots struck the
man in the pit of the stomach, and he lived only about
a quarter of an hour. No magistrate in England has a
right to arrest or examine the captain, unless by a
warrant from the Secretary of State, on the charge of
murder. After his statement to me, the mother of the
slain man went to the police officer, and accused him

of killing her son. Two or three days since, moreover, two of the sailors came before me, and gave their account of the matter; and it looked very differently from that of the captain. According to them, the man had no idea of attacking the captain, and was so drunk that he could not keep himself upright without assistance. One of those two men was actually holding him up when the captain fired two barrels of his pistol, one immediately after the other, and lodged two balls in the pit of his stomach. The man sank down at once, saying, "Jack, I am killed,"—and died very shortly. Meanwhile the captain drove this man away, under threats of shooting him likewise. Both the seamen described the captain's conduct, both then and during the whole voyage, as outrageous, and I do not much doubt that it was so. They gave their evidence like men who wished to tell the truth, and were moved by no more than a natural indignation at the captain's wrong.

I did not much like the captain from the first—a hard, rough man, with little education, and nothing of the gentleman about him, a red face and a loud voice. He seemed a good deal excited, and talked fast and much about the event, but yet not as if it had sunk deeply into him. He observed that he "would not have had it happen for a thousand dollars," that being the amount of detriment which he conceives himself to suffer by the ineffaceable blood-stain on his hand. In my opinion it is little short of murder, if at all; but what would be murder on shore is almost a natural occurrence when done in such a hell on earth as one of these ships, in the first hours of the voyage. The men are then all drunk—some of them often in delirium tremens;

and the captain feels no safety for his life except in making himself as terrible as a fiend. It is the universal testimony that there is a worse set of sailors in these short voyages between Liverpool and America than in any other trade whatever.

There is no probability that the captain will ever be called to account for this deed. He gave, at the time, his own version of the affair in his log-book; and this was signed by the entire crew, with the exception of one man, who had hidden himself in the hold in terror of the captain. His mates will sustain his side of the question; and none of the sailors would be within reach of the American courts, even should they be sought for.

. . . . .

October 1st.—On Thursday I went with Mr. Ticknor to Chester by railway. It is quite an indescribable old town, and I feel at last as if I had had a glimpse of old England. The wall encloses a large space within the town, but there are numerous houses and streets not included within its precincts. Some of the principal streets pass under the ancient gateways; and at the side there are flights of steps, giving access to the summit. Around the top of the whole wall, a circuit of about two miles, there runs a walk, well paved with flagstones, and broad enough for three persons to walk abreast. On one side—that towards the country—there is a parapet of red freestone, three or four feet high. On the other side there are houses, rising up immediately from the wall, so that they seem a part of it. The height of it, I suppose, may be thirty or forty feet, and, in some parts, you look down from the parapet into orchards, where there are tall apple-trees, and men on the branches, gathering fruit, and women and children among the grass, filling bags or baskets. There are prospects of the surrounding country among the buildings outside the wall; at one point, a view of the river Dee, with an old bridge of arches. It is all very strange, very quaint, very curious to see how the town has overflowed its barrier, and how, like many institutions here, the ancient wall still exists, but is turned to quite another purpose than what it was meant for— so far as it serves any purpose at all. There are three or four towers in the course of the circuit; the most interesting being one from the top of which King Charles I. is said to have seen the rout of his army by the Parliamentarians. We ascended the short flight of steps that led up into the tower, where an old man pointed out the site of the battle-field, now thickly studded with buildings, and told us what we had already learned from the guide-book. After this we went into the cathedral, which I will perhaps describe on some other occasion, when I shall have seen more of it, and to better advantage. The cloisters gave us the strongest impression of antiquity; the stone arches being so worn and blackened by time. Still an American must always have imagined a better cathedral than this. There were some immense windows of painted glass, but all modern. In the chapter-house we found a coal fire burning in a grate, and a large heap of old books— the library of the cathedral—in a discreditable state of decay—mildewed, rotten, neglected for years. The sexton told us that they were to be arranged and better ordered. Over the door, inside, hung two faded and tattered banners, being those of the Cheshire regiment.

The most utterly indescribable feature of Chester is the Rows, which every traveller has attempted to describe. At the height of several feet above some of the oldest streets, a walk runs through the front of the houses, which project over it. Back of the walk there are shops; on the outer side is a space of two or three yards, where the shopmen place their tables, and stands, and show-cases; overhead, just high enough for persons to stand erect, a ceiling. At frequent intervals little narrow passages go winding in among the houses, which all along are closely conjoined, and seem to have no access or exit, except through the shops, or into these narrow passages, where you can touch each side with your elbows, and the top with your hand. We penetrated into one or two of them, and they smelt anciently and disagreeably. At one of the doors stood a pale-looking, but cheerful and good-natured woman, who told us that she had come to that house when first married, twenty-one years before, and had lived there ever since; and that she felt as if she had been buried through the best years of her life. She allowed us to peep into her kitchen and parlour,—small, dingy, dismal, but yet not wholly destitute of a home look. She said that she had seen two or three coffins in a day, during cholera times, carried out of that narrow passage into which her door opened. These avenues put me in mind of those which run through ant-hills, or those which a mole makes underground. This fashion of Rows does not appear to be going out; and, for aught I can see, it may last hundreds of years longer. When a house becomes so old as to be untenantable, it is rebuilt, and the new one is fashioned like the old, so far as regards the walk running through its front.

4*

Many of the shops are very good, and even elegant, and these Rows are the favourite places of business in Chester. Indeed, they have many advantages, the passengers being sheltered from the rain, and there being within the shops that dimmer light by which tradesmen like to exhibit their wares.

A large proportion of the edifices in the Rows must be comparatively modern; but there are some very ancient ones, with oaken frames visible on the exterior. The Row, passing through these houses, is railed with oak, so old that it has turned black, and grown to be as hard as stone, which it might be mistaken for, if one did not see where names and initials have been cut into it with knives at some bygone period. Overhead, cross-beams project through the ceiling so low as almost to hit the head. On the front of one of these buildings was the inscription, "GOD'S PROVIDENCE IS MINE INHERITANCE," said to have been put there by the occupant of the house two hundred years ago, when the plague spared this one house only in the whole city. Not improbably the inscription has operated as a safeguard to prevent the demolition of the house hitherto; but a shopman of an adjacent dwelling told us that it was soon to be taken down.

Here and there, about some of the streets through which the Rows do not run, we saw houses of very aged aspect, with steep, peaked gables. The front gable-end was supported on stone pillars, and the sidewalk passed beneath. Most of these old houses seemed to be taverns,—the Black Bear, the Green Dragon, and such names. We thought of dining at one of them, but, on inspection, they looked rather too dingy and close, and of questionable neatness. So we went to the

Royal Hotel, where we probably fared just as badly at much more expense, and where there was a particularly gruff and crabbed old waiter, who, I suppose, thought himself free to display his surliness because we arrived at the hotel on foot. For my part, I love to see John Bull show himself. I must go again and again and again to Chester, for I suppose there is not a more curious place in the world.

Mr. Ticknor, who has been staying at Rock Park with us since Tuesday, has steamed away in the *Canada* this morning. His departure seems to make me feel more abroad, more dissevered from my native country, than before.

October 3rd.—Saturday evening, at six, I went to dine with Mr. Aiken, a wealthy merchant here, to meet two of the sons of Burns. There was a party of ten or twelve, Mr. Aiken and his two daughters included. The two sons of Burns have both been in the Indian army, and have attained the ranks of Colonel and Major; one having spent thirty, and the other twenty-seven, years in India. They are now old gentlemen of sixty and upwards, the elder with a grey head, the younger with a perfectly white one,—rather under than above the middle stature, and with a British roundness of figure,—plain, respectable, intelligent-looking persons, with quiet manners. I saw no resemblance in either of them to any portrait of their father. After the ladies left the table, I sat next to the Major, the younger of the two, and had a good deal of talk with him. He seemed a very kindly and social man, and was quite ready to speak about his father, nor was he at all reluctant to let it be seen how much he valued the glory of being descended from the poet. By-and-by, at Mr. Aiken's instance, he sang one of Burns's songs,—the one about "Annie" and the "Rigs o' barley." He sings in a perfectly simple style, so that it is little more than a recitative, and yet the effect is very good as to humour, sense, and pathos. After rejoining the ladies, he sang another, "A posie for my ain dear May," and likewise "A man's a man for a' that." My admiration of his father, and partly, perhaps, my being an American, gained me some favour with him, and he promised to give me what he considered the best engraving of Burns, and some other remembrance of him. The Major is that son of Burns who spent an evening at Abbotsford with Sir Walter Scott, when, as Lockhart writes, "the children sang the ballads of their sires." He spoke with vast indignation of a recent edition of his father's works by Robert Chambers, in which the latter appears to have wronged the poet by some misstatements. . . . . I liked them both and they liked me, and asked me to go and see them at Cheltenham, where they reside. We broke up at about midnight.

The members of this dinner-party were of the more liberal tone of thinking here in Liverpool. The Colonel and Major seemed to be of similar principles; and the eyes of the latter glowed, when he sang his father's noble verse, "The rank is but the guinea's stamp," &c. It would have been too pitiable if Burns had left a son who could not feel the spirit of that verse.

October 8th.—Coming to my office, two or three mornings ago, I found Mrs. ——, the mother of Mr. ——, the insane young man of whom I had taken charge. She is a lady of fifty or thereabouts, and not very remarkable any way, nor particularly ladylike. However, she was just come off a rapid journey, having travelled from Naples, with three small children, without taking rest, since my letter reached her. A son* of about twenty had come with her to the Consulate. She was, of course, infinitely grieved about the young man's insanity, and had two or three bursts of tears while we talked the matter over. She said he was the hope of her life,—the best, purest, most innocent child that ever was, and wholly free from every kind of vice. . . . . But it appears that he had a previous attack of insanity, lasting three months, about three years ago.

After I had told her all I knew about him, including my personal observations at a visit a week or two since, we drove in a cab to the Asylum. It must have been a dismal moment to the poor lady, as we entered the gateway through a tall, prison-like wall. Being ushered into the parlour, the governor soon appeared, and informed us that Mr. —— had had a relapse within a few days, and was not now so well as when I saw him. He complains of unjust confinement, and seems to consider himself, if I rightly understand, under persecution for political reasons. The governor, however, proposed to call him down, and I took my leave, feeling that it would be indelicate to be present at his first interview with his mother. So here ended my guardianship of the poor young fellow.

In the afternoon I called at the Waterloo Hotel, where Mrs. —— was staying, and found her in the coffee-room with the children. She had determined to take a lodging in the vicinity of the Asylum, and was

* This proved to be her new husband.

going to remove thither as soon as the children had had something to eat. They seemed to be pleasant and well-behaved children, and struck me more favourably than the mother, whom I suspect to be rather a foolish woman, although her present grief makes her appear in a more respectable light than at other times. She seemed anxious to impress me with the respectability and distinction of her connections in America, and I had observed the same tendency in the insane patient, at my interview with him. However, she has undoubtedly a mother's love for this poor shatterbrain, and this may weigh against the folly of her marrying an incongruously youthful second husband, and many other follies.

This was day before yesterday, and I have heard nothing of her since. The same day I had applications for assistance in two other domestic affairs; one from an Irishman, naturalised in America, who wished me to get him a passage thither, and to take charge of his wife and family here, at my own private expense, until he could remit funds to carry them across. Another was from an Irishman, who had a power of attorney from a countrywoman of his in America, to find and take charge of an infant whom she had left in the Liverpool workhouse two years ago. I have a great mind to keep a list of all the business I am consulted about and employed in. It would be very curious. Among other things, all penniless Americans, or pretenders to Americanism, look upon me as their banker; and I could ruin myself any week, if I had not laid down a rule to consider every applicant for assistance an impostor until he prove himself a true and responsible man,—which it is very difficult to do. Yesterday there limped in a very respectable-looking old man, who described himself as a citizen of Baltimore, who had been on a trip to England and elsewhere, and, being detained longer than he expected, and having had an attack of rheumatism, was now short of funds to pay his passage home, and hoped that I would supply the deficiency. He had quite a plain, homely, though respectable manner, and, for aught I know, was the very honestest man alive; but as he could produce no kind of proof of his character and responsibility, I very quietly explained the impossibility of my helping him. I advised him to try to obtain a passage on board of some Baltimore ship, the master of which might be acquainted with him, or, at all events, take his word for payment after arrival. This he seemed inclined to do, and took his leave. There was a decided aspect of simplicity about this old man, and yet I rather judge him to be an impostor.

It is easy enough to refuse money to strangers and unknown people, or whenever there may be any question about identity; but it will not be so easy when I am asked for money by persons whom I know, but do not like to trust. They shall meet the eternal "No," however.

October 13th.—In Ormerod's history of Chester it is mentioned that Randal, Earl of Chester, having made an inroad into Wales about 1225, the Welshmen gathered in mass against him, and drove him into the castle of Nothelert in Flintshire. The Earl sent for succour to the Constable of Chester, Roger Lacy, surnamed "Hell," on account of his fierceness. It was then fair-time at Chester, and the constable collected a

miscellaneous rabble of fiddlers, players, cobblers, tailors,
and all manner of debauched people, and led them to
the relief of the Earl. At sight of this strange army
the Welshmen fled; and for ever after the Earl assigned
to the Constable of Chester power over all fiddlers,
shoemakers, &c., within the bounds of Cheshire. The
constable retained for himself and his heirs the control
of the shoemakers; and made over to his own steward,
Dutton, that of the fiddlers and players; and for many
hundreds of years afterwards the Duttons of Dutton
retained the power. On Midsummer-day, they used to
ride through Chester, attended by all the minstrels playing on their several instruments, to the church of St.
John, and there renew their licenses. It is a good
theme for a legend. Sir Peter Leycester, writing in
Charles II.'s time, copies the Latin deed from the constable to Dutton; rightly translated, it seems to mean
"the magisterial power over all the lewd people . . . .
in the whole of Cheshire," but the custom grew into
what is above stated. In the time of Henry VII., the
Duttons claimed, by prescriptive right, that the Cheshire minstrels should deliver them, at the feast of St.
John, four bottles of wine and a lance, and that each
separate minstrel should pay fourpence halfpenny.....

Another account says Ralph Dutton was the constable's son-in-law, and "a lusty youth."

October 19th.—Coming to the ferry this morning a
few minutes before the boat arrived from town, I went
into the ferry-house, a small stone edifice, and found
there an Irishman, his wife, and three children, the
oldest eight or nine years old, and all girls. There
was a good fire burning in the room, and the family

was clustered round it, apparently enjoying the warmth very much; but when I went in, both husband and wife very hospitably asked me to come to the fire, although there was not more than room at it for their own party. I declined, on the plea that I was warm enough, and then the woman said that they were very cold, having been long on the road. The man was grey-haired and grey-bearded, clad in an old drab overcoat, and laden with a huge bag, which seemed to contain bedclothing or something of the kind. The woman was pale, with a thin, anxious, wrinkled face, but with a good and kind expression. The children were quite pretty, with delicate faces, and a look of patience and endurance in them, but yet as if they had suffered as little as they possibly could. The two elder were cuddled up close to the father, the youngest, about four years old, sat in its mother's lap, and she had taken off its small shoes and stockings, and was warming its feet at the fire. Their little voices had a sweet and kindly sound as they talked in low tones to their parents and one another. They all looked very shabby, and yet had a decency about them; and it was touching to see how they made themselves at home at this casual fireside, and got all the comfort they could out of the circumstances. By-and-by two or three market-women came in, and looked pleasantly at them, and said a word or two to the children.

They did not beg of me, as I supposed they would; but after looking at them awhile, I pulled out a piece of silver, and handed it to one of the little girls. She took it very readily, as if she partly expected it, and then the father and mother thanked me, and said they had been travelling a long distance, and had nothing to subsist upon, except what they picked up on the road. They found it impossible to live in England, and were now on their way to Liverpool, hoping to get a passage back to Ireland, where, I suppose, extreme poverty is rather better off than here. I heard the little girl say that she should buy bread with the money. There is not much that can be caught in the description of this scene; but it made me understand, better than before, how poor people feel, wandering about in such destitute circumstances, and how they suffer, and yet how they have a life not quite miserable, after all, and how family love goes along with them. Soon the boat arrived at the pier, and we all went on board; and as I sat in the cabin, looking up through a broken pane in the skylight, I saw the woman's thin face, with its anxious, motherly aspect; and the youngest child in her arms, shrinking from the chill wind, but yet not impatiently; and the eldest of the girls standing close by, with her expression of childish endurance, but yet so bright and intelligent that it would evidently take but a few days to make a happy and playful child of her. I got into the interior of this poor family, and understand, through sympathy, more of them than I can tell. I am getting to possess some of the English indifference as to beggars and poor people; but still, whenever I come face to face with them, and have any intercourse, it seems as if they ought to be the better for me. I wish, instead of sixpence, I had given the poor family ten shillings, and denied it to a begging subscriptionist, who has just fleeced me to that amount. How silly a man feels in this latter predicament!

I have had a good many visitors at the Consulate

from the United States within a short time,—among
others, Mr. D. D. Barnard, our late minister to Berlin,
returning homeward to-day by the *Arctic;* and Mr.
Sickles, Secretary of Legation to London, a fine-looking, intelligent, gentlemanly young man. . . . . With
him came Judge Douglas, the chosen man of Young
America. He is very short, extremely short, but has
an uncommonly good head, and uncommon dignity
without seeming to aim at it, being free and simple in
manners. I judge him to be a very able man, with
the Western sociability and free-fellowship. Generally,
I see no reason to be ashamed of my countrymen who
come out here in public position, or otherwise assuming
the rank of gentlemen.

. . . . . .

October 20*th.*— One sees incidents in the streets
here, occasionally, which could not be seen in an
American city. For instance, a week or two since, I
was passing a quiet-looking, elderly gentleman, when,
all of a sudden, without any apparent provocation, he
uplifted his stick, and struck a black-gowned boy a
smart blow on the shoulders. The boy looked at him
wofully and resentfully, but said nothing, nor can I
imagine why the thing was done. In Tythebarne
Street to-day I saw a woman suddenly assault a man,
clutch at his hair, and cuff him about the ears. The
man, who was of decent aspect enough, immediately
took to his heels, full speed, and the woman ran after
him, and, as far as I could discern the pair, the chase
continued.

. . . . . .

October 22*nd.*—At a dinner party at Mr. Holland's,
last evening, a gentleman, in instance of Charles

Dickens's unweariability, said that during some theatrical performances in Liverpool, he acted in play and farce, spent the rest of the night making speeches, feasting, and drinking at table, and ended at seven o'clock in the morning by jumping leap-frog over the backs of the whole company.

In Moore's diary, he mentions a beautiful Guernsey lily having been given to his wife, and says that the flower was originally from Guernsey. A ship from there had been wrecked on the coast of Japan, having many of the lilies on board, and the next year the flowers appeared,—springing up, I suppose, on the wave-beaten strand.

Wishing to send a letter to a dead man, who may be supposed to have gone to Tophet,—throw it into the fire.

Sir Arthur Aston had his brains beaten out with his own wooden leg, at the storming of Fredagh, in Ireland, by Cromwell.

In the county of Cheshire, many centuries ago, there lived a half-idiot, named Nixon, who had the gift of prophecy, and made many predictions about places, families, and important public events, since fulfilled. He seems to have fallen into fits of insensibility previous to uttering his prophecies.

The family of Mainwaring (pronounced Mannering), of Bromborough, had an ass's head for a crest.

"Richard Dawson, being sick of the plague, and perceiving he must die, rose out of his bed and made his grave, and caused his nephew to cast straw into the grave, which was not far from the house, and went and laid him down in the said grave, and caused clothes to be laid upon him, and so departed out of this world. This he did because he was a strong man, and heavier than his said nephew and a serving-wench were able to bury. He died about the 24th of August. Thus was I credibly told he did, 1625." This was in the township of Malpas, recorded in the parish register.

At Bickley Hall, taken down a few years ago, used to be shown the room where the body of the Earl of Leicester was laid for a whole twelvemonth,—1659 to 1660,—he having been kept unburied all that time, owing to a dispute which of his heirs should pay his funeral expenses.

November 5th.—We all, together with Mr. Squarey, went to Chester last Sunday, and attended the cathedral service. A great deal of ceremony, and not unimposing, but rather tedious before it was finished,—occupying two hours or more. The Bishop was present, but did nothing except to pronounce the benediction. In America, the sermon is the principal thing; but here all this magnificent ceremonial of prayer and chanted responses and psalms and anthems was the setting to a short, meagre discourse, which would not have been considered of any account among the elaborate, intellectual efforts of New England ministers. While this was going on, the light came through the stained glass windows and fell upon the congregation, tingeing them with crimson.

After service we wandered about the aisles, and looked at the tombs and monuments,—the oldest of which was that of some nameless abbot, with a staff and mitre half obliterated from his tomb, which was under a shallow arch on one side of the cathedral. There were also marbles on the walls, and lettered stones in the pavement under our feet; but chiefly, if not entirely, of modern date. We lunched at the Royal Hotel, and then walked round the city walls, also crossing the bridge of one great arch over the Dee, and penetrating as far into Wales as the entrance of the Marquis of Westminster's Park at Eaton. It was, I think, the most lovely day as regards weather that I have seen in England.

I passed, to-day, a man chanting a ballad in a street about a recent murder, in a voice that had innumerable cracks in it, and was most lugubrious. The other day I saw a man who was reading in a loud voice what seemed to be an account of the late riots and loss of life in Wigan. He walked slowly along the street as he read, surrounded by a small crowd of men, women, and children; and close by his elbow stalked a policeman, as if guarding against a disturbance.

November 14th.—There is a heavy, dun fog on the river and over the city to-day, the very gloomiest atmosphere that ever I was acquainted with. On the river the steamboats strike gongs or ring bells to give warning of their approach. There are lamps burning in the counting-rooms and lobbies of the warehouses and they gleam distinctly through the windows.

* * * * *

The other day, at the entrance of the market-house, I saw a woman sitting in a small hand-waggon, ap-

parently for the purpose of receiving alms. There was
no attendant at hand; but I noticed that one or two
persons who passed by seemed to inquire whether she
wished her waggon to be moved. Perhaps this is her
mode of making progress about the city, by the volun-
tary aid of boys and other people who help to drag
her. There is something in this—I don't yet well
know what—that has impressed me, as if I could make
a romance out of the idea of a woman living in this
manner a public life, and moving about by such means.

November 29th.—Mr. H. A. B—— told me of his
friend Mr. —— (who was formerly *attaché* to the British
Legation at Washington, and whom I saw at Concord),
that his father, a clergyman, married a second wife.
After the marriage, the noise of a coffin being nightly
carried down the stairs was heard in the parsonage. It
could be distinguished when the coffin reached a certain broad landing and rested on it. Finally, his father
had to remove to another residence. Besides this, Mr.
—— had had another ghostly experience,—having seen
a dim apparition of an uncle at the precise instant
when the latter died in a distant place. The *attaché*
is a credible and honourable fellow, and talks of these
matters as if he positively believed them. But Ghost-
land lies beyond the jurisdiction of veracity.

In a garden near Chester, in taking down a summer-house, a tomb was discovered beneath it, with a
Latin inscription to the memory of an old doctor of
medicine, William Bentley, who had owned the place
long ago, and died in 1680. And his dust and bones had
lain beneath all the merry times in the summer-house.

December 1st.—It is curious to observe how many methods people put in practice here to pick up a halfpenny. Yesterday I saw a man standing bareheaded and barelegged in the mud and misty weather, playing on a fife, in hopes to get a circle of auditors. Nobody, however, seemed to take any notice. Very often a whole band of musicians will strike up,—passing a hat round after playing a tune or two. On board the ferry, until the coldest weather began, there were always some wretched musicians, with an old fiddle, an old clarionet, and an old verdigrised brass bugle, performing during the passage, and, as the boat neared the shore, sending round one of their number to gather contributions in the hollow of the brass bugle. They were a very shabby set, and must have made a very scanty living at best. Sometimes it was a boy with an accordion, and his sister, a smart little girl, with a timbrel,—which, being so shattered that she could not play on it, she used only to collect halfpence in. Ballad-singers, or rather chanters or croakers, are often to be met with in the streets, but hand-organ players are not more frequent than in our cities.

I still observe little girls and other children barelegged and barefooted on the wet side-walks. There certainly never was anything so dismal as the November weather has been; never any real sunshine; almost always a mist; sometimes a dense fog, like slightly rarefied wool, pervading the atmosphere.

An epitaph on a person buried on a hillside in Cheshire, together with some others, supposed to have died of the plague, and therefore not admitted into the churchyards:—

> "Think it not strange our bones ly here,
> Thine may ly thou knowst not where.
> "ELIZABETH HAMPSON."

These graves were near the remains of two rude stone crosses, the purpose of which was not certainly known, although they were supposed to be boundary marks. Probably, as the plague-corpses were debarred from sanctified ground, the vicinity of these crosses was chosen as having a sort of sanctity.

"Bang beggar,"—an old Cheshire term for a parish beadle.

Hawthorne Hall, Cheshire, Macclesfield Hundred, Parish of Wilmslow, and within the hamlet of Morley. It was vested at an early period in the Lathoms of Irlam, Lancaster County, and passed through the Leighs to the Pages of Earlshaw. Thomas Leigh Page sold it to Mr. Ralph Bower of Wilmslow, whose children owned it in 1817. The Leighs built a chancel in the church of Wilmslow, where some of them are buried, their arms painted in the windows. The hall is an "ancient, respectable mansion of brick."

December 2nd.—Yesterday, a chill, misty December day, yet I saw a woman barefooted in the street, not to speak of children.

Cold and uncertain as the weather is, there is still a great deal of small trade carried on in the open air. Women and men sit in the streets with a stock of combs and such small things to sell, the women knitting as if they sat by a fireside. Cheap crockery is laid out in the street, so far out that without any great deviation from the regular carriage-track a wheel might pass straight through it. Stalls of apples are innumerable, but the apples are not fit for a pig. In some streets, herrings are very abundant, laid out on boards. Coals seem to be for sale by the wheelbarrow-full. Here and there you see children with some small article for sale,—as, for instance, a girl with two linen caps. A somewhat overladen cart of coal was passing along, and some small quantity of the coal fell off; no sooner had the wheels passed than several women and children gathered to the spot, like hens and chickens round a handful of corn, and picked it up in their aprons. We have nothing similar to these street women in our country.

December 10*th*.—I don't know any place that brings all classes into contiguity on equal ground so completely as the waiting-room at Rock Ferry on these frosty days. The room is not more than eight feet square, with walls of stone, and wooden benches ranged round them, and an open stove in one corner, generally well furnished with coal. It is almost always crowded, and I rather suspect that many persons, who have no fireside elsewhere, creep in here and spend the most comfortable part of their day.

This morning, when I looked into the room, there were one or two gentlemen and other respectable persons; but in the best place, close to the fire, and crouching almost into it, was an elderly beggar, with the raggedest of overcoats, two great rents in the shoulders of it disclosing the dingy lining, all bepatched with various stuff covered with dirt, and on his shoes and trousers the mud of an interminable pilgrimage. Owing to the posture in which he sat, I could not see his face, but only the battered crown and rim of the very shabbiest hat that ever was worn. Regardless of the presence of women (which, indeed, Englishmen seldom do regard when they wish to smoke), he was smoking a pipe of vile tobacco; but, after all, this was fortunate, because the man himself was not personally fragrant. He was terribly squalid,—terribly; and when I had a glimpse of his face, it well befitted the rest of his development, —grizzled, wrinkled, weather-beaten, yet sallow, and down-looking, with a watchful kind of eye turning upon everybody and everything, meeting the glances of other people rather boldly, yet soon shrinking away; a long thin nose, a grey beard of a week's growth; hair not much mixed with grey, but rusty and lifeless;—a miserable object; but it was curious to see how he was not ashamed of himself, but seemed to feel that he was one of the estates of the kingdom, and had as much right to live as other men. He did just as he pleased, took the best place by the fire, nor would have cared though a nobleman were forced to stand aside for him. When the steamer's bell rang, he shouldered a large and heavy pack, like a pilgrim with his burden of sin, but certainly journeying to hell instead of heaven. On board he looked round for the best position, at first stationing himself near the boiler-pipe; but, finding the deck damp under-foot, he went to the cabin door, and took his stand on the stairs, protected from the wind, but very incommodiously placed for those who wished to pass. All this was done without any bravado or forced impudence, but in the most quiet way, merely because he was seeking his own comfort, and considered that he had a right to seek it. It was an Englishman's spirit; but in our country, I imagine, a beggar considers himself a kind of outlaw, and would hardly assume the privileges of a man in any place of public resort. Here beggary is a system, and beggars are a numerous class, and make themselves, in a certain way, respected as such. Nobody evinced the slightest disapprobation of the man's proceedings. In America, I think, we should see many aristocratic airs on such provocation, and probably the ferry people would there have rudely thrust the beggar aside; giving him a shilling, however, which no Englishman would ever think of doing. There would also have been a great deal of fun made of his squalid and ragged figure; whereas nobody smiled at him this morning, nor in any way showed the slightest disrespect. This is good; but it is the result of a state of things by no means good.

For many days there has been a great deal of fog on the river, and the boats have groped their way along, continually striking their bells, while, on all sides, there are responses of bell and gong; and the vessels at anchor look shadow-like as we glide past them, and the master of one steamer shouts a warning to the master of another which he meets. The Englishmen, who hate to run any risk without an equivalent object, show a good deal of caution and timidity on these foggy days.

December 13*th.*—Chill, frosty weather; such an atmosphere as forebodes snow in New England, and there has been a little here. Yet I saw a barefooted young woman yesterday. The feet of these poor creatures have exactly the red complexion of their hands, acquired by constant exposure to the cold air.

At the ferry-room this morning, was a small, thin, anxious-looking woman, with a bundle, seeming in rather poor circumstances, but decently dressed, and eyeing other women, I thought, with an expression of slight ill-will and distrust; also, an elderly, stout, grey-haired woman, of respectable aspect, and two young lady-like persons, quite pretty, one of whom was reading a shilling volume of James's "Arabella Stuart." They talked to one another with that up-and-down intonation which English ladies practise, and which strikes an unaccustomed ear as rather affected, especially in women of size and mass. It is very different from an American lady's mode of talking: there is the difference between colour and no colour; the tone variegates it. One of these young ladies spoke to me, making some remark about the weather,—the first instance I have met with of a gentlewoman's speaking to an unintroduced gentleman. Besides these, a middle-aged man of the lower class, and also a gentleman's out-door servant, clad in a drab great-coat, corduroy breeches, and drab cloth gaiters buttoned from the knee to the ankle. He complained to the other man of the cold weather; said that a glass of whisky, every half-hour, would keep a man comfortable; and, accidentally hitting his coarse foot against one of the young lady's feet, said, "Beg pardon, ma'am,"—which she acknowledged with a slight movement of the head. Somehow or other, different classes seem to encounter one another in an easier manner than with us; the shock is less palpable. I suppose the reason is that the distinctions are real, and therefore need not be continually asserted.

. . . . .

Nervous and excitable persons need to talk a great deal, by way of letting off their steam.

On board the Rock Ferry steamer, a gentleman coming into the cabin, a voice addresses him from a dark corner, "How do you do, sir?"—"Speak again!" says the gentleman. No answer from the dark corner; and the gentleman repeats, "Speak again!" The speaker now comes out of the dark corner, and sits down in a place where he can be seen. "Ah!" cries the gentleman, "very well, I thank you. How do you do? I did not recognise your voice." Observable, the English caution, shown in the gentleman's not vouchsafing to say, "Very well, thank you!" till he knew his man.

What was the after life of the young man, whom Jesus, looking on, "loved," and bade him sell all that he had, and give to the poor, and take up his cross and follow him? Something very deep and beautiful might be made out of this.

December 31st.—Among the beggars of Liverpool, the hardest to encounter is a man without any legs, and, if I mistake not, likewise deficient in arms. You see him before you all at once, as if he had sprouted half-way out of the earth, and would sink down and reappear in some other place the moment he has done with you. His countenance is large, fresh, and very intelligent; but his great power lies in his fixed gaze, which is inconceivably difficult to bear. He never once removes his eye from you till you are quite past his range; and you feel it all the same, although you do not meet his glance. He is perfectly respectful; but the intentness and directness of his silent appeal is far worse than any impudence. In fact, it is the very flower of impudence. I would rather go a mile about than pass before his battery. I feel wronged by him, and yet unutterably ashamed. There must be great force in the man to produce such an effect. There is nothing of the customary squalidness of beggary about him, but remarkable trimness and cleanliness. A girl of twenty or thereabouts, who vagabondizes about the city on her hands and knees, possesses, to a considerable degree, the same characteristics. I think they hit their victims the more effectually from being below the common level of vision.

January 3rd, 1854.—Night before last there was a fall of snow, about three or four inches, and, following it, a pretty hard frost. On the river, the vessels at anchor showed the snow along their yards, and on every ledge where it could lie. A blue sky and sunshine overhead, and apparently a clear atmosphere close at hand; but in the distance a mistiness became perceptible, obscuring the shores of the river, and making the vessels look dim and uncertain. The steamers were ploughing along, smoking their pipes through the frosty air. On the landing stage and in the streets, hard-trodden snow, looking more like my New England home than anything I have yet seen. Last night the thermometer fell as low as 13°, nor probably is it above 20° to-day. No such frost has been known in England these forty years! and Mr. Wilding tells me that he never saw so much snow before.

January 6th.—I saw, yesterday, stopping at a cabinetmaker's shop in Church Street, a coach with four beautiful white horses, and a postilion on each near-horse; behind, in the dickey, a footman; and on the box a coachman, all dressed in livery. The coach-panel bore a coat of arms with a coronet, and I presume it must have been the equipage of the Earl of Derby. A crowd of people stood round, gazing at the coach and horses; and when any of them spoke, it was in a lower tone than usual. I doubt not they all had a kind of enjoyment of the spectacle, for these English are strangely proud of having a class above them.

* * *

Every Englishman runs to the *Times* with his little grievance, as a child runs to his mother.

I was sent for to the police court the other morning, in the case of an American sailor accused of robbing a shipmate at sea. A large room, with a great coal fire burning on one side, and above it the portrait of Mr. Rushton, deceased, a magistrate of many years' continuance. A long table, with chairs, and a witness-box. One of the borough magistrates, a merchant of the city, sat at the head of the table, with paper and pen and ink before him; but the real judge was the clerk of the court, whose professional knowledge and experience governed all the proceedings. In the short time while I was waiting, two cases were tried, in the first of which the prisoner was discharged. The second case was of a woman,—a thin, sallow, hard-looking, careworn, rather young woman,—for stealing a pair of slippers out of a shop. The trial occupied five minutes or less, and she was sentenced to twenty-one days' imprisonment,—whereupon, without speaking, she looked up wildly first into one policeman's face, then into another's, at the same time wringing her hands with no theatric gesture, but because her torment took this outward shape,—and was led away. The Yankee sailor was then brought up,—an intelligent, but ruffian-like fellow,—and as the case was out of the jurisdiction of the English magistrates, and as it was not worth while to get him sent over to America for trial, he was forthwith discharged. He stole a comforter.

If mankind were all intellect, they would be continually changing, so that one age would be entirely unlike another. The great conservative is the heart, which remains the same in all ages; so that commonplaces of a thousand years' standing are as effective as ever.

. . . . .

Monday, February 20*th*.—At the police court on Saturday, I attended the case of the second mate and four seamen of the *John and Albert*, for assaulting, beating, and stabbing the chief mate. The chief mate has been in the hospital ever since the assault, and was brought into the court to-day to give evidence— a man of thirty, black hair, black eyes, a dark complexion, disagreeable expression; sallow, emaciated, feeble, apparently in pain, one arm disabled. He sat bent and drawn upward, and had evidently been severely hurt, and was not yet fit to be out of bed. He had some brandy and water to enable him to sustain himself. He gave his evidence very clearly, beginning (sailor-like) with telling in what quarter the wind was at the time of the assault, and which sail was taken in. His testimony bore on one man only, at whom he

cast a vindictive look; but I think he told the truth as
far as he knew and remembered it. Of the prisoners
the second mate was a mere youth, with long sandy
hair, and an intelligent and not unprepossessing face,
dressed as neatly as a three or four weeks' capture,
with small or no means, could well allow, in a frock-
coat, and with clean linen,—the only linen or cotton
shirt in the company. The other four were rude, brutish
sailors, in flannel or red-baize shirts. Three of them
appeared to give themselves little concern; but the
fourth, a red-haired and red-bearded man,—Paraman
by name,—evidently felt the pressure of the case upon
himself. He was the one whom the mate swore to
have given him the first blow; and there was other
evidence of his having been stabbed with a knife. The
captain of the ship, the pilot, the cook, and the steward,
all gave their evidence; and the general bearing of it
was, that the chief mate had a devilish temper, and
had misused the second mate and crew, that the four
seamen had attacked him, and that Paraman had
stabbed him; while all but the steward concurred in
saying that the second mate had taken no part in the
affray. The steward, however, swore to having seen
him strike the chief mate with a wooden marlinspike,
which was broken by the blow. The magistrate dis-
missed all but Paraman, whom I am to send to America
for trial. In my opinion the chief mate got pretty nearly
what he deserved under the code of natural justice.
While business was going forward, the magistrate, Mr.
Mansfield, talked about a fancy ball at which he had
been present the evening before, and of other matters
grave and gay. It was very informal; we sat at the
table, or stood with our backs to the fire; policemen

came and went; witnesses were sworn on the greasiest copy of the Gospels I ever saw, polluted by hundreds and thousands of perjured kisses; and for hours the prisoners were kept standing at the foot of the table, interested to the full extent of their capacity, while all others were indifferent. At the close of the case, the police officers and witnesses applied to me about their expenses.

Yesterday I took a walk with my wife and two children to Bebbington church. A beautifully sunny morning. My wife and U. attended church, J. and I continued our walk. When we were at a little distance from the church, the bells suddenly chimed out with a most cheerful sound, and sunny as the morning. It is a pity we have no chimes of bells, to give the church-ward summons, at home. People were standing about the ancient church-porch and among the tombstones. In the course of our walk, we passed many old thatched cottages, built of stone, and with what looked like a cow-house or pigsty at one end, making part of the cottage; also an old stone farm-house, which may have been a residence of gentility in its day. We passed, too, a small Methodist chapel, making one of a row of low brick edifices. There was a sound of prayer within. I never saw a more unbeautiful place of worship; and it had not even a separate existence for itself, the adjoining tenement being an ale-house.

The grass along the wayside was green, with a few daisies. There was green holly in the hedges, and we passed through a wood, up some of the tree-trunks of which ran clustering ivy.

February 23rd.—There came to see me the other

day a young gentleman with a moustache and a blue
cloak, who announced himself as William Allingham,
and handed me a copy of his poems, a thin volume,
with paper covers, published by Routledge. I thought
I remembered hearing his name, but had never seen
any of his works. His face was intelligent, dark,
pleasing, and not at all John-Bullish. He said that he
had been employed in the Customs in Ireland, and was
now going to London to live by literature—to be connected with some newspaper, I imagine. He had been
in London before, and was acquainted with some of the
principal literary people—among others Tennyson and
Carlyle. He seemed to have been on rather intimate
terms with Tennyson..... We talked awhile in my
dingy and dusky Consulate, and he then took leave.
His manners are good, and he appears to possess independence of mind.....

Yesterday I saw a British regiment march down to
George's Pier, to embark in the *Niagara* for Malta.
The troops had nothing very remarkable about them;
but the thousands of ragged and squalid wretches, who
thronged the pier and streets to gaze on them, were
what I had not seen before in such masses. This was
the first populace I have beheld; for even the Irish, on
the other side of the water, acquire a respectability of
aspect. John Bull is going with his whole heart into
the Turkish war. He is very foolish. Whatever the
Czar may propose to himself, it is for the interest of
democracy that he should not be easily put down. The
regiment, on its way to embark, carried the Queen's
colours, and, side by side with them, the banner of the
28th—yellow, with the names of the Peninsular and

other battles in which it had been engaged inscribed on it in a double column. It is a very distinguished regiment; and Mr. Henry Bright mentioned as one of its distinctions, that Washington had formerly been an officer in it. I never heard of this.

February 27th.—We walked to Woodside in the pleasant forenoon, and thence crossed to Liverpool. On our way to Woodside, we saw the remains of the old Birkenhead Priory, built of the common red free-stone, much time-worn, with ivy creeping over it, and birds evidently at home in its old crevices. These ruins are pretty extensive, and seem to be the remains of a quadrangle. A handsome modern church, likewise of the same red freestone, has been built on part of the site occupied by the Priory; and the organ was sounding within, while we walked about the premises. On some of the ancient arches, there were grotesquely carved stone faces. The old walls have been sufficiently restored to make them secure, without destroying their venerable aspect. It is a very interesting spot; and so much the more so because a modern town, with its brick and stone houses, its flags and pavements, has sprung up about the ruins, which were new a thousand years ago. The station of the Chester railway is within a hundred yards. Formerly the monks of this Priory kept the only ferry that then existed on the Mersey.

At a dinner at Mr. Bramley Moore's a little while ago, we had a prairie-hen from the West of America. It was a very delicate bird, and a gentleman carved it most skilfully to a dozen guests, and had still a second slice to offer to them.

Aboard the ferry-boat yesterday, there was a labouring man eating oysters. He took them one by one from his pocket in interminable succession, opened them with his jack-knife, swallowed each one, threw the shell overboard, and then sought for another. Having concluded his meal, he took out a clay tobacco-pipe, filled it, lighted it with a match, and smoked it,—all this, while the other passengers were looking at him, and with a perfect coolness and independence, such as no one man can ever feel in America. Here a man does not seem to consider what other people will think of his conduct, but only whether it suits his own convenience to do so and so. It may be the better way.

A French military man, a veteran of all Napoleon's wars, is now living, with a false leg and arm, both movable by springs, false teeth, a false eye, a silver nose with a flesh-coloured covering, and a silver plate replacing part of the skull. He has the cross of the Legion of Honour.

March 13*th*.—On Saturday I went with Mr. B. to the Dingle, a pleasant domain on the banks of the Mersey, almost opposite to Rock Ferry. Walking home, we looked into Mr. Thom's Unitarian chapel, Mr. B.'s family's place of worship. There is a little graveyard connected with the chapel, a most uninviting and unpicturesque square of ground, perhaps thirty or forty yards across, in the midst of back fronts of city buildings. About half the space was occupied by flat tombstones, level with the ground, the remainder being yet vacant. Nevertheless, there were perhaps more names of men generally known to the world on these few tombstones than in any other churchyard in Liverpool, —Roscoe, Blanco White, and the Rev. William Enfield, whose name has a classical sound in my ears, because, when a little boy, I used to read his "Speaker" at school. In the vestry of the chapel there were many books, chiefly old theological works, in ancient print and binding, much mildewed and injured by the damp. The body of the chapel is neat, but plain, and, being not very large, has a kind of social and family aspect, as if the clergyman and his people must needs have intimate relations among themselves. The Unitarian sect in Liverpool have, as a body, great wealth and respectability.

Yesterday I walked with my wife and children to the brow of a hill overlooking Birkenhead and Tranmere, and commanding a fine view of the river, and Liverpool beyond. All round about new and neat residences for city people are springing up, with fine names,—Eldon Terrace, Rose Cottage, Belvoir Villa, &c., &c., with little patches of ornamented garden or lawn in front, and heaps of curious rock-work, with which the English are ridiculously fond of adorning their front yards. I rather think 'the middling classes —meaning shopkeepers, and other respectabilities of that level—are better lodged here than in America; and, what I did not expect, the houses are a great deal newer than in our new country. Of course, this can only be the case in places circumstanced like Liverpool and its suburbs. But, scattered among these modern villas, there are old stone cottages of the rudest structure, and doubtless hundreds of years old, with thatched roofs, into which the grass has rooted itself, and now looks verdant. These cottages are in themselves as ugly as possible, resembling a large kind of pigsty; but often, by dint of the verdure on their thatch, and the shrubbery clustering about them, they look picturesque.

The old-fashioned flowers in the gardens of New England—blue-bells, crocuses, primroses, foxglove, and many others—appear to be wild flowers here on English soil. There is something very touching and pretty in this fact, that the Puritans should have carried their field and hedge flowers, and nurtured them in their gardens, until, to us, they seem entirely the product of cultivation.

March 16th.—Yesterday, at the coroner's court, attending the inquest on a black sailor who died on board an American vessel, after her arrival at this port. The court-room is capable of accommodating perhaps fifty people, dingy, with a pyramidal skylight above, and a single window on one side, opening into a gloomy back court. A private room, also lighted with a pyramidal skylight, is behind the court-room, into which I was asked, and found the coroner, a grey-headed, grave, intelligent, broad, red-faced man, with an air of some authority, well mannered and dignified, but not exactly a gentleman,—dressed in a blue coat, with a black cravat, showing a shirt-collar above it. Considering how many and what a variety of cases of the ugliest death are constantly coming before him, he was much more cheerful than could be expected, and had a kind of formality and orderliness which I suppose balances the exceptionalities with which he has to deal. In the private room with him was likewise the surgeon, who professionally attends the court. We chatted about suicide and such matters—the surgeon, the coroner, and I—until the American case was ready, when we adjourned to the court-room, and the coroner began the examination. The American captain was a rude, uncouth Down-Easter, about thirty years old, and sat on a bench, doubled and bent into an indescribable attitude, out of which he occasionally straightened himself, all the time toying with a ruler, or some such article. The case was one of no interest; the man had been frost-bitten, and died from natural causes, so that no censure was deserved or passed upon the captain. The jury, who had been examining the body, were at first inclined to think that the man had not been frost-bitten, but that his feet had been immersed in boiling water; but, on explanation by the surgeon, readily yielded their opinion, and gave the verdict which the coroner put into their mouths, exculpating the captain from all blame. In fact, it is utterly impossible that a jury of chance individuals should not be entirely governed by the judgment of so experienced and weighty a man as the coroner. In the court-room were two or three police officers in uniform, and some other officials, a very few idle spectators, and a few witnesses waiting to be examined. And while the case was going forward, a poor-looking woman came in, and I heard her, in an undertone, telling an attendant of a death that had just occurred. The attendant received the communication in a very quiet and matter-of-course way, said that it should be attended to, and the woman retired.

The Diary of a Coroner would be a work likely to meet with large popular acceptance. A dark passage-way, only a few yards in extent, leads from the liveliest street in Liverpool to this coroner's court-room, where all the discussion is about murder and suicide. It seems, that, after a verdict of suicide, the corpse can only be buried at midnight, without religious rites.

"His lines are cast in pleasant places,"—applied to a successful angler.

A woman's chastity consists, like an onion, of a series of coats. You may strip off the outer ones without doing much mischief, perhaps none at all; but you keep taking off one after another, in expectation of coming to the inner nucleus, including the whole value of the matter. It proves, however, that there is no such nucleus, and that chastity is diffused through the whole series of coats, is lessened with the removal of each, and vanishes with the final one, which you supposed would introduce you to the hidden pearl.

March 23rd. — Mr. B. and I took a cab Saturday afternoon, and drove out of the city in the direction of Knowsley. On our way we saw many gentlemen's or rich people's places, some of them dignified with the title of Halls,—with lodges at their gates, and standing considerably removed from the road. The greater part of them were built of brick,—a material with which I have not been accustomed to associate ideas of grandeur; but it was much in use here in Lancashire in the Elizabethan age,—more, I think, than now. The suburban residences, however, are of much later date than Elizabeth's time. Among other places, Mr. B. called at The Hazels, the residence of Sir Thomas Birch, a kinsman of his. It is a large brick mansion, and has old trees and shrubbery about it, the latter very fine and verdant,—hazels, holly, rhododendron, &c. Mr. B. went in, and shortly afterwards Sir Thomas Birch came out,—a very frank and hospitable gentleman,—and pressed me to enter and take luncheon, which latter hospitality I declined.

. . . . .

His house is in very nice order. He had a good many pictures, and, amongst them, a small portrait of his mother, painted by Sir Thomas Lawrence, when a youth. It is unfinished, and when the painter was at the height of his fame, he was asked to finish it. But Lawrence, after looking at the picture, refused to retouch it, saying that there was a merit in this early sketch which he could no longer attain. It was really a very beautiful picture of a lovely woman.

Sir Thomas Birch proposed to go with us and get us admittance into Knowsley Park, where we could not possibly find entrance without his aid. So we went to the stables, where the old groom had already shown hospitality to our cabman, by giving his horse some provender, and himself some beer. There seemed to be a kindly and familiar sort of intercourse between the old servant and the Baronet,—each of them, I presume, looking on their connection as indissoluble.

The gate-warden of Knowsley Park was an old woman, who readily gave us admittance at Sir Thomas Birch's request. The family of the Earl of Derby is not now at the Park. . . . . It was a very bad time of year to see it; the trees just showing the earliest symptoms of vitality, while whole acres of ground were covered with large, dry, brown ferns,—which I suppose are very beautiful when green. Two or three hares scampered out of these ferns, and sat on their

hind legs looking about them, as we drove by. A sheet
of water had been drawn off, in order to deepen its
bed. The oaks did not seem to me so magnificent as
they should be in an ancient noble property like this.
A century does not accomplish so much for a tree in
this slow region as it does in ours. I think, however,
that they were more individual and picturesque, with
more character in their contorted trunks; therein somewhat resembling apple-trees. Our forest-trees have a
great sameness of character, like our people,—because
one and the other grow too closely.

In one part of the Park we came to a small tower,
for what purpose I know not, unless as an observatory;
and near it was a marble statue on a high pedestal.
The statue had been long exposed to the weather, and
was overgrown and ingrained with moss and lichens,
so that its classic beauty was in some sort gothicized.
A half-mile or so from this point, we saw the mansion
of Knowsley, in the midst of a very fine prospect, with
a tolerably high ridge of hills in the distance. The
house itself is exceedingly vast, a front and two wings,
with suites of rooms, I suppose, interminable. The
oldest part, Sir Thomas Birch told us, is a tower of
the time of Henry VII. Nevertheless, the effect is not
overwhelming, because the edifice looks low in proportion to its great extent over the ground; and besides,
a good deal of it is built of brick, with white window-
frames, so that, looking at separate parts, I might think
them American structures, without the smart addition
of green venetian blinds, so universal with us. Portions, however, were built of red freestone; and if I had
looked at it longer, no doubt I should have admired it
more. We merely drove round it from the rear to the

front. It stands in my memory rather like a college or a hospital, than as the ancestral residence of a great English noble.

We left the Park in another direction, and passed through a part of Lord Sefton's property, by a private road.

By-the-bye, we saw half a dozen policemen, in their blue coats and embroidered collars, after entering Knowsley Park; but the Earl's own servants would probably have supplied their place, had the family been at home. The mansion of Croxteth, the seat of Lord Sefton, stands near the public road, and, though large, looked of rather narrow compass after Knowsley.

. . . . .

The rooks were talking together very loquaciously in the high tops of the trees near Sir Thomas Birch's house, it being now their building-time. It was a very pleasant sound, the noise being comfortably softened by the remote height. Sir Thomas said that more than half a century ago the rooks used to inhabit another grove of lofty trees, close in front of the house; but being noisy, and not altogether cleanly in their habits, the ladies of the family grew weary of them, and wished to remove them. Accordingly, the colony was driven away, and made their present settlement in a grove behind the house. Ever since that time not a rook has built in the ancient grove; every year, however, one or another pair of young rooks attempt to build among the deserted tree-tops, but the old rooks tear the new nest to pieces as often as it is put together. Thus, either the memory of aged individual rooks or an authenticated tradition in their society has preserved the idea that the old grove is forbidden and inauspicious to them.

. . . . .

A son of General Arnold, named William Fitch Arnold, and born in 1794, now possesses the estate of Little Missenden Abbey, Bucks County, and is a magistrate for that county. He was formerly Captain of the 19th Lancers. He has now two sons and four daughters. The other three sons of General Arnold, all older than this one, and all military men, do not appear to have left children; but a daughter married to Colonel Phipps, of the Mulgrave family, has a son and two daughters. I question whether any of our true-hearted revolutionary heroes have left a more prosperous progeny than this arch-traitor. I should like to know their feelings with respect to their ancestor.

April 3rd.—I walked with J., two days ago, to Eastham, a village on the road to Chester, and five or six miles from Rock Ferry. On our way we passed through a village, in the centre of which was a small stone pillar, standing on a pedestal of several steps, on which children were sitting and playing. I take it to have been an old Catholic cross; at least, I know not what else it is. It seemed very ancient. Eastham is the finest old English village I have seen, with many antique houses, and with altogether a rural and picturesque aspect, unlike anything in America, and yet possessing a familiar look, as if it were something I had dreamed about. There were thatched stone cottages intermixed with houses of a better kind, and likewise a gateway and gravelled walk, that perhaps gave admittance to the Squire's mansion. It was not

merely one long, wide street, as in most New England
villages, but there were several crooked ways, gathering the whole settlement into a pretty small compass.
In the midst of it stood a venerable church of the common red freestone, with a most reverend air, considerably smaller than that of Bebbington, but more beautiful, and looking quite as old. There was ivy on its
spire and elsewhere. It looked very quiet and peaceful,
and as if it had received the people into its low
arched door every Sabbath for many centuries. There
were many tombstones about it, some level with the
ground, some raised on blocks of stone, on low pillars,
moss-grown and weather-worn; and probably these
were but the successors of other stones that had quite
crumbled away, or been buried by the accumulation
of dead men's dust above them. In the centre of the
churchyard stood an old yew-tree, with immense trunk,
which was all decayed within, so that it is a wonder
how the tree retains any life,—which, nevertheless, it
does. It was called "the old Yew of Eastham" six
hundred years ago!

After passing through the churchyard, we saw the
village inn on the other side. The doors were fastened,
but a girl peeped out of the window at us, and let us
in, ushering us into a very neat parlour. There was
a cheerful fire in the grate, a straw carpet on the floor,
a mahogany sideboard, and a mahogany table in the
middle of the room; and on the walls, the portraits of
mine host (no doubt) and of his wife and daughters,
—a very nice parlour, and looking like what I might
have found in a country tavern at home, only this was
an ancient house, and there is nothing at home like
the glimpse, from the window, of the church, and its

red, ivy-grown tower. I ordered some lunch, being waited on by the girl, who was very neat, intelligent, and comely, and more respectful than a New England maid. As we came out of the inn, some village urchins left their play, and ran to me begging, calling me "Master!" They turned at once from play to begging, and, as I gave them nothing, they turned to their play again.

This village is too far from Liverpool to have been much injured as yet by the novelty of cockney residences, which have grown up almost everywhere else, so far as I have visited. About a mile from it, however, is the landing-place of a steamer (which runs regularly, except in the winter months), where a large, new hotel is built. The grounds about it are extensive and well wooded. We got some biscuits at the hotel, and I gave the waiter (a splendid gentleman in black) four halfpence, being the surplus of a shilling. He bowed and thanked me very humbly. An American does not easily bring his mind to the small measure of English liberality to servants; if anything is to be given, we are ashamed not to give more, especially to clerical-looking persons, in black suits and white neckcloths.

. . . . . .

I stood on the Exchange at noon, to-day, to see the 88th Regiment, the Connaught Rangers, marching down to embark for the East. They were a body of young, healthy, and cheerful-looking men, and looked greatly better than the dirty crowd that thronged to gaze at them. The royal banner of England, quartering the lion, the leopard, and the harp, waved on the town-house, and looked gorgeous and venerable. Here and there a woman exchanged greetings with an individual soldier, as he marched along, and gentlemen shook hands with officers with whom they happened to be acquainted. Being a stranger in the land, it seemed as if I could see the future in the present better than if I had been an Englishman; so I questioned with myself how many of these ruddy-cheeked young fellows, marching so stoutly away, would ever tread English ground again. The populace did not evince any enthusiasm, yet there could not possibly be a war to which the country could assent more fully than to this. I somewhat doubt whether the English populace really feels a vital interest in the nation.

Some years ago, a piece of rude marble sculpture, representing St. George and the Dragon, was found over the fireplace of a cottage near Rock Ferry, on the road to Chester. It was plastered over with pipe-clay, and its existence was unknown to the cottagers until a lady noticed the projection and asked what it was. It was supposed to have originally adorned the walls of the Priory at Birkenhead. It measured fourteen and a half by nine inches, in which space were the heads of a king and queen, with uplifted hands, in prayer; their daughters also in prayer, and looking very grim; a lamb, the slain dragon, and St. George, proudly prancing on what looks like a donkey, brandishing a sword over his head.

The following is a legend inscribed on the inner margin of a curious old box:—

"From Birkenhead into Hilbree
A squirrel might leap from tree to tree."

I do not know where Hilbree is; but all round Birkenhead a squirrel would scarcely find a single tree to climb upon. All is pavement and brick buildings now.

Good Friday.—The English and Irish think it good to plant on this day, because it was the day when our Saviour's body was laid in the grave. Seeds, therefore, are certain to rise again.

At dinner the other day, Mrs. —— mentioned the origin of Franklin's adoption of the customary civil dress, when going to court as a diplomatist. It was simply that his tailor had disappointed him of his court suit, and he wore his plain one with great reluctance, because he had no other. Afterwards, gaining great success and praise by his mishap, he continued to wear it from policy.

The grandmother of Mrs. —— died fifty years ago, at the age of twenty-eight. She had great personal charms, and among them a head of beautiful chestnut hair. After her burial in a family tomb, the coffin of one of her children was laid on her own, so that the lid seems to have decayed, or been broken from this cause; at any rate, this was the case when the tomb was opened, about a year ago. The grandmother's coffin was then found to be filled with beautiful, glossy, living chestnut ringlets, into which her whole substance seems to have been transformed, for there was nothing else but these shining curls, the growth of half a century in the tomb. An old man, with a ringlet of his youthful mistress treasured on his heart, might be supposed to witness this wonderful thing.

Madam ———, who is now at my house, and very infirm, though not old, was once carried to the grave, and on the point of being buried. It was in Barbary, where her husband was Consul-General. He was greatly attached to her, and told the pall-bearers at the grave that he must see her once more. When her face was uncovered he thought he discerned signs of life, and felt a warmth. Finally she revived, and for many years afterwards supposed the funeral procession to have been a dream; she having been partially conscious throughout, and having felt the wind blowing on her, and lifting the shroud from her feet,—for I presume she was to be buried in oriental style, without a coffin. Long after, in London, when she was speaking of this dream, her husband told her the facts, and she fainted away. Whenever it is now mentioned, her face turns white. Mr. ———, her son, was born on ship-board, on the coast of Spain, and claims four nationalities,—those of Spain, England, Ireland, and the United States; his father being Irish, his mother a native of England, himself a naturalized citizen of the United States, and his father having registered his birth and baptism in a Catholic church of Gibraltar, which gives him Spanish privileges. He has hereditary claims to a Spanish countship. His infancy was spent in Barbary, and his lips first lisped in Arabic. There has been an unsettled and wandering character in his whole life.

The grandfather of Madam ———, who was a British officer, once horsewhipped Paul Jones—Jones being a poltroon. How singular it is that the personal courage of famous warriors should be so often called in question!

May 20th.—I went yesterday to a hospital to take

the oath of a mate to a protest. He had met with a
severe accident by a fall on shipboard. The hospital is
a large edifice of red freestone, with wide, airy passages, resounding with footsteps passing through them.
A porter was waiting in the vestibule. Mr. Wilding
and myself were shown to the parlour, in the first instance—a neat, plainly furnished room, with newspapers
and pamphlets lying on the table and sofas. Soon the
surgeon of the house came—a brisk, alacritous, civil,
cheerful young man—by whom we were shown to the
apartment where the mate was lying. As we went
through the principal passage, a man was borne along
in a chair, looking very pale, rather wild, and altogether as if he had just been through great tribulation,
and hardly knew as yet whereabouts he was. I noticed
that his left arm was but a stump, and seemed done
up in red baize—at all events it was of a scarlet hue.
The surgeon shook his right hand cheerily, and he was
carried on. This was a patient who had just had his
arm cut off. He had been a rough person apparently,
but now there was a kind of tenderness about him,
through pain and helplessness.

In the chamber where the mate lay, there were
seven beds, all of them occupied by persons who had
met with accidents. In the centre of the room was a
stationary pine table, about the length of a man, intended, I suppose, to stretch patients upon for necessary operations. The furniture of the beds was plain
and homely. I thought that the faces of the patients
all looked remarkably intelligent, though they were
evidently men of the lower classes. Suffering had
educated them morally and intellectually. They gazed
curiously at Mr. Wilding and me, but nobody said a

word. In the bed next to the mate lay a little boy with a broken thigh. The surgeon observed that children generally did well with accidents; and this boy certainly looked very bright and cheerful. There was nothing particularly interesting about the mate.

After finishing our business, the surgeon showed us into another room of the surgical ward, likewise devoted to cases of accident and injury. All the beds were occupied, and in two of them lay two American sailors who had recently been stabbed. They had been severely hurt, but were doing very well. The surgeon thought that it was a good arrangement to have several cases together, and that the patients kept up one another's spirits—being often merry together. Smiles and laughter may operate favourably enough from bed to bed; but dying groans, I should think, must be somewhat of a discouragement. Nevertheless, the previous habits and modes of life of such people as compose the more numerous class of patients in a hospital must be considered before deciding this matter. It is very possible that their misery likes such bed-fellows as it here finds.

As we were taking our leave, the surgeon asked us if we should not like to see the operating-room; and before we could reply he threw open a door, and behold, there was a roll of linen "garments rolled in blood," and a bloody fragment of a human arm! The surgeon glanced at me, and smiled kindly, but as if pitying my discomposure.

Gervase Elwes, son of Sir Gervase Elwes, Baronet, of Stoke, Suffolk, married Isabella, daughter of Sir Thomas Hervey, Knight, and sister of the first Earl of

Bristol. This Gervase died before his father, but left a son, Henry, who succeeded to the Baronetcy. Sir Henry died without issue, and was succeeded by his sister's son, John Maggott Twining, who assumed the name of Elwes. He was the famous miser, and must have had Hawthorne blood in him, through his grandfather, Gervase, whose mother was a Hawthorne. It was to this Gervase that my ancestor, William Hawthorne, devised some land in Massachusetts, "if he would come over, and enjoy it." My ancestor calls him his nephew.

June 12*th*.—Barry Cornwall, Mr. Procter, called on me a week or more ago, but I happened not to be in the office. Saturday last he called again, and as I had crossed to Rock Park he followed me thither. A plain, middle-sized, English-looking gentleman, elderly, with short white hair, and particularly quiet in his manners. He talks in a somewhat low tone without emphasis, scarcely distinct. . . . . His head has a good outline, and would look well in marble. I liked him very well. He talked unaffectedly, showing an author's regard to his reputation, and was evidently pleased to hear of his American celebrity. He said that in his younger days he was a scientific pugilist, and once took a journey to have a sparring encounter with the Game Chicken. Certainly, no one would have looked for a pugilist in this subdued old gentleman. He is now Commissioner of Lunacy, and makes periodical circuits through the country, attending to the business of his office. He is slightly deaf, and this may be the cause of his unaccented utterance—owing to his not being able to regulate his voice exactly by his own ear. . . . . He is a

good man, and much better expressed by his real name,
Procter, than by his poetical one, Barry Cornwall. . . . .
He took my hand in both of his at parting. . . . .

June 17*th.*—At eleven, at this season (and how
much longer I know not), there is still a twilight. If
we could only have such dry, deliciously warm even-
ings as we used to have in our own land, what enjoyment there might be in these interminable twilights!
But here we close the window-shutters, and make ourselves cosey by a coal fire.

All three of the children, and, I think, my wife and
myself, are going through the hooping-cough. The
east wind of this season and region is most horrible.
There have been no really warm days; for though the
sunshine is sometimes hot, there is never any diffused
heat throughout the air. On passing from the sunshine
into the shade, we immediately feel too cool.

June 20*th.*—The vagabond musicians about town
are very numerous. On board the steam ferry-boats,
I have heretofore spoken of them. They infest them
from May to November, for very little gain apparently.
A shilling a day per man must be the utmost of their
emolument. It is rather sad to see somewhat respectable old men engaged in this way, with two or three
younger associates. Their instruments look much the
worse for wear, and even my unmusical ear can distinguish more discord than harmony. They appear to
be a very quiet and harmless people. Sometimes there
is a woman playing on a fiddle, while her husband
blows a wind instrument. In the streets it is not unusual to find a band of half-a-dozen performers, who,

without any provocation or reason whatever, sound their brazen instruments till the houses re-echo. Sometimes one passes a man who stands whistling a tune most unweariably, though I never saw anybody give him anything. The ballad-singers are the strangest, from the total lack of any music in their cracked voices. Sometimes you see a space cleared in the street, and a foreigner playing, while a girl—weather-beaten, tanned, and wholly uncomely in face and shabby in attire—dances ballets. The common people look on, and never criticise or treat any of these poor devils unkindly or uncivilly; but I do not observe that they give them anything.

A crowd—or, at all events, a moderate-sized group—is much more easily drawn together here than with us. The people have a good deal of idle and momentary curiosity, and are always ready to stop when another person has stopped, so as to see what has attracted his attention. I hardly ever pause to look at a shop-window without being immediately incommoded by boys and men, who stop likewise, and would forthwith throng the pavement if I did not move on.

June 30th.—If it is not known how and when a man dies, it makes a ghost of him for many years thereafter, perhaps for centuries. King Arthur is an example; also the Emperor Frederic, and other famous men, who were thought to be alive ages after their disappearance. So with private individuals. I had an uncle John, who went a voyage to sea about the beginning of the war of 1812, and has never returned to this hour. But as long as his mother lived, as many as twenty years, she never gave up the hope of his return, and was constantly hearing stories of persons whose description answered to his. Some people actually affirmed that they had seen him in various parts of the world. Thus, so far as her belief was concerned, he still walked the earth. And even to this day I never see his name, which is no very uncommon one, without thinking that this may be the lost uncle.

Thus, too, the French Dauphin still exists, or a kind of ghost of him; the three Tells, too, in the cavern of Uri.

July 6th.—Mr. Cecil, the other day, was saying that England could produce as fine peaches as any other country. I asked what was the particular excellence of a peach, and he answered, "Its cooling and refreshing quality, like that of a melon!" Just think of this idea of the richest, most luscious, of all fruits! But the untravelled Englishman has no more idea of what fruit is than of what sunshine is; he thinks he has tasted the first and felt the last, but they are both alike watery. I heard a lady in Lord Street talking about the "broiling sun," when I was almost in a shiver. They keep up their animal heat by means of wine and ale, else they could not bear this climate.

July 19th.—A week ago I made a little tour in North Wales with Mr. Bright. We left Birkenhead by railway for Chester at two o'clock; thence for Bangor; thence by carriage over the Menai bridge to Beaumaris. At Beaumaris, a fine old castle—quite coming up to my idea of what an old castle should be. A grey, ivy-hung exterior wall, with large round towers at intervals; within this another wall, the place of the portcullis between; and again, within the second wall the castle itself, with a spacious green court-yard in front. The outer wall is so thick that a passage runs in it all round the castle, which covers a space of three acres. This passage gives access to a chapel, still very perfect, and to various apartments in the towers, —all exceedingly dismal, and giving very unpleasant impressions of the way in which the garrison of the castle lived. The main castle is entirely roofless, but the hall and other rooms are pointed out by the guide, and the whole is tapestried with abundant ivy, so that my impression is of grey walls, with here and there a vast green curtain; a carpet of green over the floors of halls and apartments; and festoons around all the outer battlement, with an uneven and rather perilous footpath running along the top. There is a fine vista through the castle itself, and the two gateways of the two encompassing walls. The passage within the wall is very rude, both underfoot and on each side, with various ascents and descents of rough steps,—sometimes so low that your head is in danger; and dark, except where a little light comes through a loophole or window in the thickness of the wall. In front of the castle a tennis-court was fitted up, by laying a smooth pavement on the ground, and casing the walls with tin or zinc, if I recollect aright. All this was open to the sky; and when we were there, some young men of the town were playing at the game. There are but very few of these tennis-courts in England; and this old castle was a very strange place for one.

The castle is the property of Sir Richard Bulkely, whose seat is in the vicinity, and who owns a great part of the island of Anglesea, on which Beaumaris lies. The hotel where we stopped was the Bulkely Arms, and Sir Richard has a kind of feudal influence in the town.

In the morning we walked along a delightful road, bordering on the Menai Straits, to Bangor Ferry. It was really a very pleasant road, overhung by a growth of young wood, exceedingly green and fresh. English trees are green all about their stems, owing to the creeping plants that overrun them. There were some flowers in the hedges, such as we cultivate in gardens. At the ferry, there was a whitewashed cottage; a woman or two, some children, and a fisherman-like personage, walking to and fro before the door. The scenery of the strait is very beautiful and picturesque, and directly opposite to us lay Bangor,—the strait being here almost a mile across. An American ship from Boston lay in the middle of it. The ferryboat was just putting off from the Bangor side, and, by the aid of a sail, soon neared the shore.

At Bangor we went to a handsome hotel, and hired a carriage and two horses for some Welsh place, the name of which I forget; neither can I remember a single name of the places through which we posted that day, nor could I spell them if I heard them pronounced, nor pronounce them if I saw them spelt. It was a circuit of about forty miles, bringing us to Conway at last. I remember a great slate quarry; and also that many of the cottages, in the first part of our drive, were built of blocks of slate. The mountains were very bold, thrusting themselves up abruptly in peaks, —not of the dumpling formation, which is somewhat too prevalent among the New England mountains. At one point we saw Snowdon, with its bifold summit. We also visited the smaller waterfall (this is a translation of an unpronounceable Welsh name), which is the largest in Wales. It was a very beautiful rapid, and the guidebook considers it equal in sublimity to Niagara. Likewise there were one or two lakes which the guidebook greatly admired, but which to me, who remembered a hundred sheets of blue water in New England, seemed nothing more than sullen and dreary puddles, with bare banks, and wholly destitute of beauty. I think they were nowhere more than a hundred yards across. But the hills were certainly very good, and, though generally bare of trees, their outlines thereby were rendered the stronger and more striking.

Many of the Welsh women, particularly the elder ones, wear black beaver hats, high-crowned, and almost precisely like men's. It makes them look ugly and witch-like. Welsh is still the prevalent language, and the only one spoken by a great many of the inhabitants. I have had Welsh people in my office, on official business, with whom I could not communicate except through an interpreter.

At some unutterable village we went into a little church, where we saw an old stone image of a warrior, lying on his back, with his hands clasped. It was the natural son (if I remember rightly) of David, Prince of Wales, and was doubtless the better part of a thousand years old. There was likewise a stone coffin of still greater age; some person of rank and renown had mouldered to dust within it, but it was now open and empty. Also, there were monumental brasses on the walls, engraved with portraits of a gentleman and lady in the costumes of Elizabeth's time. Also, on one of the pews, a brass record of some persons who slept in the vault beneath; so that, every Sunday, the survivors and descendants kneel and worship directly over their dead ancestors. In the churchyard, on a flat tombstone, there was the representation of a harp. I supposed that it must be the resting-place of a bard; but the inscription was in memory of a merchant, and a skilful manufacturer of harps.

This was a very delightful town. We saw a great many things which it is now too late to describe, the sharpness of the first impression being gone; but I think I can produce something of the sentiment of it hereafter.

We arrived at Conway late in the afternoon, to take the rail for Chester. I must see Conway, with its old grey wall and its unrivalled castle, again. It was better than Beaumaris, and I never saw anything more picturesque than the prospect from the castle wall towards the sea. We reached Chester at 10 P.M. The next morning, Mr. Bright left for Liverpool before I was awake. I visited the Cathedral, where the organ was sounding, sauntered through the Rows, bought some playthings for the children, and left for home soon after twelve.

Liverpool, August 8th.—Visiting the Zoological Gardens the other day with J., it occurred to me what a fantastic kind of life a person connected with them might be depicted as leading,—a child, for instance. The grounds are very extensive, and include arrangements for all kinds of exhibitions calculated to attract the idle people of a great city. In one enclosure is a bear, who climbs a pole to get cake and gingerbread from the spectators. Elsewhere, a circular building, with compartments for lions, wolves, and tigers. In another part of the garden is a colony of monkeys, the skeleton of an elephant, birds of all kinds. Swans and various rare water-fowl were swimming on a piece of water, which was green, by-the-bye, and when the fowls dived they stirred up black mud. A stork was parading along the margin, with melancholy strides of its long legs, and came slowly towards us, as if for companionship. In one apartment was an obstreperously noisy society of parrots and macaws, most gorgeous and diversified of hue. These different colonies of birds and beasts were scattered about in various parts of the grounds, so that you came upon them unexpectedly. Also, there were archery and shooting grounds, and a swing. A theatre, also, at which a rehearsal was going on,—we standing at one of the doors, and looking in towards the dusky stage where the company, in their ordinary dresses, were rehearsing something that had a good deal of dance and action in it. In the open air there was an arrangement of painted scenery representing a wide expanse of mountains, with a city at their feet, and before it the sea, with actual water, and large vessels upon it, the vessels having only the side that would be presented to the spectator. But the scenery was so good that at a first casual glance I almost mistook it for reality. There was a refreshment-room, with drinks and cakes and pastry, but, so far as I saw, no substantial victual. About in the centre of the garden there was an actual homely-looking, small dwelling-house, where perhaps the overlookers of the place live. Now this might be wrought, in an imaginative description, into a pleasant sort of a fool's paradise, where all sorts of unreal delights should cluster round some suitable personage; and it would relieve, in a very odd and effective way, the stern realities of life on the outside of the garden walls. I saw a little girl, simply dressed, who seemed to have her *habitat* within the grounds. There was also a daguerreotypist, with his wife and family, carrying on his business in a shanty, and perhaps having his home in its inner room. He seemed to be an honest, intelligent, pleasant young man, and his wife a pleasant woman; and I had J.'s daguerreotype taken for three shillings, in a little gilded frame. In the description of the garden, the velvet turf, of a charming verdure, and the shrubbery and shadowy walks and large trees, and the slopes and inequalities of ground, must not be forgotten. In one place there was a maze and labyrinth, where a person might wander a long while in the vain endeavour to get out, although all the time looking at the exterior garden, over the low hedges that border the walks of the maze. And this is like the inappreciable difficulties that often beset us in life.

I will see it again before long, and get some additional record of it.

August 10*th*.—We went to the Isle of Man a few weeks ago, where S. and the children spent a fortnight. I spent two Sundays with them.

I never saw anything prettier than the little church of Kirk Madden there. It stands in a perfect seclusion of shadowy trees,—a plain little church, that would not be at all remarkable in another situation, but is most picturesque in its solitude and bowery environ-

ment. The churchyard is quite full and overflowing
with graves, and extends down the gentle slope of a
hill, with a dark mass of shadow above it. Some of
the tombstones are flat on the ground, some erect, or
laid horizontally on low pillars or masonry. There
were no very old dates on any of these stones; for the
climate soon effaces inscriptions, and makes a stone of
fifty years look as old as one of five hundred,—unless
it be slate, or something harder than the usual red
freestone. There was an old Runic monument, however, near the centre of the churchyard, that had some
strange sculpture on it, and an inscription still legible
by persons learned in such matters. Against the tower
of the church, too, there is a circular stone, with carving on it, said to be of immemorial antiquity. There
is likewise a tall marble monument, as much as fifty
feet high, erected some years ago to the memory of
one of the Athol family by his brother-officers of a
local regiment of which he was colonel. At one of
the side entrances of the church, and forming the
threshold within the thickness of the wall, so that the
feet of all who enter must tread on it, is a flat tombstone of somebody who felt himself a sinner, no doubt,
and desired to be thus trampled upon. The stone is
much worn.

The structure is extremely plain inside and very
small. On the walls, over the pews, are several monumental sculptures,—a quite elaborate one to a Colonel
Murray, of the Coldstream Guards; his military profession being designated by banners and swords in
marble. Another was to a farmer.

On one side of the church tower there was a little
penthouse, or lean-to,—merely a stone roof, about three

or four feet high, and supported by a single pillar,—beneath which was once deposited the bier.

I have let too much time pass before attempting to record my impressions of the Isle of Man; but, as regards this church, no description can come up to its quiet beauty, its seclusion, and its every requisite for an English country church.

Last Sunday I went to Eastham, and, entering the churchyard, sat down on a tombstone under the yew-tree which has been known for centuries as the Great Tree of Eastham. Some of the village people were sitting on the graves near the door; and an old woman came towards me, and said, in a low, kindly, admonishing tone, that I must not let the sexton see me, because he would not allow any one to be there in sacrament-time. I inquired why she and her companions were there, and she said they were waiting for the sacrament. So I thanked her, gave her a sixpence, and departed. Close under the eaves I saw two upright stones, in memory of two old servants of the Stanley family,—one over ninety, and the other over eighty years of age.

August 12*th*.—J. and I went to Birkenhead Park yesterday. There is a large ornamental gateway to the Park, and the grounds within are neatly laid out, with borders of shrubbery. There is a sheet of water, with swans and other aquatic fowl, which swim about, and are fed with dainties by the visitors. Nothing can be more beautiful than a swan. It is the ideal of a goose,—a goose beautified and beatified. There were not a great many visitors, but some children were dancing on the green, and a few lover-like people straying about. I think the English behave better than the Americans at similar places.

There was a *camera-obscura*, very wretchedly indistinct. At the refreshment-room were ginger beer and British wines.

August 21*st.*—I was in the Crown Court on Saturday, sitting in the sheriff's seat. The judge was Baron ———, an old gentleman of sixty, with very large, long features. His wig helped him to look like some strange kind of animal,—very queer, but yet with a sagacious, and, on the whole, beneficent aspect. During the session some mischievous young barrister occupied himself with sketching the judge in pencil; and, being handed about, it found its way to me. It was very like and very laughable, but hardly caricatured. The judicial wig is an exceedingly odd affair; and as it covers both ears, it would seem intended to prevent his Lordship, and justice in his person, from hearing any of the case on either side, that thereby he may decide the better. It is like the old idea of blindfolding the statue of Justice.

It seems to me there is less formality, less distance between the judge, jury, witnesses, and bar, in the English courts than in our own. The judge takes a very active part in the trial, constantly asking a question of the witness on the stand, making remarks on the conduct of the trial, putting in his word on all occasions, and allowing his own sense of the matter in hand to be pretty plainly seen; so that, before the trial is over, and long before his own charge is delivered, he must have exercised a very powerful influence over the minds of the jury. All this is done, not without dignity, yet in a familiar kind of way. It is a sort of paternal supervision of the whole matter, quite unlike the cold awfulness of an American judge. But all this may be owing partly to the personal characteristics of Baron ———. It appeared to me, however, that, from the closer relations of all parties, truth was likely to be arrived at and justice to be done. As an innocent man, I should not be afraid to be tried by Baron ———.

EATON HALL.

August 24th.—I went to Eaton Hall yesterday with my wife and Mr. G. P. Bradford, *viâ* Chester. On our way, at the latter place, we visited St. John's church. It is built of the same red freestone as the Cathedral, and looked exceedingly antique and venerable; this kind of stone, from its softness, and its liability to be acted upon by the weather, being liable to an early decay. Nevertheless, I believe the church was built above a thousand years ago,—some parts of it, at least,—and the surface of the tower and walls is worn away and hollowed in shallow sweeps by the hand of Time. There were broken niches in several places, where statues had formerly stood. All, except two or three, had fallen or crumbled away, and those which remained were much damaged. The face and details of the figure were almost obliterated. There were many gravestones round the church, but none of them of any antiquity. Probably, as the names become indistinguishable on the older stones, the graves are dug over again, and filled with new occupants and covered with new stones, or perhaps with the old ones newly inscribed.

Closely connected with the church was the clergyman's house, a comfortable-looking residence; and likewise in the churchyard, with tombstones all about it, even almost at the threshold, so that the doorstep itself might have been a tombstone, was another house, of respectable size and aspect. We surmised that this might be the sexton's dwelling, but it proved not to be so; and a woman answering our knock, directed us to the place where he might be found. So Mr. Bradford and I went in search of him, leaving S. seated on a tombstone. The sexton was a jolly-looking, ruddy-faced man, a mechanic of some sort, apparently, and he followed us to the churchyard with much alacrity. We found S. standing at a gateway, which opened into the most ancient, and now quite ruinous, part of the church, the present edifice covering much less ground than it did some centuries ago. We went through this gateway, and found ourselves in an enclosure of venerable walls, open to the sky, with old Norman arches standing about, beneath the loftiest of which the sexton told us the high altar used to stand. Of course there were weeds and ivy growing in the crevices, but not so abundantly as I have seen them elsewhere. The sexton pointed out a piece of a statue that had once stood in one of the niches, and which he himself, I think, had dug up from several feet below the earth; also, in a niche of the walls, high above our heads, he showed us an ancient wooden coffin, hewn out of a solid log of oak, the hollow being made rudely in the shape of a human figure. This, too, had been dug up, and nobody knew how old it was. While we looked at all this solemn old trumpery, the curate, quite a young man, stood at the back door of his house, elevated considerably above the ruins, with his young wife (I presume) and a friend or two, chattering cheerfully among themselves. It was pleasant to see them there. After examining the ruins, we went inside of the church, and found it a dim and dusky old place, quite paved over with tombstones, not an inch of space being left in the aisles or near the altar, or in any nook or corner, uncovered by a tombstone. There were also mural monuments and escutcheons, and close against the wall lay the mutilated statue of a Crusader, with his legs crossed, in the style which one has so often read about. The old fellow seemed to have been represented in chain armour; but he had been more battered and bruised since death than even during his pugnacious life, and his nose was almost knocked away. This figure had been dug up many years ago, and nobody knows whom it was meant to commemorate.

The nave of the church is supported by two rows of Saxon pillars, not very lofty, but six feet six inches (so the sexton says) in diameter. They are covered with plaster, which was laid on ages ago, and is now so hard and smooth that I took the pillars to be really composed of solid shafts of grey stone. But, at one end of the church, the plaster had been removed from two of the pillars, in order to discover whether they were still sound enough to support the building; and they proved to be made of blocks of red freestone, just as sound as when it came from the quarry; for though this stone soon crumbles in the open air, it is as good as indestructible when sheltered from the weather. It looked very strange to see the fresh hue of these two pillars amidst the dingy antiquity of the rest of the structure.

The body of the church is covered with pews, the wooden enclosures of which seemed of antique fashion. There were also modern stoves; but the sexton said it was very cold there in spite of the stoves. It had, I must say, a disagreeable odour pervading it, in which the dead people of long ago had doubtless some share, —a musty odour, by no means amounting to a stench, but unpleasant, and, I should think, unwholesome. Old wood-work, and old stones, and antiquity of all kinds, moral and physical, go to make up this smell. I observed it in the Cathedral, and Chester generally has it, especially under the Rows. After all, the necessary damp and lack of sunshine, in such a shadowy old church as this, have probably more to do with it than the dead people have; although I did think the odour was particularly strong over some of the tombstones. Not having shillings to give the sexton, we were forced to give him half-a-crown.

The church of St. John is outside of the city walls. Entering the East gate, we walked awhile under the Rows, bought our tickets for Eaton Hall and its gardens, and likewise some playthings for the children; for this old city of Chester seems to me to possess an unusual number of toy-shops. Finally we took a cab, and drove to the Hall, about four miles distant, nearly the whole of the way lying through the wooded Park. There are many sorts of trees, making up a wilderness, which looked not unlike the woods of our own Concord, only less wild. The English oak is not a handsome tree, being short and sturdy, with a round, thick mass of foliage, lying all within its own bounds. It was a showery day. Had there been any sunshine, there might doubtless have been many beautiful effects of light and shadow in these woods. We saw one or two herds of deer, quietly feeding, a hundred yards or so distant. They appeared to be somewhat wilder than cattle, but, I think, not much wilder than sheep. Their ancestors have probably been in a half-domesticated state, receiving food at the hands of man, in winter, for centuries. There is a kind of poetry in this, quite as much as if they were really wild deer, such as their forefathers were, when Hugh Lupus used to hunt them.

Our miserable cab drew up at the steps of Eaton Hall, and, ascending under the portico, the door swung silently open, and we were received very civilly by two old men,—one, a tall footman in livery; the other, of higher grade, in plain clothes. The entrance-hall is very spacious, and the floor is tesselated or somehow inlaid with marble. There was statuary in marble on the floor, and in niches stood several figures in antique armour, of various dates; some with lances, and others with battle-axes and swords. There was a two-handed sword, as much as six feet long; but not nearly so ponderous as I have supposed this kind of weapon to be, from reading of it. I could easily have brandished it.

I don't think I am a good sight-seer; at least, I soon get satisfied with looking at set sights, and wish to go on to the next.

The plainly dressed old man now led us into a long corridor, which goes, I think, the whole length of the house, about five hundred feet, arched all the way, and lengthened interminably by a looking-glass at the end, in which I saw our own party approaching like a party of strangers. But I have so often seen this effect produced in dry-goods stores and elsewhere, that I was not much impressed. There were family portraits and other pictures, and likewise pieces of statuary, along this arched corridor; and it communicated with a chapel with a scriptural altar-piece, copied from Rubens, and a picture of St. Michael and the Dragon, and two, or perhaps three, richly painted windows. Everything here is entirely new and fresh, this part having been repaired, and never yet inhabited by the family. This bran-newness makes it much less effective than if it had been lived in; and I felt pretty much as if I were strolling through any other renewed house. After all, the utmost force of man can do positively very little towards making grand things or beautiful things. The imagination can do so much more, merely on shutting one's eyes, that the actual effect seems meagre; so that a new house, unassociated with the past, is exceedingly unsatisfactory, especially when you have heard that the wealth and skill of man has here done its best. Besides, the rooms, as we saw them, did not look by any means their best, the carpets not being down, and the furniture being covered with protective envelopes. However, rooms cannot be seen to advantage by daylight; it being altogether essential to the effect, that they should be illuminated by artificial light, which takes them somewhat out of the region of bare reality. Nevertheless, there was undoubtedly great splendour,—for the details of which I refer to the guide-book. Among the family portraits, there was one of a lady famous for her beautiful hand; and she was holding it up to notice in the funniest way,—and very beautiful it certainly was. The private apartments of the family were not shown us. I should think it impossible for the owner of this house to imbue

it with his personality to such a degree as to feel it to
be his home. It must be like a small lobster in a shell
much too large for him.

After seeing what was to be seen of the rooms, we
visited the gardens, in which are noble conservatories
and hot-houses, containing all manner of rare and
beautiful flowers, and tropical fruits. I noticed some
large pines, looking as if they were really made of gold.
The gardener (under-gardener I suppose he was) who
showed this part of the spectacle was very intelligent
as well as kindly, and seemed to take an interest in his
business. He gave S. a purple everlasting flower, which
will endure a great many years, as a memento of our
visit to Eaton Hall. Finally, we took a view of the
front of the edifice, which is very fine, and much more
satisfactory than the interior, and returned to Chester.

We strolled about under the unsavoury Rows, sometimes scudding from side to side of the street, through
the shower; took lunch in a confectioner's shop, and
drove to the railway station in time for the three o'clock
train. It looked picturesque to see two little girls, hand
in hand, racing along the ancient passages of the Rows;
but Chester has a very evil smell.

At the railroad station, S. saw a small edition of
"Twice-Told Tales," forming a volume of the Cottage
Library; and, opening it, there was the queerest imaginable portrait of myself,—so very queer that we could
not but buy it. The shilling edition of "The Scarlet
Letter" and "Seven Gables" is at all the book-stalls
and shop-windows; but so is "The Lamplighter," and
still more trashy books.

August 26*th*.—All past affairs, all home conclusions,

all people whom I have known in America and meet again here, are strangely compelled to undergo a new trial. It is not that they suffer by comparison with circumstances of English life and forms of English manhood or womanhood; but, being free from my old surroundings, and the inevitable prejudices of home, I decide upon them absolutely.

I think I neglected to record that I saw Miss Martineau a few weeks since. She is a large, robust, elderly woman, and plainly dressed; but withal she has so kind, cheerful, and intelligent a face, that she is pleasanter to look at than most beauties. Her hair is of a decided grey, and she does not shrink from calling herself old. She is the most continual talker I ever heard; it is really like the babbling of a brook, and very lively and sensible too; and all the while she talks, she moves the bowl of her ear-trumpet from one auditor to another, so that it becomes quite an organ of intelligence and sympathy between her and yourself. The ear-trumpet seems a sensible part of her, like the antennæ of some insects. If you have any little remark to make, you drop it in; and she helps you to make remarks by this delicate little appeal of the trumpet, as she slightly directs it towards you; and if you have nothing to say, the appeal is not strong enough to embarrass you. All her talk was about herself and her affairs; but it did not seem like egotism, because it was so cheerful and free from morbidness. And this woman is said to be Atheistical! I will not think so, were it only for her sake. What! only a few weeds to spring out of her mortality, instead of her intellect and sympathies flowering and fruiting for ever!

* * * * *

September 13*th.*—My family went to Rhyl last Thursday, and on Saturday I joined them there, in company with O'Sullivan, who arrived in the *Bahama* from Lisbon that morning. We went by way of Chester, and found S. waiting for us at the Rhyl station. Rhyl is a most uninteresting place—a collection of new lodging-houses and hotels, on a long sand-beach, which the tide leaves bare almost to the horizon. The sand is by no means a marble pavement, but sinks under the foot, and makes very heavy walking; but there is a promenade in front of the principal range of houses, looking on the sea, whereon we have rather better footing. Almost all the houses were full, and S. had taken a parlour and two bed-rooms, and is living after the English fashion, providing her own table, lights, fuel, and everything. It is very awkward to our American notions; but there is an independence about it, which I think must make it agreeable on better acquaintance. But the place is certainly destitute of attraction, and life seems to pass very heavily. The English do not appear to have a turn for amusing themselves.

Sunday was a bright and hot day, and in the forenoon I set out on a walk, not well knowing whither, over a very dusty road, with not a particle of shade along its dead level. The Welsh mountains were before me, at the distance of three or four miles—long ridgy hills, descending pretty abruptly upon the plain; on either side of the road, here and there, an old white-washed, thatched stone cottage, or a stone farm-house, with an aspect of some antiquity. I never suffered so much before, on this side of the water, from heat and dust, and should probably have turned back had I not espied the round towers and walls of an old castle at some distance before me. Having looked at a guide-book, previously to setting out, I knew that this must be Rhyddlan Castle, about three miles from Rhyl; so I plodded on, and by-and-by entered an antiquated village, on one side of which the castle stood. This Welsh village is very much like the English villages, with narrow streets and mean houses or cottages, built in blocks, and here and there a larger house standing alone; everything far more compact than in our rural villages, and with no grassy street-margin nor trees; aged and dirty also, with dirty children staring at the passenger, and an undue supply of mean inns; most, or many of the men in breeches, and some of the women, especially the elder ones, in black beaver hats. The streets were paved with round pebbles, and looked squalid and ugly.

The children and grown people stared lazily at me as I passed, but showed no such alert and vivacious curiosity as a community of Yankees would have done. I turned up a street that led me to the castle, which looked very picturesque close at hand—more so than at a distance, because the towers and walls have not a sufficiently broken outline against the sky. There are several round towers at the angles of the wall very large in their circles, built of grey stone, crumbling, ivy-grown, everything that one thinks of in an old ruin. I could not get into the inner space of the castle without climbing over a fence, or clambering down into the moat; so I contented myself with walking round it, and viewing it from the outside. Through the gateway I saw a cow feeding on the green grass in the inner court of the castle. In one of the walls there was a large triangular gap, where perhaps the assailants had made a breach. Of course, there were weeds on the ruinous top of the towers, and along the summit of the wall. This was the first castle built by Edward I. in Wales, and he resided here during the erection of Conway Castle, and here Queen Eleanor gave birth to a princess. Some few years since a meeting of Welsh bards was held within it.

After viewing it awhile, and listening to the babble of some children who lay on the grass near by, I resumed my walk, and meeting a Welshman in the village street, I asked him my nearest way back to Rhyl. "Dim Sassonach," said he, after a pause. How odd that an hour or two on the railway should have brought me amongst a people speak no English! Just below the castle, there is an arched stone bridge over the river Clwyd, and the best view of the edifice is from hence. It stands on a gentle eminence, commanding the passage of the river, and two twin round towers rise close beside one another, whence, I suppose, archers have often drawn their bows against the wild Welshmen, on the river-banks. Behind was the line of mountains; and this was the point of defence between the hill country and the lowlands. On the bridge stood a good many idle Welshmen, leaning over the parapet, and looking at some small vessels that had come up the river from the sea. There was the frame of a new vessel on the stocks near by.

As I returned, on my way home, I again inquired my way of a man in breeches, who, I found, could speak English very well. He was kind, and took pains to direct me, giving me the choice of three ways, viz., the one by which I came, another across the fields, and a third by the embankment along the riverside. I chose the latter, and so followed the course of the Clwyd, which is very ugly, with a tidal flow and wide marshy banks. On its farther side was Rhyddlan marsh, where a battle was fought between the Welsh and Saxons a thousand years ago. I have forgotten to mention that the castle and its vicinity was the scene of the famous battle of the fiddlers, between De Blandeville, Earl of Chester, and the Welsh, about the time of the Conqueror.

CONWAY CASTLE.

September 13*th*.—On Monday we went with O'Sullivan to Conway by rail. Certainly this must be the most perfect specimen of a ruinous old castle in the whole world; it quite fills up one's idea. We first walked round the exterior of the wall, at the base of which are hovels, with dirty children playing about them, and pigs rambling along, and squalid women visible in the doorways; but all these things melt into the picturesqueness of the scene, and do not harm it. The whole town of Conway is built in what was once the castle yard, and the whole circuit of the wall is still standing in a delightful state of decay. At the angles, and at regular intervals, there are round towers, having half their circle on the outside of the walls, and half within. Most of these towers have a great crack pervading them irregularly from top to bottom; the ivy hangs upon them,—the weeds grow on the tops. Gateways, three or four of them, open through the walls, and streets proceed from them into the town. At some points, very old cottages or small houses are close against the sides, and, old as they are, they must have been built after the whole structure was a ruin. In one place I saw the sign of an ale-house painted on the grey stones of one of the old round towers. As we entered one of the gates, after making the entire circuit, we saw an omnibus coming down the street towards us, with its horn sounding. Llandudno was its place of destination; and, knowing no more about it than that it was four miles off, we took our seats. Llandudno is a watering village at the base of the Great Orme's Head, at the mouth of the Conway River. In this omnibus there were two pleasant-looking girls, who talked Welsh together—a guttural, childish kind of a babble. Afterwards we got into conversation with them, and found them very agreeable. One of them was reading Tupper's "Proverbial Philosophy." On reaching Llandudno, S. waited at the hotel, while O'Sullivan, U., and I ascended the Great Orme's Head. There are copper-mines here, and we heard of a large cave, with stalactites, but did not go so far as that. We found the old shaft of a mine, however, and threw stones down it, and counted twenty before we heard them strike the bottom. At the base of the Head, on the side opposite the village, we saw a small church with a broken roof, and horizontal gravestones of slate within the stone enclosure around it. The view from the hill was most beautiful—a blue summer sea, with the distant trail of smoke from a steamer, and many snowy sails; in another direction the mountains, near and distant, some of them with clouds below their peaks.

We went to one of the mines which are still worked, and boys came running to meet us with specimens of the copper ore for sale. The miners were not now hoisting ore from the shaft, but were washing and selecting the valuable fragments from great heaps of crumbled stone and earth. All about this spot there are shafts and well-holes, looking fearfully deep and black, and without the slightest protection, so that we might just as easily have walked into them as not. Having examined these matters sufficiently, we descended the hill towards the village, meeting parties of visitors mounted on donkeys, which is a much more sensible way of ascending in a hot day than to walk. On the sides and summit of the hill we found yellow gorse,—heath of two colours, I think, and very beautiful,—and here and there a harebell. Owing to the long-continued dry weather, the grass was getting withered and brown, though not so much so as on American hill-pastures at this season. Returning to the village, we all went into a confectioner's shop, and made a good luncheon. The two prettiest young ladies whom I have seen in England came into the shop and ate cakes while we were there. They appeared to be living together in a lodging-house, and ordered some of their housekeeping articles from the confectioner. Next we went into the village bazaar,—a sort of tent or open shop, full of knickknacks and gewgaws, and bought some playthings for the children. At half-past one we took our seats in the omnibus, to return to Conway.

We had as yet only seen the castle wall and the exterior of the castle; now we were to see the inside. Right at the foot of it an old woman has her stand for the sale of lithographic views of Conway and other places; but these views are ridiculously inadequate, so that we did not buy any of them. The admittance into the castle is by a wooden door of modern construction, and the present seneschal is, I believe, the sexton of a church. He remembered me as having been there a month or two ago; and probably, considering that I was already initiated, or else because he had many other visitors, he left us to wander about the castle at will. It is altogether impossible to describe Conway Castle. Nothing ever can have been so perfect in its own style, and for its own purposes, when it was first built; and now nothing else can be so perfect as a picture of ivy-grown, peaceful ruin. The banqueting-hall, all open to the sky and with thick curtains of ivy tapestrying the walls, and grass and weeds growing on the arches that overpass it, is indescribably beautiful. The hearthstones of the great old fireplaces, all about the castle, seem to be favourite spots for weeds to grow. There are eight large round towers, and out of four of them, I think, rise smaller towers, ascending to a much greater height, and once containing winding staircases, all of which are now broken, and inaccessible from below, though, in at least one of the towers, the stairs seemed perfect, high aloft. It must have been the rudest violence that broke down these stairs; for each step was a thick and heavy slab of stone, built into the wall of the tower. There is no such thing as a roof in any part: towers, hall, kitchen, all are open to the sky. One round tower, directly overhanging the railway, is so shattered by the falling away of the lower part, that you can look quite up into it and through it, while sitting in the cars; and yet it has stood thus, without falling into complete ruin, for more than two hundred years. I think that it was in this tower that we found the castle oven, an immense cavern, big enough to bake bread for an army. The railway passes exactly at the base of the high rock on which this part of the castle is situated, and goes into the town through a great arch that has been opened in the castle wall. The tubular bridge across the Conway has been built in a style that accords with the old architecture, and I observed that one little sprig of ivy had rooted itself in the new structure.

There are numberless intricate passages in the thickness of the castle walls, forming communications between tower and tower,—damp, chill passages, with rough stone on either hand, darksome, and very likely leading to dark pitfalls. The thickness of the walls is amazing; and the people of those days must have been content with very scanty light, so small were the apertures,—sometimes merely slits and loopholes, glimmering through many feet of thickness of stone. One of the towers was said to have been the residence of Queen Eleanor; and this was better lighted than the others, containing an oriel window, looking out of a little oratory as it seemed to be, with groined arches and traces of ornamental sculpture, so that we could dress up some imperfect image of a queenly chamber, though the tower was roofless and floorless. There was another pleasant little windowed nook, close beside the oratory, where the queen might have sat sewing or looking down the river Conway at the picturesque headlands towards the sea. We imagined her stately figure in antique robes, standing beneath the groined arches of the oratory. There seem to have been three chambers, one above another, in these towers, and the one in which was the embowed window was the middle one. I suppose the diameter of each of these circular rooms could not have been more than twenty feet on the inside. All traces of wood-work and iron-work are quite gone from the whole castle. These are said to have

been taken away by Lord Conway in the reign of
Charles II. There is a grassy space under the windows
of Queen Eleanor's tower,—a sort of outwork of the
castle, where probably, when no enemy was near, the
queen used to take the open air in summer afternoons
like this. Here we sat down on the grass of the ruined
wall, and agreed that nothing in the world could be so
beautiful and picturesque as Conway Castle, and that
never could there have been so fit a time to see it as
this sunny, quiet, lovely afternoon. Sunshine adapts
itself to the character of a ruin in a wonderful way; it
does not "flout the ruins grey," as Scott says, but
sympathizes with their decay, and saddens itself for
their sake. It beautifies the ivy too.

We saw, at the corner of this grass plot around
Queen Eleanor's tower, a real *trunk* of a tree of ivy,
with so stalwart a stem, and such a vigorous grasp of
its strong branches, that it would be a very efficient
support to the wall, were it otherwise inclined to fall.
Oh that we could have ivy in America! What is there
to beautify us when our time of ruin comes?

Before departing, we made the entire circuit of the
castle on its walls, and O'Sullivan and I climbed by
a ladder to the top of one of the towers. While there,
we looked down into the street beneath, and saw a
photographist preparing to take a view of the castle,
and calling out to some little girl in some niche or
on some pinnacle of the walls to stand still that he
might catch her figure and face. I think it added to
the impressiveness of the old castle, to see the streets
and the kitchen gardens and the homely dwellings
that had grown up within the precincts of this feudal
fortress, and the people of to-day following their little

businesses about it. This does not destroy the charm; but tourists and idle visitors do impair it. The earnest life of to-day, however, petty and homely as it may be, has a right to its place alongside of what is left of the life of other days; and if it be vulgar itself, it does not vulgarize the scene. But tourists do vulgarize it; and I suppose we did so, just like others.

We took the train back to Rhyl, where we arrived at about four o'clock, and, having dined, we again took the rail for Chester, and thence to Rock Park (that is, O'Sullivan and I), and reached home at about eleven o'clock.

Yesterday, September 13th, I began to wear a watch from Bennett's, 65, Cheapside, London. W. C. Bennett warrants it as the best watch which they can produce. If it prove as good and as durable as he prophecies, J. will find it a perfect time-keeper long after his father has done with Time. If I had not thought of his wearing it hereafter, I should have been content with a much inferior one. No. 39,620.

September 20th.—I went back to Rhyl last Friday in the steamer. We arrived at the landing-place at nearly four o'clock, having started at twelve, and I walked thence to our lodgings, 18, West Parade. The children and their mother were all gone out, and I sat some time in our parlour before anybody came. The next morning I made an excursion in the omnibus as far as Ruthin, passing through Rhyddlan, St. Asaph, Denbigh, and reaching Ruthin at one o'clock. All these are very ancient places. St. Asaph has a cathedral which is not quite worthy of that name, but is a very large and stately church in excellent repair. Its square battlemented tower has a very fine appearance, crowning the clump of village houses on the hill-top, as you approach from Rhyddlan. The ascent of the hill is very steep; so it is at Denbigh and at Ruthin,—the steepest streets, indeed, that I ever climbed. Denbigh is a place of still more antique aspect than St. Asaph; it looks, I think, even older than Chester, with its gabled houses, many of their windows opening on hinges, and their fronts resting on pillars, with an open porch beneath. The castle makes an admirably ruinous figure on the hill, higher than the village. I had come hither for the purpose of inspecting it, but as it began to rain just then, I concluded to get into the omnibus and go to Ruthin. There was another steep ascent from the commencement of the long street of Ruthin, till I reached the market-place, which is of nearly triangular shape, and an exceedingly old-looking place. Houses of stone or plastered brick; one or two with timber frames; the roofs of an uneven line, and bulging out or sinking in; the slates moss-grown. Some of them have two peaks and even three in a row, fronting on the streets, and there is a stone market-house with a table of regulations. In this market-place there is said to be a stone on which King Arthur beheaded one of his enemies; but this I did not see. All these villages were very lively, as the omnibus drove in; and I rather imagine it was market-day in each of them, —there being quite a bustle of Welsh people. The old women came round the omnibus courtesying and intimating their willingness to receive alms,—witch-like women, such as one sees in pictures or reads of in romances, and very unlike anything feminine in America. Their style of dress cannot have changed

for centuries. It was quite unexpected to me to hear
Welsh so universally and familiarly spoken. Everybody spoke it. The omnibus-driver could speak but
imperfect English; there was a jabber of Welsh all
through the streets and market-places; and it flowed
out with a freedom quite different from the way in
which they expressed themselves in English. I had
had an idea that Welsh was spoken rather as a freak
and in fun than as a native language; it was so strange
to find another language the people's actual and earnest
medium of thought within so short a distance of England. But English is scarcely more known to the body
of the Welsh people than to the peasantry of France.
Moreover, they sometimes pretend to ignorance, when
they might speak it fairly enough.

I took luncheon at the hotel where the omnibus
stopped, and then went to search out the castle. It
appears to have been once extensive, but the remains
of it are now very few, except a part of the external
wall. Whatever other portion may still exist has been
built into a modern castellated mansion, which has
risen within the wide circuit of the fortress,—a handsome and spacious edifice of red freestone, with a high
tower, on which a flag was flying. The grounds were
well laid out in walks, and really I think the site of
the castle could not have been turned to better account.
I am getting tired of antiquity. It is certainly less
interesting in the long run than novelty; and so I was
well content with the fresh, warm, red hue of the
modern house, and the unworn outline of its walls,
and its cheerful, large windows; and was willing that
the old ivy-grown ruins should exist now only to contrast with the modernisms. These ancient walls, by-

the-bye, are of immense thickness. There is a passage through the interior of a portion of them, the width of this interior passage to the outer one being fifteen feet on one side, and I know not how much on the other.

It continued showery all day; and the omnibus was crowded. I had chosen the outside from Rhyl to Denbigh, but all the rest of the journey imprisoned myself within. On our way home an old lady got into the omnibus,—a lady of tremendous rotundity; and as she tumbled from the door to the farthest part of the carriage, she kept advising all the rest of the passengers to get out. "I don't think there will be much rain, gentlemen," quoth she; "you will be much more comfortable on the outside." As none of us complied, she glanced along the seats. "What! are you all Sass'nach?" she inquired. As we drove along, she talked Welsh with great fluency to one of the passengers, a young woman with a baby, and to as many others as could understand her. It has a strange, wild sound, like a language half blown away by the wind. The lady's English was very good; but she probably prided herself on her proficiency in Welsh. My excursion to-day had been along the valley of the Clwyd, a very rich and fertile tract of country.

The next day we all took a long walk on the beach, picking up shells.

On Monday we took an open carriage and drove to Rhyddlan; whence we sent back the carriage, meaning to walk home along the embankment of the river Clwyd, after inspecting the castle. The fortress is very ruinous, having been dismantled by the Parliamentarians. There are great gaps,—two, at least, in the walls that connect the round towers, of which there

were six, one on each side of a gateway in front, and
the same at a gateway towards the river, where there
is a steep descent to a wall and square tower, at the
water-side. Great pains and a great deal of gunpowder
must have been used in converting this castle into a
ruin. There were one or two fragments lying where
they had fallen more than two hundred years ago,
which, though merely a conglomeration of small stones
and mortar, were just as hard as if they had been
solid masses of granite. The substantial thickness of
the walls is composed of these agglomerated small
stones and mortar, the casing being hewn blocks of
red freestone. This is much worn away by the weather,
wherever it has been exposed to the air; but, under
shelter, it looks as if it might have been hewn only a
year or two ago. Each of the round towers had
formerly a small staircase turret rising beside and
ascending above it, in which a warder might be posted,
but they have all been so battered and shattered that
it is impossible for an uninstructed observer to make
out a satisfactory plan of them. The interior of each
tower was a small room, not more than twelve or fifteen
feet across; and of these there seem to have been three
stories, with loopholes for archery, and not much other
light than what came through them. Then there are
various passages and nooks and corners and square
recesses in the stone, some of which must have been
intended for dungeons, and the ugliest and gloomiest
dungeons imaginable, for they could not have had any
light or air. There is not the least splinter of wood-
work remaining in any part of the castle,—nothing but
bare stone, and a little plaster in one or two places on
the wall. In the front gateway we looked at the groove

on each side, in which the portcullis used to rise and fall; and in each of the contiguous round towers there was a loophole, whence an enemy on the outer side of the portcullis might be shot through with an arrow.

The inner court-yard is a parallelogram, nearly a square, and is about forty-five of my paces across. It is entirely grass-grown, and vacant, except for two or three trees that have been recently set out, and which are surrounded with palings to keep away the cows that pasture in and about the place. No window looks from the walls or towers into this court-yard; nor are there any trace of buildings having stood within the enclosure, unless it be what looks something like the flue of a chimney within one of the walls. I should suppose, however, that there must have been, when the castle was in its perfect state, a hall, a kitchen, and other commodious apartments and offices for the king and his train, such as there were at Conway and Beaumaris. But if so, all fragments have been carried away, and all hollows of the old foundations scrupulously filled up. The round towers could not have comprised all the accommodation of the castle. There is nothing more striking in these ruins than to look upward from the crumbling base, and see flights of stairs, still comparatively perfect, by which you might securely ascend to the upper heights of the tower, although all traces of a staircase have disappeared below, and the upper portion cannot be attained. On three sides of the fortress is a moat, about sixty feet wide and cased with stone. It was probably of great depth in its day, but it is now partly filled up with earth, and is quite dry and grassy throughout its whole extent. On the inner side of the moat was the outer wall of the castle, portions of which still remain. Between the outer wall and the castle itself the space is also about sixty feet.

The day was cloudy and lowering, and there were several little spatterings of rain, while we rambled about. The two children ran shouting hither and thither, and were continually clambering into dangerous places, racing along ledges of broken wall. At last they altogether disappeared for a good while; their voices, which had heretofore been plainly audible, were hushed, nor was there any answer when we began to call them, while making ready for our departure. But they finally appeared, coming out of the moat, where they had been picking and eating blackberries,—which, they said, grow very plentifully there, and which they were very reluctant to leave. Before quitting the castle, I must not forget the ivy, which makes a perfect tapestry over a large portion of the walls.

We walked about the village, which is old and ugly; small, irregular streets, contriving to be intricate, though there are few of them; mean houses, joining to each other. We saw, in the principal one, the parliament house in which Edward I. gave a Charter, or allowed rights of some kind, to his Welsh subjects. The ancient part of its wall is entirely distinguishable from what has since been built upon it.

Thence we set out to walk along the embankment, although the sky looked very threatening. The wind, however, was so strong, and had such a full sweep at us, on the top of the bank, that we decided on taking a path that led from it across the moor. But we soon had cause to repent of this; for, which way soever we turned, we found ourselves cut off by a ditch or a little stream; so that here we were, fairly astray on Rhyddlan moor, the old battle-field of the Saxons and Britons, and across which, I suppose, the fiddlers and mountebanks had marched to the relief of the Earl of Chester. Anon, too, it began to shower; and it was only after various leaps and scramblings that we made our way to a large farmhouse, and took shelter under a cart-shed. The back of the house to which we gained access was very dirty and ill kept; some dirty children peeped at us as we approached, and nobody had the civility to ask us in; so we took advantage of the first cessation of the shower to resume our way. We were shortly overtaken by a very intelligent-looking and civil man, who seemed to have come from Rhyddlan, and said he was going to Rhyl. We followed his guidance over stiles and along hedge-row paths which we never could have threaded rightly by ourselves.

By-and-by our kind guide had to stop at an intermediate farm; but he gave us full directions how to proceed, and we went on till it began to shower again pretty briskly, and we took refuge in a little bit of old stone cottage, which, small as it was, had a greater antiquity than any mansion in America. The door was open, and as we approached, we saw several children gazing at us; and their mother, a pleasant-looking woman, who seemed rather astounded at the visit that was about to befall her, tried to draw a tattered curtain over part of her interior, which she fancied even less fit to be seen than the rest. To say the truth, the house was not at all better than a pigsty; and while we sat there, a pig came familiarly to the door, thrust in his snout, and seemed surprised that he should be driven away, instead of being admitted as one of the family. The floor was of brick; there was no ceiling, but only the peaked gable overhead. The room was kitchen, parlour, and, I suppose, bedroom for the whole family; at all events, there was only the tattered curtain between us and the sleeping accommodations. The good woman either could not or would not speak a word of English, only laughing when S. said, "Dim Sassenach!" but she was kind and hospitable, and found a chair for each of us. She had been making some bread, and the dough was on the dresser. Life with these people is reduced to its simplest elements. It is only a pity that they cannot or do not choose to keep themselves cleaner. Poverty, except in cities, need not be squalid. When the shower abated a little, we gave all the pennies we had to the children, and set forth again. By-the-bye, there were several coloured prints stuck up against the walls, and there was a clock ticking in a corner, and some paper-hangings pinned upon the slanting roof.

It began to rain again before we arrived at Rhyl, and we were driven into a small tavern. After staying there awhile, we set forth between the drops; but the rain fell still heavier, so that we were pretty well damped before we got to our lodgings. After dinner, I took the rail for Chester and Rock Park, and S. and the children and maid followed the next day.

September 22nd.—I dined on Wednesday evening at Mr. John Heywood's, Norris Green. Mr. Monckton Milnes and lady were of the company. Mr. Milnes is a very agreeable, kindly man, resembling Longfellow a good deal in personal appearance; and he promotes, by his genial manners, the same pleasant intercourse which is so easily established with Longfellow. He is said to be a very kind patron of literary men, and to do a great deal of good among young and neglected people of that class. He is considered one of the best conversationists at present in society: it may very well be so; his style of talking being very simple and natural, anything but obtrusive, so that you might enjoy its agreeableness without suspecting it. He introduced me to his wife (a daughter of Lord Crewe), with whom and himself I had a good deal of talk. . . . . Mr. Milnes told me that he owns the land in Yorkshire, whence some of the pilgrims of the *Mayflower* emigrated to Plymouth, and that Elder Brewster was the postmaster of the village. . . . . He also said that in the next voyage of the *Mayflower*, after she carried the Pilgrims, she was employed in transporting a cargo of slaves from Africa,—to the West Indies, I suppose. This is a queer fact, and would be nuts for the Southerners.

MEM.—An American would never understand the passage in Bunyan about Christian and Hopeful going astray along a by-path into the grounds of Giant Despair,—from there being no stiles and by-paths in our country.

September 26th.—On Saturday evening my wife and I went to a *soirée* given by the Mayor and Mrs. Lloyd at the Town Hall to receive the Earl of Harrowby. It was quite brilliant, the public rooms being really magnificent, and adorned for the occasion with a large collection of pictures, belonging to Mr. Naylor. They were mostly, if not entirely, of modern artists,—of Turner, Wilkie, Landseer, and others of the best English painters. Turner's seemed too ethereal to have been done by mortal hands.

The British Scientific Association being now in session here, many distinguished strangers were present.

* * *

September 29th.—Mr. Monckton Milnes called on me at the Consulate day before yesterday. He is pleasant and sensible. . . . . Speaking of American politicians, I remarked that they were seldom anything but politicians, and had no literary or other culture beyond their own calling. He said the case was the same in England, and instanced Sir —— ——, who once called on him for information when an appeal had been made to him respecting two literary gentlemen. Sir —— —— had *never heard* the names of either of these gentlemen, and applied to Mr. Milnes, as being somewhat conversant with the literary class, to know whether they were distinguished, and what were their claims. The names of the two literary men were James Sheridan Knowles and Alfred Tennyson.

October 5th.—Yesterday I was present at a *déjeuner* on board the *James Barnes*, on occasion of her coming under the British flag, having been built for the Messrs. Barnes by Donald McKay of Boston. She is a splendid vessel, and magnificently fitted up, though not with consummate taste. It would be worth while that ornamental architects and upholsterers should study this branch of art, since the ship-builders seem willing to expend a good deal of money on it. In fact, I do not see that there is anywhere else so much encouragement to the exercise of ornamental art. I saw nothing to criticise in the solid and useful details of the ship; the ventilation, in particular, being free and abundant, so that the hundreds of passengers who will have their berths between decks, and at a still lower depth, will have good air and enough of it.

There were four or five hundred persons, principally Liverpool merchants and their wives, invited to the *déjeuner;* and the tables were spread between decks, the berths for passengers not being yet put in. There was not quite light enough to make the scene cheerful, it being an overcast day; and, indeed, there was an English plainness in the arrangement of the festal room, which might have been better exchanged for the flowery American taste, which I have just been criticising. With flowers, and the arrangement of flags, we should have made something very pretty of the space between decks; but there was nothing to hide the fact, that in a few days hence there would be crowded berths and sea-sick steerage passengers where we were now feasting. The cheer was very good,—cold fowl and meats; cold pies of foreign manufacture, very rich, and of mysterious composition; and champagne in plenty, with other wines for those who liked them.

I sat between two ladies, one of them Mrs.——, a pleasant young woman, who, I believe, is of American provincial nativity, and whom I therefore regarded as half a countrywoman. We talked a good deal together, and I confided to her my annoyance at the prospect of being called up to answer a toast; but she did not pity me at all, though she felt much alarm about her husband, Captain——, who was in the same predicament. Seriously, it is the most awful part of my official duty, —this necessity of making dinner-speeches at the Mayor's, and other public or semi-public tables. However, my neighbourhood to Mrs. —— was good for me, inasmuch as by laughing over the matter with her I came to

regard it in a light and ludicrous way; and so, when
the time actually came, I stood up with a careless dare-
devil feeling. The chairman toasted the President immediately after the Queen, and did me the honour to
speak of myself in a most flattering manner, something
like this: "Great by his position under the Republic,—
greater still, I am bold to say, in the Republic of letters!"
I made no reply at all to this; in truth, I forgot all
about it when I began to speak, and merely thanked
the company in behalf of the President and my countrymen, and made a few remarks with no very decided
point to them. However, they cheered and applauded,
and I took advantage of the applause to sit down, and
Mrs. —— informed me that I had succeeded admirably.
It was no success at all, to be sure; neither was it a
failure, for I had aimed at nothing, and I had exactly
hit it. But after sitting down, I was conscious of an
enjoyment in speaking to a public assembly, and felt
as if I should like to rise again. It is something like
being under fire,—a sort of excitement, not exactly
pleasure, but more piquant than most pleasures. I
have felt this before, in the same circumstances; but,
while on my legs, my impulse is to get through with
my remarks and sit down again as quickly as possible.
The next speech, I think, was by Rev. Dr. ——, the
celebrated Arctic gentleman, in reply to a toast complimentary to the clergy. He turned aside from the
matter in hand, to express his kind feelings towards
America, where he said he had been most hospitably
received, especially at Cambridge University. He also
made allusions to me, and I suppose it would have
been no more than civil in me to have answered with
a speech in acknowledgment, but I did not choose to

make another venture, so merely thanked him across the corner of the table, for he sat near me. He is a venerable-looking, white-haired gentleman, tall and slender, with a pale, intelligent, kindly face.

Other speeches were made; but from beginning to end there was not one breath of eloquence, nor even one neat sentence; and I rather think that Englishmen would purposely avoid eloquence or neatness in after-dinner speeches. It seems to be no part of their object. Yet any Englishman almost, much more generally than Americans, will stand up and talk on in a plain way, uttering one rough, ragged, and shapeless sentence after another, and will have expressed himself sensibly, though in a very rude manner, before he sits down. And this is quite satisfactory to his audience, who, indeed, are rather prejudiced against the man who speaks too glibly.

The guests began to depart shortly after three o'clock. This morning I have seen two reports of my little speech,—one exceedingly incorrect; another pretty exact, but not much to my taste, for I seem to have left out everything that would have been fittest to say.

October 6th.—The people, for several days, have been in the utmost anxiety, and latterly in the highest exultation about Sebastopol,—and all England, and Europe to boot, have been fooled by the belief that it had fallen. This, however, now turns out to be incorrect; and the public visage is somewhat grim in consequence. I am glad of it. In spite of his actual sympathies, it is impossible for a true American to be otherwise than glad. Success makes an Englishman intolerable; and, already, on the mistaken idea that the way was open to a prosperous conclusion of the war, the *Times* had begun to throw out menaces against America. I shall never love England till she sues to us for help, and, in the meantime, the fewer triumphs she obtains, the better for all parties. An Englishman in adversity is a very respectable character; he does not lose his dignity, but merely comes to a proper conception of himself. It is rather touching to an observer to see how much the universal heart is in this matter, —to see the merchants gathering round the telegraphic messages, posted on the pillars of the Exchange newsroom,—the people in the street who cannot afford to buy a paper clustering round the windows of the news-offices, where a copy is pinned up,—the groups of corporals and sergeants at the recruiting rendezvous, with a newspaper in the midst of them;—and all earnest and sombre, and feeling like one man together, whatever their rank. I seem to myself like a spy or a traitor when I meet their eyes, and am conscious that I neither hope nor fear in sympathy with them, although they look at me in full confidence of sympathy. Their heart "knoweth its own bitterness," and as for me, being a stranger and an alien, I "intermeddle not with their joy."

October 9th.—My ancestor left England in 1630. I return in 1853. I sometimes feel as if I myself had been absent these two hundred and twenty-three years, leaving England just emerging from the feudal system, and finding it, on my return, on the verge of republicanism. It brings the two far-separated points of time-very closely together, to view the matter thus.

· · · · · ·

October 16th.—A day or two ago arrived the sad news of the loss of the *Arctic* by collision with a French steamer off Newfoundland, and the loss also of three or four hundred people. I have seldom been more affected by anything quite alien from my personal and friendly concerns, than by the death of Captain Luce and his son. The boy was a delicate lad, and it is said that he had never been absent from his mother till this time, when his father had taken him to England to consult a physician about a complaint in his hip. So his father, while his ship was sinking, was obliged to decide whether he would put the poor, weakly, timorous child on board the boat, to take his hard chance of life there, or keep him to go down with himself and the ship. He chose the latter; and within half an hour, I suppose, the boy was among the child-angels. Captain Luce could not do less than die, for his own part, with the responsibility of all those lost lives upon him. He may not have been in the least to blame for the calamity, but it was certainly too heavy a one for him to survive. He was a sensible man, and a gentleman, courteous, quiet, with something almost melancholy in his address and aspect. Oftentimes he has come into my inner office to say good-bye before his departures, but I cannot precisely remember whether or no he took leave of me before this latest voyage. I never exchanged a great many words with him; but those were kind ones.

. . . . .

October 19th.—It appears to be customary for people of decent station, but in distressed circumstances, to go round among their neighbours and the public, accompanied by a friend, who explains the case. I have been accosted in the street in regard to one of these matters; and to-day there came to my office a grocer, who had become security for a friend, and who was threatened with an execution—with another grocer for supporter and advocate. The beneficiary takes very little active part in the affair, merely looking careworn, distressed, and pitiable, and throwing in a word of corroboration, or a sigh, or an acknowledgment, as the case may demand. In the present instance, the friend, a young, respectable-looking tradesman, with a Lancashire accent, spoke freely and simply of his client's misfortunes, not pressing the case unduly, but doing it full justice, and saying, at the close of the interview, that it was no pleasant business for himself. The broken grocer was an elderly man, of somewhat sickly aspect. The whole matter is very foreign to American habits. No respectable American would think of retrieving his affairs by such means, but would prefer ruin ten times over; no friend would take up his cause; no public would think it worth while to prevent the small catastrophe. And yet the custom is not without its good side, as indicating a closer feeling of brotherhood, a more efficient sense of neighbourhood, than exists among ourselves, although, perhaps, we are more careless of a fellow-creature's ruin, because ruin with us is by no means the fatal and irretrievable event that it is in England.

. . . . .

I am impressed with the ponderous and imposing look of an English legal document—an assignment of real estate in England, for instance—engrossed on an immense sheet of thickest paper, in a formal hand, beginning with "'This Indenture" in German text, and with occasional phrases of form, breaking out into large script—very long and repetitious, fortified with the Mayor of Manchester's seal, two or three inches in diameter, which is certified by a notary-public, whose signature, again, is to have my consular certificate and official seal.

November 2nd.—A young Frenchman enters, of gentlemanly aspect, with a greyish cloak or paletot overspreading his upper person, and a handsome and well-made pair of black trousers and well-fitting boots below. On sitting down, he does not throw off nor at all disturb the cloak. Eying him more closely, one discerns that he has no shirt-collar, and that what little is visible of his shirt-bosom seems not to be of to-day nor of yesterday—perhaps not even of the day before. His manners are very good; nevertheless, he is a coxcomb and a jackanapes. He avers himself a naturalized citizen of America, where he has been tutor in several families of distinction, and has been treated like a son. He left America on account of his health, and came near being tutor in the Duke of Norfolk's family, but failed for lack of testimonials; he is exceedingly capable and accomplished, but reduced in funds, and wants employment here, or the means of returning to America, where he intends to take a situation under government, which he is sure of obtaining. He mentioned a quarrel which he had recently had with an Englishman in behalf of America, and would have fought a duel had such been the custom of the country. He made the Englishman foam at the mouth, and told him that he had been twelve years at a military school, and could easily kill him. I say to him that I see little or no prospect of his getting employment here, but offer to inquire whether any situation, as clerk or otherwise, can be obtained for him in a vessel returning to America, and ask his address. He has no address. Much to my surprise, he takes his leave without requesting pecuniary aid, but hints that he shall call again.

He is a very disagreeable young fellow, like scores of others who call on me in the like situation. His English is very good for a Frenchman, and he says he speaks it the least well of five languages. He has been three years in America, and obtained his naturalization papers, he says, as a special favour, and by means of strong interest. Nothing is so absolutely odious as the sense of freedom and equality pertaining to an American grafted on the mind of a native of any other country in the world. A naturalized citizen is HATEFUL. Nobody has a right to our ideas, unless born to them.

November 9th.—I lent the above Frenchman a small sum; he advertised for employment as a teacher; and he called this morning to thank me for my aid, and says Mr. C. has engaged him for his children, at a guinea a week, and that he has also another engagement. The poor fellow seems to have been brought to a very low ebb. He has pawned everything, even to his last shirt, save the one he had on, and had been living at the rate of twopence a day. I had procured him a chance to return to America, but he was ashamed to go back in such poor circumstances, and so determined to seek better fortune here. I like him better than I did,—partly, I suppose, because I have helped him.

November 14th.—The other day I saw an elderly

gentleman walking in Dale Street, apparently in a state of mania; for as he limped along (being afflicted with lameness) he kept talking to himself, and sometimes breaking out into a threat against some casual passenger. He was a very respectable-looking man; and I remember to have seen him last summer, in the steamer, returning from the Isle of Man, where he had been staying at Castle Mona. What a strange and ugly predicament it would be for a person of quiet habits to be suddenly smitten with lunacy at noonday in a crowded street, and to walk along through a dim maze of extravagances,— partly conscious of them, but unable to resist the impulse to give way to them! A long-suppressed nature might be represented as bursting out in this way, for want of any other safety-valve.

In America, people seem to consider the government merely as a political administration; and they care nothing for the credit of it, unless it be the administration of their own political party. In England, all people, of whatever party, are anxious for the credit of their rulers. Our government, as a knot of persons, changes so entirely every four years, that the institution has come to be considered a temporary thing.

Looking at the moon the other evening, little R. said, "It blooms out in the morning!" taking the moon to be the bud of the sun.

The English are a most intolerant people. Nobody is permitted, nowadays, to have any opinion but the prevalent one. There seems to be very little difference between their educated and their ignorant classes in this respect; if any, it is to the credit of the latter, who do not show tokens of such extreme interest in the war. It is agreeable, however, to observe how all Englishmen pull together,—how each man comes forward with his little scheme for helping on the war,—how they feel themselves members of one family, talking together about their common interest, as if they were gathered around one fireside; and then what a hearty meed of honour they award to their soldiers! It is worth facing death for. Whereas, in America, when our soldiers fought as good battles, with as great proportionate loss, and far more valuable triumphs, the country seemed rather ashamed than proud of them.

Mrs. Heywood tells me that there are many Catholics among the lower classes in Lancashire and Cheshire,—probably the descendants of retainers of the old Catholic nobility and gentry, who are more numerous in these shires than in other parts of England. The present Lord Sefton's grandfather was the first of that race who became Protestant.

December 25th.—Commodore P. called to see me this morning,—a brisk, gentlemanly, off-hand, but not rough, unaffected and sensible man, looking not so elderly as he ought, on account of a very well-made wig. He is now on his return from a cruise in the East Indian seas, and goes home by the Baltic, with a prospect of being very well received on account of his treaty with Japan. I seldom meet with a man who puts himself more immediately on conversable terms than the Commodore. He soon introduced his particular business with me,— it being to inquire whether I would recommend some suitable person to prepare his

notes and materials for the publication of an account
of his voyage. He was good enough to say that he
had fixed upon me, in his own mind, for this office;
but that my public duties would of course prevent me
from engaging in it. I spoke of Herman Melville,
and one or two others; but he seems to have some
acquaintance with the literature of the day, and did
not grasp very cordially at any name that I could
think of; nor, indeed, could I recommend any one with
full confidence. It would be a very desirable task for
a young literary man, or, for that matter, for an old
one; for the world can scarcely have in reserve a less
hackneyed theme than Japan.

This is a most beautiful day of English winter;
clear and bright, with the ground a little frozen, and
the green grass along the waysides at Rock Ferry,
sprouting up through the frozen pools of yesterday's
rain. England is for ever green. On Christmas day,
the children found wall-flowers, pansies, and pinks in
the garden; and we had a beautiful rose from the
garden of the hotel, grown in the open air. Yet one
is sensible of the cold here, as much as in the zero
atmosphere of America. The chief advantage of the
English climate is that we are not tempted to heat our
rooms to so unhealthy a degree as in New England.

I think I have been happier this Christmas than
ever before,—by my own fireside, and with my wife
and children about me,—more content to enjoy what
I have,—less anxious for anything beyond it, in this
life. My early life was perhaps a good preparation for
the declining half of life; it having been such a blank
that any thereafter would compare favourably with it.
For a long, long while, I have occasionally been visited

with a singular dream; and I have an impression that
I have dreamed it ever since I have been in England.
It is, that I am still at College,—or, sometimes, even
at school,—and there is a sense that I have been there
unconscionably long, and have quite failed to make
such progress as my contemporaries have done; and I
seem to meet some of them with a feeling of shame
and depression that broods over me as I think of it,
even when awake. This dream, recurring all through
these twenty or thirty years, must be one of the effects
of that heavy seclusion in which I shut myself up for
twelve years after leaving college, when everybody
moved onward, and left me behind. How strange that
it should come now, when I may call myself famous
and prosperous!—when I am happy too!

January 3d, 1855.—The progress of the age is
trampling over the aristocratic institutions of England,
and they crumble beneath it. This war has given the
country a vast impulse towards democracy. The nobility will never hereafter, I think, assume or be permitted to rule the nation in peace, or command armies
in war, on any ground except the individual ability
which may appertain to one of their number, as well
as to a commoner. And yet the nobles were never
positively more noble than now; never, perhaps, so
chivalrous, so honourable, so highly cultivated; but,
relatively to the rest of the world, they do not main-
tain their old place. The pressure of the war has
tested and proved this fact, at home and abroad. At
this moment it would be an absurdity in the nobles to
pretend to the position which was quietly conceded to
them a year ago. This one year has done the work of

fifty ordinary ones; or, more accurately, it has made
apparent what has long been preparing itself.

January 6th.—The American ambassador called on
me to-day and stayed a good while,—an hour or two.
He is visiting at Mr. William Brown's, at Richmond
Hill, having come to this region to bring his niece,
who is to be bride's-maid at the wedding of an American
girl. I like Mr.———. He cannot exactly be called
gentlemanly in his manners, there being a sort of rusticity
about him; moreover, he has a habit of squinting
one eye, and an awkward carriage of his head; but,
withal, a dignity in his large person, and a consciousness
of high position and importance, which give him
ease and freedom. Very simple and frank in his address,
he may be as crafty as other diplomatists are said to
be; but I see only good sense and plainness of speech,
—appreciative, too, and genial enough to make himself
conversable. He talked very freely of himself and
of other public people, and of American and English
affairs. He returns to America, he says, next October,
and then retires for ever from public life, being sixty-
four years of age, and having now no desire except to
write memoirs of his times, and especially of the administration
of Mr. Polk. I suggested a doubt whether
the people would permit him to retire; and he immediately
responded to my hint as regards his prospects
for the Presidency. He said that his mind was fully
made up, and that he would never be a candidate, and
that he had expressed this decision to his friends in
such a way as to put it out of his own power to change
it. He acknowledged that he should have been glad
of the nomination for the Presidency in 1852, but that

it was now too late, and that he was too old,—and, in
short, he seemed to be quite sincere in his *nolo episcopari;*
although, really, he is the only Democrat, at this moment, whom it would not be absurd to talk of for the
office. As he talked, his face flushed, and he seemed
to feel inwardly excited. Doubtless, it was the high
vision of half his lifetime which he here relinquished.
I cannot question that he is sincere; but, of course,
should the people insist upon having him for President,
he is too good a patriot to refuse. I wonder whether
he can have had any object in saying all this to me.
He might see that it would be perfectly natural for me
to tell it to General Pierce. But it is a very vulgar
idea,—this of seeing craft and subtlety, when there is
a plain and honest aspect.

January 9th.—I dined at Mr. William Brown's
(M.P.) last evening with a large party. The whole
table and dessert service was of silver. Speaking of
Shakespeare, Mr. ——— said that the Duke of Somerset,
who is now nearly fourscore, told him that the father
of John and Charles Kemble had made all possible
research into the events of Shakespeare's life, and that
he had found reason to believe that Shakespeare attended a certain revel at Stratford, and, indulging too
much in the conviviality of the occasion, he tumbled
into a ditch on his way home, and died there! The
Kemble patriarch was an aged man when he communicated this to the Duke; and their ages, linked to
each other, would extend back a good way; scarcely
to the beginning of the last century, however. If I
mistake not, it was from the traditions of Stratford
that Kemble had learned the above. I do not remem-

her ever to have seen it in print,—which is most singular.

Miss L. has an English rather than an American aspect,—being of stronger outline than most of our young ladies, although handsomer than Englishwomen generally, extremely self-possessed and well poised, without affectation or assumption, but quietly conscious of rank, as much so as if she were an Earl's daughter. In truth, she felt pretty much as an Earl's daughter would do towards the merchants' wives and daughters who made up the feminine portion of the party.

* * * * *

I talked with her a little, and found her sensible, vivacious, and firm-textured, rather than soft and sentimental. She paid me some compliments; but I do not remember paying her any.

Mr. J.'s daughters, two pale, handsome girls, were present. One of them is to be married to a grandson of Mr. ——, who was also at the dinner. He is a small young man, with a thin and fair moustache,.... and a lady who sat next me whispered that his expectations are £6,000 per annum. It struck me, that, being a country gentleman's son, he kept himself silent and reserved, as feeling himself too good for this commercial dinner-party; but perhaps, and I rather think so, he was really shy and had nothing to say, being only twenty-one, and therefore quite a boy among Englishmen. The only man of cognizable rank present, except Mr. —— and the Mayor of Liverpool, was a Baronet, Sir Thomas Birch.

January 17th.—S. and I were invited to be present at the wedding of Mr. J.'s daughter this morning, but we were also bidden to the funeral services of Mrs. G., a young American lady; and we went to the "house of mourning," rather than to the "house of feasting." Her death was very sudden. I crossed to Rock Ferry on Saturday, and met her husband in the boat. He said his wife was rather unwell, and that he had just been sent for to see her; but he did not seem at all alarmed. And yet, on reaching home, he found her dead! The body is to be conveyed to America, and the funeral service was read over her in her house, only a few neighbours and friends being present. We were shown into a darkened room, where there was a dim gas-light burning, and a fire glimmering, and here and there a streak of sunshine struggling through the drawn curtains. Mr. G. looked pale, and quite overcome with grief,—this, I suppose, being his first sorrow,—and he has a young baby on his hands, and no doubt feels altogether forlorn in this foreign land. The clergyman entered in his canonicals, and we walked in a little procession into another room, where the coffin was placed. Mr. G. sat down and rested his head on the coffin: the clergyman read the service; then knelt down, as did most of the company, and prayed with great propriety of manner, but with no earnestness,— and we separated. Mr. G. is a small, smooth, and pretty young man, not emphasized in any way; but grief threw its awfulness about him to-day in a degree which I should not have expected.

January 20th.—Mr. Steele, a gentleman of Rock Ferry, showed me this morning a pencil-case formerly belonging to Dr. Johnson. It is six or seven inches long, of large calibre, and very clumsily manufactured of iron, perhaps plated in its better days, but now quite bare. Indeed, it looks as rough as an article of kitchen furniture. The intaglio on the end is a lion rampant. On the whole, it well became Dr. Johnson to have used such a stalwart pencil-case. It had a six-inch measure on a part of it, so that it must have been at least eight inches long. Mr. Steele says he has seen a cracked earthen teapot, of large size, in which Miss Williams used to make tea for Dr. Johnson.

God himself cannot compensate us for being born for any period short of eternity. All the misery endured here constitutes a claim for another life, and, still more, *all the happiness;* because all true happiness involves something more than the earth owns, and needs something more than a mortal capacity for the enjoyment of it.

After receiving an injury on the head, a person fancied all the rest of his life that he heard voices flouting, jeering, and upbraiding him.

February 19th.—I dined with the Mayor at the Town Hall last Friday evening. I sat next to Mr. W. J., an Irish-American merchant, who is in very good standing here. He told me that he used to be very well acquainted with General Jackson, and that he was present at the street fight between him and the Bentons, and helped to take General Jackson off the ground. Colonel Benton shot at him from behind; but it was Jesse Benton's ball that hit him and broke his arm. I did not understand him to infer any treachery or cowardice from the circumstance of Colonel Benton's shooting at Jackson from behind, but suppose it occurred in the confusion and excitement of a street fight. Mr. W. J. seems to think that, after all, the reconciliation between the old General and Benton was merely external, and that they really hated one another as before. I do not think so.

These dinners of the Mayors are rather agreeable than otherwise, except for the annoyance, in my case, of being called up to speak to a toast, and that is less disagreeable than at first. The suite of rooms at the Town House is stately and splendid, and all the Mayors, as far as I have seen, exercise hospitality in a manner worthy of the chief magistrates of a great city. They are supposed always to spend much more than their salary (which is £2,000) in these entertainments. The town provides the wines, I am told, and it might be expected that they should be particularly good,—at least, those which improve by age, for a quarter of a century should be only a moderate age for wine from the cellars of centuries-long institutions, like a corporate borough. Each Mayor might lay in a supply of the best vintage he could find, and trust his good name to posterity to the credit of that wine; and so he would be kindly and warmly remembered long after his own nose had lost its rubicundity. In point of fact, the wines seem to be good, but not remarkable. The dinner was good, and very handsomely served, with attendance enough, both in the hall below—where the door was wide open at the appointed hour, notwithstanding the cold,—and at table; some being in the rich livery of the borough, and some in plain clothes. Servants, too, were stationed at various points from the hall to the reception-room; and the last one shouted forth the

name of the entering guest. There were, I should
think, about fifty guests at this dinner. .... Two
bishops were present: the Bishops of Chester and New
South Wales, dressed in a kind of long tunics, with
black breeches and silk stockings, insomuch that I first
fancied they were Catholics. Also Dr. McNeile, in a
stiff-collared coat, looking more like a general than a
divine. There were two officers in blue uniforms; and
all the rest of us were in black, with only two white
waistcoats—my own being one—and a rare sprinkling
of white cravats. How hideously a man looks in them!
I should like to have seen such assemblages as must
have gathered in that reception-room, and walked with
stately tread to the dining-hall, in times past—the
Mayor and other civic dignities in their robes, noblemen in their state dresses, the Consul in his olive-leaf
embroidery, everybody in some sort of bedizenment—
and then the dinner would have been a magnificent
spectacle, worthy of the gilded hall, the rich table-
service, and the powdered and gold-laced servitors. At
a former dinner I remember seeing a gentleman in
small-clothes, with a dress-sword; but all formalities of
the kind are passing away. The Mayor's dinners, too,
will no doubt be extinct before many years go by. I
drove home from the Woodside Ferry in a cab with
Bishop Burke and two other gentlemen. The Bishop
is nearly seven feet high.

After writing the foregoing account of a civic
banquet, where I ate turtle-soup, salmon, woodcock,
oyster patties, and I know not what else, I have been
to the News-room and found the Exchange pavement
densely throngned with people of all ages and of all
manner of dirt and rags. They were waiting for soup-

tickets, and waiting very patiently too, without outcry or disturbance, or even sour looks—only patience and meekness in their faces. Well, I don't know that they have a right to be impatient of starvation; but still there does seem to be an insolence of riches and prosperity, which one day or another will have a downfall. And this will be a pity too.

On Saturday I went with my friend Mr. Bright to Otterpool and to Larkhill to see the skaters on the private waters of those two seats of gentlemen; and it is a wonder to behold—and it is always a new wonder to me—how comfortable Englishmen know how to make themselves; locating their dwellings far within private grounds, with secure gateways and porters' lodges, and the smoothest roads and trimmest paths, and shaven lawns, and clumps of trees, and every bit of the ground, every hill and dell, made the most of for convenience and beauty, and so well kept that even winter cannot cause disarray; and all this appropriated to the same family for generations, so that I suppose they come to believe it created exclusively and on purpose for them. And, really, the result is good and beautiful. It is a home—an institution which we Americans have not; but then I doubt whether anybody is entitled to a home in this world, in so full a sense.

The day was very cold, and the skaters seemed to enjoy themselves exceedingly. They were, I suppose, friends of the owners of the grounds, and Mr. Bright said they were treated in a jolly way, with hot luncheons. The skaters practise skating more as an art, and can perform finer manœuvres on the ice, than our New England skaters usually can, though the English have so much less opportunity for practice. A beggar-woman was haunting the grounds at Otterpool, but I saw nobody give her anything. I wonder how she got inside of the gate.

Mr. W. J. spoke of General Jackson as having come from the same part of Ireland as himself, and perhaps of the same family. I wonder whether he meant to say that the General was *born* in Ireland—that having been suspected in America.

February 21st.—Yesterday two companies of work-people came to our house in Rock Park, asking assistance, being out of work and with no resource other than charity. There were a dozen or more in each party. Their deportment was quiet and altogether unexceptionable—no rudeness, no gruffness, no menace. Indeed, such demonstrations would not have been safe, as they were followed about by two policemen; but they really seem to take their distress as their own misfortune and God's will, and impute it to nobody as a fault. This meekness is very touching, and makes one question the more whether they have all their rights. There have been disturbances, within a day or two, in Liverpool, and shops have been broken open, and robbed of bread and money; but this is said to have been done by idle vagabonds, and not by the really hungry work-people. These last submit to starvation gently and patiently, as if it were an every-day matter with them, or, at least, nothing but what lay fairly within their horoscope. I suppose, in fact, their stomachs have the physical habit that makes hunger not intolerable, because customary. If they had been used to a full meat diet, their hunger would be fierce, like that of ravenous beasts; but now they are trained to it.

I think that the feeling of an American, divided, as I am, by the ocean from his country, has a continual and immediate correspondence with the national feeling at home; and it seems to be independent of any external communication. Thus, my ideas about the Russian war vary in accordance with the state of the public mind at home, so that I am conscious whereabouts public sympathy is.

March 7th.—J. and I walked to Tranmere, and passed an old house which I suppose to be Tranmere Hall. Our way to it was up a hollow lane, with a bank and hedge on each side, and with a few thatched stone cottages, centuries old, their ridge-poles crooked and the stones time-worn, scattered along. At one point there was a wide, deep well, hewn out of the solid red freestone, and with steps, also hewn in solid rock, leading down to it. These steps were much hollowed by the feet of those who had come to the well; and they reach beneath the water, which is very high. The well probably supplied water to the old cotters and retainers of Tranmere Hall five hundred years ago. The Hall stands on the verge of a long hill which stretches behind Tranmere and as far as Birkenhead.

It is an old grey stone edifice, with a good many gables, and windows with mullions, and some of them extending the whole breadth of the gable. In some parts of the house, the windows seem to have been built up: probably in the days when daylight was

taxed. The form of the Hall is multiplex, the roofs
sloping down and intersecting one another, so as to
make the general result indescribable. There were
two sun-dials on different sides of the house, both the
dial-plates of which were of stone; and on one the
figures, so far as I could see, were quite worn off, but
the gnomon still cast the shadow over it in such a way
that I could judge that it was about noon. The other
dial had some half-worn hour-marks, but no gnomon.
The chinks of the stones of the house were very weedy,
and the building looked quaint and venerable; but it
is now converted into a farm-house, with the farm-yard
and outbuildings closely appended. A village, too,
has grown up about it, so that it seems out of place
among modern stuccoed dwellings, such as are erected
for tradesmen and other moderate people who have
their residences in the neighbourhood of a great city.
Among these there are a few thatched cottages, the
homeliest domiciles that ever mortals lived in, belonging to the old estate. Directly across the street is a
wayside inn, "licensed to sell wine, spirits, ale, and
tobacco." The street itself has been laid out since the
land grew valuable by the increase of Liverpool and
Birkenhead; for the old Hall would never have been
built on the verge of a public way.

March 27th.—I attended court to-day, at St. George's
Hall, with my wife, Mr. Bright, and Mr. Channing,
sitting in the High Sheriff's seat. It was the civil
side, and Mr. Justice Cresswell presided. The lawyers,
as far as aspect goes, seemed to me inferior to an
American bar, judging from their countenances, whether
as intellectual men or gentlemen. Their wigs and

gowns do not impose on the spectator, though they
strike him as an imposition. Their date is past. Mr.
Warren, of "Ten Thousand a Year," was in court,—a
pale, thin, intelligent face, evidently a nervous man,
more unquiet than anybody else in court,—always restless in his seat, whispering to his neighbours, settling
his wig, perhaps with an idea that people single him
out. St. George's Hall—the interior hall itself, I mean
—is a spacious, lofty, and most rich and noble apartment, and very satisfactory. The pavement is made
of mosaic tiles, and has a beautiful effect.

April 7th.—I dined at Mr. J. P. Heywood's on
Thursday, and met there Mr. and Mrs. —— of Smithell's
Hall. The hall is an old edifice of some five hundred
years, and Mrs. —— says there is a bloody footstep
at the foot of the great staircase. The tradition is
that a certain martyr, in Bloody Mary's time, being
examined before the occupant of the Hall, and committed to prison, stamped his foot, in earnest protest
against the injustice with which he was treated. Blood
issued from his foot, which slid along the stone pavement, leaving a long footmark printed in blood. And
there it has remained ever since, in spite of the scrub-
bings of all succeeding generations. Mrs. —— spoke
of it with much solemnity, real or affected. She says
that they now cover the bloody impress with a carpet,
being unable to remove it. In the History of Lancashire,
which I looked at last night, there is quite a different
account,—according to which the footstep is not a
bloody one, but is a slight cavity or inequality in the
surface of the stone, somewhat in the shape of a man's
foot with a peaked shoe. The martyr's name was

George Marsh. He was a curate, and was afterwards burnt. Mrs. —— asked me to go and see the Hall and the footmark; and as it is in Lancashire, and not a great way off, and a curious old place, perhaps I may.

April 12*th.*—The Earl of ——, whom I saw the other day at St. George's Hall, has a somewhat elderly look,—a pale and rather thin face, which strikes one as remarkably short, or compressed from top to bottom. Nevertheless, it has great intelligence, and sensitiveness too, I should think, but a cold, disagreeable expression. I should take him to be a man of not very pleasant temper,—not genial. He has no physical presence nor dignity, yet one sees him to be a person of rank and consequence. But, after all, there is nothing about him which it need have taken centuries of illustrious nobility to produce, especially in a man of remarkable ability, as Lord —— certainly is. S., who attended court all through the Hapgood trial, and saw Lord —— for hours together every day, has come to conclusions quite different from mine. She thinks him a perfectly natural person, without any assumption, any self-consciousness, any scorn of the lower world. She was delighted with his ready appreciation and feeling of what was passing around him,—his quick enjoyment of a joke,—the simplicity and unaffectedness of his emotion at whatever incidents excited his interest,—the genial acknowledgment of sympathy, causing him to look round and exchange glances with those near him, who were not his individual friends, but barristers and other casual persons. He seemed to her all that a nobleman ought to be, entirely simple and free from pretence and self-assertion, which persons of lower rank can hardly help bedevilling themselves with. I saw him only for a very few moments, so cannot put my observation against hers, especially as I was influenced by what I had heard the Liverpool people say of him.

I do not know whether I have mentioned that the handsomest man I have seen in England was a young footman of Mr. Heywood's. In his rich livery, he was a perfect Joseph Andrews.

In my Romance, the original emigrant to America may have carried away with him a family secret, whereby it was in his power, had he so chosen, to have brought about the ruin of the family. This secret he transmits to his American progeny, by whom it is inherited throughout all the intervening generations. At last, the hero of the Romance comes to England, and finds, that, by means of this secret, he still has it in his power to procure the downfall of the family. It would be something similar to the story of Meleager, whose fate depended on the firebrand that his mother had snatched from the flames.

April 24*th.*—On Saturday I was present at a *déjeuner* on board the *Donald McKay;* the principal guest being Mr. Layard, M.P. There were several hundred people, quite filling the between-decks of the ship, which was converted into a saloon for the occasion. I sat next to Mr. Layard, at the head of the table, and so had a good opportunity of seeing and getting acquainted with him. He is a man in early middle age,—of middle stature, with an open, frank, intelligent, kindly face. His forehead is not expansive, but is prominent in the perceptive regions, and retreats a good deal. His mouth is full,—I liked him from the first. He was very kind and complimentary to me, and made me promise to go and see him in London.

It would have been a very pleasant entertainment, only that my pleasure in it was much marred by having to acknowledge a toast in honour of the President. However, such things do not trouble me nearly so much as they used to do, and I came through it tolerably enough. Mr. Layard's speech was the great affair of the day. He speaks with much fluency (though he assured me that he had to put great force upon himself to speak publicly), and, as he warms up, seems to engage with his whole moral and physical man,—quite possessed with what he has to say. His evident earnestness and good faith make him eloquent, and stand him instead of oratorical graces. His views of the position of England and the prospects of the war were as dark as well could be; and his speech was exceedingly to the purpose, full of common sense, and with not one word of clap-trap. Judging from its effect upon the audience, he spoke the voice of the whole English people,—although an English baronet, who sat next below me, seemed to dissent, or at least to think that it was not exactly the thing for a stranger to hear. It concluded amidst great cheering. Mr. Layard appears to be a true Englishman, with a moral force and strength of character, and earnestness of purpose, and fulness of common sense, such as have always served England's turn in her past successes; but rather fit for resistance than progress. No doubt, he is a good and very able man; but I question whether he could get England out of the difficulties which he sees so clearly, or could do much better than Lord Palmerston, whom he so decries.

* * * *

April 25*th.*—Taking the deposition of sailors yesterday, in a case of alleged ill-usage by the officers of a vessel, one of the witnesses was an old seaman of sixty. In reply to some testimony of his, the captain said, "You were the oldest man in the ship, and we honoured you as such." The mate also said that he never could have thought of striking an old man like that. Indeed, the poor old fellow had a kind of dignity and venerableness about him, though he confessed to having been drunk, and seems to have been a mischief-maker,—what they call a sea-preacher,—promoting discontent and grumbling. He must have been a very handsome man in his youth, having regular features of a noble and beautiful cast. His beard was grey; but his dark hair had hardly a streak of white, and was abundant all over his head. He was deaf, and seemed to sit in a kind of seclusion, unless when loudly questioned or appealed to. Once he broke forth from a deep silence thus,—"I defy any man!" and then was silent again. It had a strange effect, this general defiance, which he meant, I suppose, in answer to some accusation that he thought was made against him. His general behaviour throughout the examination was very decorous and proper; and he said he had never but once hitherto been before a Consul, and that was in 1819, when a mate had ill-used him, and, "being a young man then, I gave him a beating,"—whereupon his face gleamed with a quiet smile, like faint sunshine on an old ruin. "By many a tempest has his beard been shook;" and I suppose he must soon go into a workhouse, and thence, shortly, to his grave. He is now in a hospital, having, as the surgeon certifies, some ribs fractured; but there does not appear to have been any violence used upon him aboard the ship of such a nature as to cause this injury, though he swears it was a blow from a rope, and nothing else. What struck me in the case was the respect and rank that his age seemed to give him, in the view of the officers; and how, as the captain's expression signified, it lifted him out of his low position, and made him a person to be honoured. The dignity of his manner is perhaps partly owing to the ancient mariner, with his long experience, being an oracle among the forecastle men.

May 3rd.—It rains to-day, after a very long period of east wind and dry weather. The east wind here, blowing across the island, seems to be the least damp of all the winds; but it is full of malice and mischief, of an indescribably evil temper, and stabs one like a cold, poisoned dagger. I never spent so disagreeable a spring as this, although almost every day for a month has been bright.

Friday, May 11th.—A few weeks ago, a sailor, a most pitiable object, came to my office to complain of cruelty from his captain and mate. They had beaten him shamefully, of which he bore grievous marks about his face and eyes, and bruises on his head and other parts of his person; and finally the ship had sailed, leaving him behind. I never in my life saw so forlorn a fellow, so ragged, so wretched; and even his wits seemed to have been beaten out of him, if perchance

he ever had any. He got an order for the hospital;
and there he has been, off and on, ever since, till yesterday, when I received a message that he was dying,
and wished to see the Consul; so I went with Mr.
Wilding to the hospital. We were ushered into the
waiting-room, — a kind of parlour, with a fire in the
grate, and a centre-table, whereon lay one or two medical journals, with wood engravings; and there was a
young man, who seemed to be an official of the house,
reading. Shortly the surgeon appeared, — a brisk,
cheerful, kindly sort of person, whom I have met there
on previous visits. He told us that the man was dying,
and probably would not be able to communicate anything, but, nevertheless, ushered us up to the highest
floor, and into the room where he lay. It was a large,
oblong room, with ten or twelve beds in it, each occupied by a patient. The surgeon said that the hospital
was often so crowded that they were compelled to lay
some of the patients on the floor. The man whom we
came to see lay on his bed in a little recess formed by
a projecting window; so that there was a kind of seclusion for him to die in. He seemed quite insensible to
outward things, and took no notice of our approach,
nor responded to what was said to him, — lying on his
side, breathing with short gasps, — his apparent disease
being inflammation of the chest, although the surgeon
said that he might be found to have sustained internal
injury by bruises. He was restless, tossing his head
continually, mostly with his eyes shut, and much compressed and screwed up, but sometimes opening them;
and then they looked brighter and darker than when I
first saw them. I think his face was not at any time
so stupid as at his first interview with me; but what-

ever intelligence he had was rather inward than outward, as if there might be life and consciousness at a depth within, while as to external matters he was in a mist. The surgeon felt his wrist, and said that there was absolutely no pulsation, and that he might die at any moment, or might perhaps live an hour, but that there was no prospect of his being able to communicate with me. He was quite restless, nevertheless, and sometimes half raised himself in bed, sometimes turned himself quite over, and then lay gasping for an instant. His woollen shirt being thrust up on his arm, there appeared a tattooing of a ship and anchor, and other nautical emblems, on both of them, which another sailor-patient, on examining them, said must have been done years ago. This might be of some importance, because the dying man had told me, when I first saw him, that he was no sailor, but a farmer, and that, this being his first voyage, he had been beaten by the captain for not doing a sailor's duty, which he had had no opportunity of learning. These sea-emblems indicated that he was probably a seaman of some years' service.

While we stood in the little recess, such of the other patients as were convalescent gathered near the foot of the bed; and the nurse came and looked on, and hovered about us,— a sharp-eyed, intelligent woman of middle age, with a careful and kind expression, neglecting nothing that was for the patient's good, yet taking his death as coolly as any other incident in her daily business. Certainly, it was a very forlorn death-bed; and I felt—what I have heretofore been inclined to doubt—that it might be a comfort to have persons whom one loves, to go with us to the threshold of the other world, and leave us only when we are fairly across it. This poor fellow had a wife and two children on the other side of the water.

At first he did not utter any sound; but by-and-by he moaned a little, and gave tokens of being more sensible to outward concerns,—not quite so misty and dreamy as hitherto. We had been talking all the while—myself in a whisper, but the surgeon in his ordinary tones—about his state, without his paying any attention. But now the surgeon put his mouth down to the man's face and said, "Do you know that you are dying?" At this the patient's head began to move upon the pillow; and I thought at first that it was only the restlessness that he had shown all along; but soon it appeared to be an expression of emphatic dissent, a negative shake of the head. He shook it with all his might, and groaned and mumbled, so that it was very evident how miserably reluctant he was to die. Soon after this he absolutely spoke. "Oh, I want you to get me well! I want to get away from here!" in a groaning and moaning utterance. The surgeon's question had revived him, but to no purpose; for, being told that the Consul had come to see him, and asked whether he had anything to communicate, he said only, "Oh, I want him to get me well!" and the whole life that was left in him seemed to be unwillingness to die. This did not last long; for he soon relapsed into his first state, only with his face a little more pinched and screwed up, and his eyes strangely sunken and lost in his head; and the surgeon said that there would be no use in my remaining. So I took my leave. Mr. Wilding had brought a deposition of the man's evidence, which he had clearly made at the Consulate, for him to sign, and this we left with the surgeon, in case there should be such an interval of consciousness and intelligence before death as to make it possible for him to sign it. But of this there is no probability.

* * * * *

I have just received a note from the hospital, stating, that the sailor, Daniel Smith, died about three quarters of an hour after I saw him.

May 18*th*.—The above-mentioned Daniel Smith had about him a bundle of letters, which I have examined. They are all very yellow, stained with sea-water, smelling of bad tobacco-smoke, and much worn at the folds. Never were such ill-written letters, nor such incredibly fantastic spelling. They seem to be from various members of his family,—most of them from a brother, who purports to have been a deck-hand in the coasting and steamboat trade between Charleston and other ports; others from female relations; one from his father, in which he inquires how long his son has been in jail, and when the trial is to come on,—the offence, however, of which he was accused not being indicated. But from the tenor of his brother's letters, it would appear that he was a small farmer in the interior of South Carolina, sending butter, eggs, and poultry to be sold in Charleston by his brother, and receiving the returns in articles purchased there. This was his own account of himself; and he affirmed, in his deposition before me, that he had never had any purpose of shipping for Liverpool, or anywhere else; but that, going on board the ship to bring a man's trunk ashore, he was compelled to remain and serve as a sailor. This was a hard fate, certainly, and a strange thing to happen in the United States at this day,—that a free citizen should be absolutely kidnapped, carried to a foreign country, treated with savage cruelty during the voyage, and left to die on his arrival. Yet all this has unquestionably been done, and will probably go unpunished.

. . . . .

The seed of the long-stapled cotton, now cultivated in America, was sent there in 1786 from the Bahama Islands, by some of the royalist refugees, who had settled there. The inferior short-stapled cotton had been previously cultivated for domestic purposes. The seeds of every other variety have been tried without success. The kind now grown was first introduced into Georgia. Thus to the refugees America owes as much of her prosperity as is due to the cotton-crops, and much of whatever harm is to result from slavery.

May 22nd.—Captain J. says that he saw, in his late voyage to Australia and India, a vessel commanded by an Englishman, who had with him his wife and thirteen children. This ship was the home of the family, and they had no other. The thirteen children had all been born on board, and had been brought up on board, and knew nothing of dry land, except by occasionally setting foot on it.

Captain J. is a very agreeable specimen of the American shipmaster,—a pleasant, gentlemanly man, not at all refined, and yet with fine and honourable sensibilities. Very easy in his manners and conversation, yet gentle,—talking on freely, and not much minding grammar; but finding a sufficient and picturesque expression for what he wishes to say; very cheerful and vivacious; accessible to feeling, as yesterday, when talking about the recent death of his mother. His voice faltered, and the tears came into his eyes, though before and afterwards he smiled merrily, and made us smile; fond of his wife, and carrying her about the world with him, and blending her with all his enjoyments; an excellent and sagacious man of business; liberal in his expenditure; proud of his ship and flag; always well dressed, with some little touch of sailor-like flashiness, but not a whit too much; slender in figure, with a handsome face, and rather profuse brown beard and whiskers; active and alert; about thirty-two. A daguerreotype sketch of any conversation of his would do him no justice, for its slang, its grammatical mistakes, its mistaken words (as "portable" for "portly"), would represent a vulgar man, whereas the impression he leaves is by no means that of vulgarity; but he is a character quite perfect within itself, fit for the deck and the cabin, and agreeable in the drawing-room, though not amenable altogether to its rules. Being so perfectly natural, he is more of a gentleman for those little violations of rule, which most men, with his opportunities, might escape.

The men whose appeals to the Consul's charity are the hardest to be denied, are those who have no country,—Hungarians, Poles, Cubans, Spanish-Americans, and French republicans. All exiles for liberty come to me, as if the representative of America were their representative. Yesterday, came an old French soldier, and showed his wounds; to-day, a Spaniard, a friend of Lopez,—bringing his little daughter with him. He said he was starving, and looked so. The little girl

was in good condition enough, and decently dressed.—
May 23rd.

May 30th.—The two past days have been Whitsuntide holidays; and they have been celebrated at Tranmere in a manner very similar to that of the old "Election" in Massachusetts, as I remember it a good many years ago, though the festival has now almost or quite died out. Whitsuntide was kept up on our side of the water, I am convinced, under pretence of rejoicings at the election of Governor. It occurred at precisely the same period of the year,—the same week; the only difference being, that Monday and Tuesday are the Whitsun festival days, whereas, in Massachusetts, Wednesday was "Election day," and the acme of the merry-making.

I passed through Tranmere yesterday forenoon, and lingered awhile to see the sports. The greatest peculiarity of the crowd, to my eye, was that they seemed not to have any best clothes, and therefore had put on no holiday suits,—a grimy people, as at all times, heavy, obtuse, with thick beer in their blood. Coarse, rough-complexioned women and girls were intermingled, —the girls with no maiden trimness in their attire, large and blowsy. Nobody seemed to have been washed that day. All the enjoyment was of an exceedingly sombre character, so far as I saw it, though there was a richer variety of sports than at similar festivals in America. There were wooden horses revolving in circles, to be ridden a certain number of rounds for a penny; also swinging cars gorgeously painted, and the newest named after Lord Raglan; and four cars balancing one another, and turned by a winch; and people with targets and rifles,—the principal aim being to hit an apple bobbing on a string before the target; other guns for shooting at the distance of a foot or two, for a prize of filberts; and a game much in fashion, of throwing heavy sticks at earthen mugs suspended on lines, three throws for a penny. Also, there was a posture-master, showing his art in the centre of a ring of miscellaneous spectators, and handing round his hat after going through all his attitudes. The collection amounted to only one halfpenny, and, to eke it out, I threw in three more. There were some large booths with tables placed the whole length, at which sat men and women drinking and smoking pipes; orange-girls, a great many, selling the worst possible oranges, which had evidently been boiled to give them a show of freshness. There were likewise two very large structures, the walls made of boards roughly patched together, and roofed with canvas, which seemed to have withstood a thousand storms. Theatres were there, and in front there were pictures of scenes which were to be represented within; the price of admission being twopence to one theatre, and a penny to the other. But small as the price of tickets was, I could not see that anybody bought them. Behind the theatres, close to the board wall, and perhaps serving as the general dressing-room, was a large windowed waggon, in which I suppose the company travel and live together. Never, to my imagination, was the mysterious glory that has surrounded theatrical representation ever since my childhood brought down into such dingy reality as this. The tragedy queens were the same coarse and homely women and girls that surrounded me on the green. Some of the people had evidently been drinking more than was good for them; but their drunkenness was silent and stolid, with no madness in it. No ebullition of any sort was apparent.

May 31st.—Last Sunday week, for the first time, I heard the note of the cuckoo. "Cuck-oo—cuck-oo," it says, repeating the word twice, not in a brilliant metallic tone, but low and flute-like, without the excessive sweetness of the flute,—without an excess of saccharine juice in the sound. There are said to be always two cuckoos seen together. The note is very soft and pleasant. The larks I have not yet heard in the sky; though it is not infrequent to hear one singing in a cage in the streets of Liverpool.

. . .

Brewers' draymen are allowed to drink as much of their master's beverage as they like, and they grow very brawny and corpulent, resembling their own horses in size, and presenting, one would suppose, perfect pictures of physical comfort and well-being. But the least bruise, or even the hurt of a finger, is liable to turn to gangrene or erysipelas, and become fatal.

When the wind blows violently, however clear the sky, the English say, "It is a stormy day." And, on the other hand, when the air is still, and it does not actually rain, however dark and lowering the sky may be, they say, "The weather is fine!"

June 2nd.—The English women of the lower classes have a grace of their own, not seen in each individual, but nevertheless belonging to their order, which is not to be found in American women of the corresponding class. The other day, in the police court, a girl was put into the witness-box, whose native graces of this sort impressed me a good deal. She was coarse, and her dress was none of the cleanest, and nowise smart. She appeared to have been up all night, too, drinking at the Tranmere wake, and had since ridden in a cart, covered up with a rug. She described herself as a servant-girl, out of place; and her charm lay in all her manifestations,—her tones, her gestures, her look, her way of speaking and what she said, being so appropriate and natural in a girl of that class; nothing affected; no proper grace thrown away by attempting to appear lady-like,—which an American girl *would* have attempted,—and she would also have succeeded in a certain degree. If each class would but keep within itself, and show its respect for itself by aiming at nothing beyond, they would all be more respectable. But this kind of fitness is evidently not to be expected in the future; and something else must be substituted for it.

These scenes at the police court are often well worth witnessing. The controlling genius of the court, except when the stipendiary magistrate presides, is the clerk, who is a man learned in the law. Nominally the cases are decided by the aldermen, who sit in rotation; but at every important point there comes a nod or a whisper from the clerk; and it is that whisper which sets the defendant free or sends him to prison. Nevertheless, I suppose the alderman's common sense and native shrewdness are not without their efficacy in producing a general tendency towards the right; and, no doubt, the decisions of the police court are quite as often just as those of any other court whatever.

. . . . .

June 11th.—I walked with J. yesterday to Bebbington church. When I first saw this church, nearly two years since, it seemed to me the fulfilment of my ideal of an old English country church. It is not so satisfactory now, although certainly a venerable edifice. There used some time ago to be ivy all over the tower; and at my first view of it, there was still a little remaining on the upper parts of the spire. But the main roots, I believe, were destroyed, and pains were taken to clear away the whole of the ivy, so that now it is quite bare,—nothing but homely grey stone, with marks of age, but no beauty. The most curious thing about the church is the font. It is a massive pile, composed of five or six layers of freestone in an octagon shape, placed in the angle formed by the projecting side porch and the wall of the church, and standing under a stained glass window. The base is six or seven feet across, and it is built solidly up in successive steps, to the height of about six feet,—an octagonal pyramid, with the basin of the font crowning the pile hewn out of the solid stone, and about a foot in diameter and the same in depth. There was water in it from the recent rains,—water just from heaven, and therefore as holy as any water it ever held in old Romish times. The aspect of this aged font is extremely venerable, with moss in the basin and all over the stones; grass, and weeds of various kinds, and little shrubs, rooted in the chinks of the stones and between the successive steps.

At each entrance of Rock Park, where we live, there is a small Gothic structure of stone, each inhabited by a policeman and his family; very small dwellings indeed, with the main apartment opening directly out-of-doors; and when the door is open, one can see the household fire, the good wife at work, perhaps the table set, and a throng of children clustering round, and generally overflowing the threshold. The policeman walks about the Park in stately fashion, with his silver-laced blue uniform and snow-white gloves, touching his hat to gentlemen who reside in the Park. In his public capacity he has rather an awful aspect, but privately he is a humble man enough, glad of any little job, and of old clothes for his many children, or, I believe, for himself. One of the two policemen is a shoemaker and cobbler. His pay, officially, is somewhere about a guinea a-week.

The Park, just now, is very agreeable to look at, shadowy with trees and shrubs, and with glimpses of green leaves and flower-gardens through the branches and twigs that line the iron fences. After a shower the hawthorn blossoms are delightfully fragrant. Golden tassels of the laburnum are abundant.

I may have mentioned elsewhere the traditional prophecy, that, when the ivy should reach the top of Bebbington spire, the tower was doomed to fall. It has still, therefore, a chance of standing for centuries. Mr. Turner tells me that the font now used is inside of the church, but the one outside is of unknown antiquity, and that it was customary, in papistical times, to have the font without the church.

· · · · ·

There is a little boy often on board the Rock Ferry steamer with an accordion,—an instrument I detest; but nevertheless it becomes tolerable in his hands, not so much for its music, as for the earnestness and interest with which he plays it. His body and the accordion together become one musical instrument on which his soul plays tunes, for he sways and vibrates with the music from head to foot and throughout his frame, half closing his eyes and uplifting his face, as painters represent St. Cecilia and other famous musicians; and sometimes he swings his accordion in the air, as if in a perfect rapture. After all, my ears, though not very nice, are somewhat tortured by his melodies, especially when confined within the cabin. The boy is ten years old, perhaps, and rather pretty; clean, too, and neatly dressed, very unlike all other street and vagabond children whom I have seen in Liverpool. People give him their halfpence more readily than to any other musicians who infest the boat.

J., the other day, was describing a soldier-crab to his mother, he being much interested in natural history, and endeavouring to give as strong an idea as possible of its warlike characteristics, and power to harm those who molest it. Little R. sat by, quietly listening and sewing, and at last, lifting her head, she remarked, "I hope God did not hurt hisself, when he was making him!"

LEAMINGTON.

June 21st.—We left Rock Ferry and Liverpool on Monday the 18th by the rail for this place; a very dim and rainy day, so that we had no pleasant prospects of the country; neither would the scenery along the Great Western Railway have been in any case very striking, though sunshine would have made the abundant verdure and foliage warm and genial. But a railway naturally finds its way through all the common places of a country, and is certainly a most unsatisfactory mode of travelling, the only object being to arrive. However, we had a whole carriage to ourselves, and the children enjoyed the earlier part of the journey very much. We skirted Shrewsbury, and I think I saw the old tower of a church near the station, perhaps the same that struck Falstaff's "long hour." As we left the town I saw the Wrekin, a round, pointed hill of regular shape, and remembered the old toast, "'To all friends round the Wrekin!" As we approached Birmingham, the country began to look somewhat Brummagemish, with, its manufacturing chimneys, and pennons of flame quivering out of their tops; its forges, and great heaps of mineral refuse; its smokiness and other ugly symptoms. Of Birmingham itself we saw little or nothing, except the mean and new brick lodging-houses, on the outskirts of the town. Passing through Warwick, we had a glimpse of the castle,—an ivied wall and two turrets, rising out of embosoming foliage; one's very idea of an old castle. We reached Leamington at a little past six, and drove to the Clarendon Hotel,—a very spacious and stately house, by far the most splendid hotel I have yet seen in England. The landlady, a courteous old lady in black, showed my wife our rooms, and we established ourselves in an immensely large and lofty parlour, with red curtains and ponderous furniture, perhaps a very little out of date. The waiter brought me the book of arrivals, containing the names of all visitors for from three to five years back. During two years I estimated that there had been about three hundred and fifty persons only, and while we were there, I saw nobody but ourselves to support the great hotel. Among the names were those of princes, earls, countesses, and baronets; and when the people of the house heard from R.'s nurse that I too was a man of office, and held the title of Honourable in my own country, they greatly regretted that I entered myself as plain "Mister" in the book. We found this hotel very comfortable, and might doubtless have made it luxurious, had we chosen to go to five times the expense of similar luxuries in America; but we merely ordered comfortable things, and so came off at no very extravagant rate,—and with great honour, at all events, in the estimation of the waiter.

During the afternoon we found lodgings, and established ourselves in them before dark.

. . . . .

This English custom of lodgings, of which we had some experience at Rhyl last year, has its advantages; but is rather uncomfortable for strangers, who, in first settling themselves down, find that they must undertake all the responsibility of housekeeping at an instant's warning, and cannot get even a cup of tea till they have made arrangements with the grocer. Soon, however, there comes a sense of being at home, and by our exclusive selves, which never can be attained at hotels nor boarding-houses. Our house is well situated and respectably furnished, with the dinginess, however, which is inseparable from lodging-houses,—as if others had used these things before and would use them again after we had gone,—a well-enough adaptation, but a lack of peculiar appropriateness; and I think one puts off real enjoyment from a sense of not being truly fitted.

. . . . .

July 1st.—On Friday I took the rail with J. for Coventry. It was a bright and very warm day, oppressively so, indeed; though I think that there is never in this English climate the pervading warmth of an

American summer day. The sunshine may be excessively hot, but an overshadowing cloud or the shade of a tree or of a building at once affords relief; and if the slightest breeze stirs, you feel the latent freshness of the air.

Coventry is some nine or ten miles from Leamington. The approach to it from the railway presents nothing very striking,—a few church towers, and one or two tall steeples; and the houses first seen are of modern and unnoticeable aspect. Getting into the interior of the town, however, you find the streets very crooked, and some of them very narrow. I saw one place where it seemed possible to shake hands from one jutting, storied old house to another. There were whole streets of the same kind of houses, one story impending over another, such as used to be familiar to me in Salem, and in some streets of Boston. In fact, the whole aspect of the town—its irregularity and continual indirectness—reminded me very much of Boston, as I used to see it, in rare visits thither, when a child.

These Coventry houses, however, many of them, are much larger than any of similar style that I have seen elsewhere, and they spread into greater bulk as they ascend, by means of one story jutting over the other. Probably the New-Englanders continued to follow this fashion of architecture after it had been abandoned in the mother-country. The old house built by Philip English, in Salem, dated about 1692, was in this style, —many gabled, and impending. Here the edifices of such architecture seem to be Elizabethan, and of earlier date. A woman in Stratford told us that the rooms, very low on the ground floor, grew loftier from story to story to the attic. The fashion of windows, in Coventry,

is such as I have not hitherto seen. In the highest story,
a window of the ordinary height extends along the
whole breadth of the house, ten, fifteen, perhaps twenty
feet, just like any other window of a common-place
house, except for this inordinate width. One does not
easily see what the inhabitants want of so much window-
light; but the fashion is very general; and in modern
houses, or houses that have been modernized, this style
of window is retained. Thus young people who grow
up amidst old people contract quaint and old-fashioned
manners and aspect.

I imagine that these ancient towns—such as Chester
and Stratford, Warwick and Coventry—contain even
a great deal more antiquity than meets the eye. You
see many modern fronts; but if you peep or penetrate
inside, you find an antique arrangement,—old rafters,
intricate passages, and ancient staircases, which have
put on merely a new outside, and are likely still to
prove good for the usual date of a new house. They
put such an immense and stalwart ponderosity into
their frameworks, that I suppose a house of Elizabeth's
time, if renewed, has at least an equal chance of dura-
bility with one that is new in every part. All the
hotels in Coventry, so far as I noticed them, are old,
with new fronts; and they have an archway for the
admission of vehicles into the court-yard, and doors
opening into the rooms of the building on each side
of the arch. Maids and waiters are seen darting across
the arched passage from door to door, and it requires
a guide (in my case, at least) to show you the way to
the coffee-room or the bar. I have never been up-stairs in
any of them, but can conceive of infinite bewilderment
of zigzag corridors between staircase and chamber.

It was fair-day in Coventry, and this gave what no doubt is an unusual bustle to the streets. In fact, I have not seen such crowded and busy streets in any English town; various kinds of merchandise being for sale in the open air, and auctioneers disposing of miscellaneous wares, pretty much as they do at musters and other gatherings in the United States. The oratory of the American auctioneer, however, greatly surpasses that of the Englishman in vivacity and fun. But this movement and throng, together with the white glow of the sun on the pavements, make the scene, in my recollection, assume an American aspect, and this is strange in so antique and quaint a town as Coventry.

We rambled about without any definite aim, but found our way, I believe, to most of the objects that are worth seeing. St. Michael's church was most magnificent,—so old, yet enduring; so huge, so rich; with such intricate minuteness in its finish, that, look as long as you will at it, you can always discover something new directly before your eyes. I admire this in Gothic architecture,—that you cannot master it all at once, that it is not a naked outline; but, as deep and rich as human nature itself, always revealing new ideas. It is as if the builder had built himself and his age up into it, and as if the edifice had life. Grecian temples are less interesting to me, being so cold and crystalline. I think this is the only church I have seen where there are any statues still left standing in the niches of the exterior walls. We did not go inside. The steeple of St. Michael's is three hundred and three feet high, and no doubt the clouds often envelop the tip of the spire. Trinity, another church, with a tall spire, stands near St. Michael's, but did not attract me so much; though I, perhaps, might have admired it equally, had I seen it first or alone. We certainly know nothing of church-building in America, and of all English things that I have seen, methinks the churches disappoint me least. I feel, too, that there is something much more wonderful in them than I have yet had time to know and experience.

In the course of the forenoon, searching about everywhere in quest of Gothic architecture, we found our way into St. Mary's Hall. The doors were wide open; it seemed to be public,—there was a notice on the wall desiring visitors to give nothing to attendants for showing it, and so we walked in. I observed, in the guide-books, that we should have obtained an order for admission from some member of the town council; but we had none, and found no need of it. An old woman, and afterwards an old man, both of whom seemed to be at home on the premises, told us that we might enter, and troubled neither themselves nor us any further.

St. Mary's Hall is now the property of the Corporation of Coventry, and seems to be the place where the Mayor and Council hold their meetings. It was built by one of the old guilds or fraternities of merchants and tradesmen..... The woman shut the kitchen door when I approached, so that I did not see the great fire-places and huge cooking-utensils which are said to be there. Whether these are ever used nowadays, and whether the Mayor of Coventry gives such hospitable banquets as the Mayor of Liverpool, I do not know.

We went to the Red Lion, and had a luncheon of cold lamb and cold pigeon-pie. This is the best way of dining at English hotels,—to call the meal a luncheon, in which case you will get as good or better a variety than if it were a dinner, and at less than half the cost. Having lunched, we again wandered about town, and entered a quadrangle of gabled houses, with a church and its churchyard on one side. This proved to be St. John's church, and a part of the houses were the locality of Bond's Hospital, for the reception of ten poor men, and the remainder was devoted to the Bablake School. Into this latter I peered, with a real American intrusiveness, which I never found in myself before, but which I must now assume, or miss a great many things which I am anxious to see. Running along the front of the house, under the jut of the impending story, there was a cloistered walk, with windows opening on the quadrangle. An arched oaken door, with long iron hinges, admitted us into a school-room about twenty feet square, paved with brick tiles, blue and red. Adjoining this there is a larger school-room, which we did not enter, but peeped at, through one of the inner windows, from the cloistered walk. In the room which we entered, there were seven scholars' desks, and an immense arched fire-place, with seats on each side, under the chimney, on a stone slab resting on a brick pedestal. The opening of the fire-place was at least twelve feet in width. On one side of the room were pegs for fifty-two boys' hats and clothes, and there was a boy's coat, of peculiar cut, hanging on a peg, with the number "50" in brass upon it. The coat looked ragged and shabby. An old school-book was lying on one of the desks, much tattered, and without a title; but it seemed

to treat wholly of Saints' days and festivals of the
Church. A flight of stairs, with a heavy balustrade of
carved oak, ascended to a gallery, about eight or nine
feet from the lower floor, which runs along two sides
of the room, looking down upon it. The room is
without a ceiling, and rises into a peaked gable, about
twenty feet high. There is a large clock in it, and it
is lighted by two windows, each about ten feet wide,—
one in the gallery, and the other beneath it. Two
benches or settles, with backs, stood one on each side
of the fire-place. An old woman in black passed through
the room while I was making my observations, and
looked at me, but said nothing. The school was founded
in 1563, by Thomas Whealby, Mayor of Coventry; the
revenue is about £900, and admits children of the work-
ing-classes at eleven years old, clothes and provides
for them, and finally apprentices them for seven years.
We saw some of the boys playing in the quadrangle,
dressed in long blue coats or gowns, with cloth caps
on their heads. I know not how the atmosphere of
antiquity, and massive continuance from age to age,
which was the charm to me in this scene of a charity-
school-room, can be thrown over it in description. After
noting down these matters, I looked into the quiet
precincts of Bond's Hospital, which, no doubt, was
more than equally interesting; but the old men were
lounging about or lolling at length, looking very drowsy,
and I had not the heart nor the face to intrude among
them. There is something altogether strange to an
American in these charitable institutions,—in the preservation of antique modes and customs which is effected
by them, insomuch that, doubtless without at all intending it, the founders have succeeded in preserving a

model of their own long-past age down into the midst of ours, and how much later nobody can know.

We were now rather tired, and went to the railroad, intending to go home; but we got into the wrong train, and were carried by express, with hurricane speed, to Brandon, where we alighted, and waited a good while for the return train to Coventry. At Coventry again we had more than an hour to wait, and therefore wandered wearily up into the city, and took another look at its bustling streets, in which there seems to be a good emblem of what England itself really is,—with a great deal of antiquity in it, and which is now chiefly a modification of the old. The new things are based and supported on the sturdy old things, and often limited and impeded by them; but this antiquity is so massive that there seems to be no means of getting rid of it without tearing society to pieces.

July 2nd.—To-day I shall set out on my return to Liverpool, leaving my family here.

TO THE LAKES.

July 4th.—I left Leamington on Monday, shortly after twelve, having been accompanied to the railway station by U. and J., whom I sent away before the train started. While I was waiting, a rather gentlemanly, well-to-do, English-looking man sat down by me, and began to talk of the Crimea, of human affairs in general, of God and his providence, of the coming troubles of the world, and of spiritualism, in a strange free way for an Englishman, or, indeed, for any man. It was easy to see that he was an enthusiast of some

hue or other. He being bound for Birmingham and I
for Rugby, we soon had to part; but he asked my
name, and told me his own, which I did not much
attend to, and immediately forgot.

[Here follows a long account of a visit to Lichfield
and Uttoxeter, condensed in "Our Old Home."]

July 6th.—The day after my arrival, by way of
Lichfield and Uttoxeter, to Liverpool, the door of the
Consulate opened, and in came the very sociable personage who accosted me at the railway station at Leamington. He was on his way towards Edinburgh, to
deliver a course of lectures or a lecture, and had called,
he said, to talk with me about spiritualism, being desirous of having the judgment of a sincere mind on
the subject. In his own mind, I should suppose, he
is past the stage of doubt and inquiry; for he told me
that in every action of his life he is governed by the
counsels received from the spiritual world through a
medium. I did not inquire whether this medium (who
is a small boy) had suggested his visit to me. My remarks to him were quite of a sceptical character in
regard to the faith to which he had surrendered himself. He had formerly lived in America, and had had
a son born there. He gave me a pamphlet written by
himself, on the cure of consumption and other diseases
by antiseptic remedies. I hope he will not bore me
any more, though he seems to be a very sincere and
good man; but these enthusiasts who adopt such extravagant ideas appear to me to lack imagination, instead
of being misled by it, as they are generally supposed
to be.

NEWBY BRIDGE.—FOOT OF WINDERMERE.

July 13th.—I left Liverpool on Saturday last, by the London and North-Western Railway, for Leamington, spent Sunday there, and started on Monday for the English lakes, with the whole family. We should not have taken this journey just now, but I had an official engagement which it was convenient to combine with a pleasure-excursion. The first night we arrived at Chester, and put up at the Albion Hotel, where we found ourselves very comfortable. We took the rail at twelve the next day, and went as far as Milnethorpe station, where we engaged seats in an old-fashioned stage-coach, and came to Newby Bridge. I suppose there are not many of these coaches now running on any road in Great Britain; but this appears to be the genuine machine, in all respects, and especially in the round, ruddy coachman, well moistened with ale, good-natured, courteous, and with a proper sense of his dignity and important position. U., J., and I mounted atop, S., nurse, and R. got inside, and we bowled off merrily towards the heart of the hills. It was more than half-past nine when we arrived at Newby Bridge, and alighted at the Swan Hotel, where we now are.

It is a very agreeable place; not striking as to scenery, but with a pleasant rural aspect. A stone bridge of five arches crosses the river Severn (which is the communication between Windermere Lake and Morecambe Bay) close to the house, which sits low and well sheltered in the lap of hills,—an old-fashioned inn, where the landlord and his people have a simple and friendly way of dealing with their guests, and yet provide them with all sorts of facilities for being comfortable. They load our supper and breakfast tables with trout, cold beef, ham, toast, and muffins; and give us three fair courses for dinner, and excellent wine, the cost of all which remains to be seen. This is not one of the celebrated stations among the lakes; but twice a day the stage-coach passes from Milnethorpe towards Ulverston, and twice returns, and three times a little steamer passes to and fro between our hotel and the head of the lake. Young ladies, in broad-brimmed hats, stroll about, or row on the river in the light shallops, of which there are abundance; sportsmen sit on the benches under the windows of the hotel, arranging their fishing-tackle; phaetons and post-chaises, with postilions in scarlet jackets and white breeches, with one high-topped boot, and the other leathered far up on the leg to guard against friction between the horses, dash up to the door. Morning and night comes the stage-coach, and we inspect the outside passengers, almost face to face with us, from our parlour windows, up one pair of stairs. Little boys, and J. among them, spend hours on hours fishing in the clear, shallow river for the perch, chubs, and minnows that may be seen flashing, like gleams of light, over the flat stones with which the bottom is paved. I cannot answer for the other boys, but J. catches nothing.

There are a good many trees on the hills and round about, and pleasant roads loitering along by the gentle river-side, and it has been so sunny and warm since we came here that we shall have quite a genial recollection of the place, if we leave it before the skies have time to frown. The day after we came, we climbed a high and pretty steep hill, through a path shadowed with trees and shrubbery, up to a tower, from the summit of which we had a wide view of mountain scenery and the greater part of Windermere. This lake is a lovely little pool among the hills, long and narrow, beautifully indented with tiny bays and headlands; and when we saw it, it was one smile (as broad a smile as its narrowness allowed) with really brilliant sunshine. All the scenery we have yet met with is in excellent taste, and keeps itself within very proper bounds,—never getting too wild and rugged to shock the sensibilities of cultivated people, as American scenery is apt to do. On the rudest surface of English earth, there is seen the effect of centuries of civilisation, so that you do not quite get at naked Nature anywhere. And then every point of beauty is so well known, and has been described so much, that one must needs look through other people's eyes, and feel as if he were seeing a picture rather than a reality. Man has, in short, entire possession of Nature here, and I should think young men might sometimes yearn for a fresher draught. But an American likes it.

FURNESS ABBEY.

Yesterday, July 12th, we took a phaeton and went to Furness Abbey,—a drive of about sixteen miles, passing along the course of the Leam to Morecambe Bay, and through Ulverston and other villages. These villages all look antique, and the smallest of them generally are formed of such close, contiguous clusters of houses, and have such narrow and crooked streets, that they give you an idea of a metropolis in miniature. The houses along the road (of which there are not many, except in the villages) are almost invariably old, built of stone, and covered with a light grey plaster; generally they have a little flower-garden in front, and often honeysuckles, roses, or some other sweet and pretty rustic adornment, are flowering over the porch. I have hardly had such images of simple, quiet, rustic comfort and beauty as from the look of these houses; and the whole impression of our winding and undulating road, bordered by hedges, luxuriantly green, and not too closely clipped, accords with this aspect. There is nothing arid in an English landscape; and one cannot but fancy that the same may be true of English rural life. The people look wholesome and well-to-do,—not specimens of hard, dry, sunburnt muscle, like our yeomen,—and are kind and civil to strangers, sometimes making a little inclination of the head in passing. Miss Martineau, however, does not seem to think well of their mental and moral condition.

We reached Furness Abbey about twelve. There is a railway station close by the ruins; and a new hotel stands within the precincts of the abbey grounds; and continually there is the shriek, the whiz, the rumble, the bell-ringing, denoting the arrival of the trains; and passengers alight, and step at once (as their choice may be) into the refreshment-room, to get a glass of ale or a cigar,—or upon the gravelled paths of the lawn, leading to the old broken walls and arches of the abbey. The ruins are extensive, and the enclosure of the abbey is stated to have covered a space of sixty-five acres. It is impossible to describe them. The most interesting part is that which was formerly the church, and which, though now roofless, is still surrounded by walls, and retains the remnants of the pillars that formerly supported the intermingling curves of the arches. The

floor is all overgrown with grass, strewn with fragments
and capitals of pillars. It was a great and stately
edifice, the length of the nave and choir having been
nearly three hundred feet, and that of the transept
more than half as much. The pillars along the nave
were alternately a round, solid one and a clustered one.
Now, what remains of some of them is even with the
ground; others present a stump just high enough to
form a seat; and others are, perhaps, a man's height
from the ground,—and all are mossy, and with grass
and weeds rooted into their chinks, and here and there
a tuft of flowers, giving its tender little beauty to their
decay. The material of the edifice is a soft red stone,
and it is now extensively overgrown with a lichen of
a very light grey hue, which, at a little distance, makes
the walls look as if they had long ago been whitewashed, and now had partially returned to their original
colour. The arches of the nave and transept were
noble and immense; there were four of them together,
supporting a tower which has long since disappeared,
—arches loftier than I ever conceived to have been
made by man. Very possibly, in some cathedral that
I have seen, or am yet to see, there may be arches as
stately as these; but I doubt whether they can ever
show to such advantage in a perfect edifice as they do
in this ruin,—most of them broken, only one, as far
as I recollect, still completing its sweep. In this state
they suggest a greater majesty and beauty than any
finished human work can show; the crumbling traces
of the half-obliterated design producing somewhat of
the effect of the first idea of anything admirable, when
it dawns upon the mind of an artist or a poet,—an

idea which, do what he may, he is sure to fall short of in his attempt to embody it.

In the middle of the choir is a much dilapidated monument of a cross-legged knight (a crusader, of course) in armour, very rudely executed; and, against the wall, lie two or three more bruised and battered warriors, with square helmets on their heads and visors down. Nothing can be uglier than these figures; the sculpture of those days seems to have been far behind the architecture. And yet they knew how to put a grotesque expression into the faces of their images, and we saw some fantastic shapes and heads at the lower points of arches which would do to copy into *Punch*. In the chancel, just at the point below where the high altar stands, was the burial-place of the old Barons of Kendal. The broken crusader, perhaps, represents one of them; and some of their stalwart bones might be found by digging down. Against the wall of the choir, near the vacant space where the altar was, are some stone seats with canopies richly carved in stone, all quite perfectly preserved, where the priests used to sit at intervals, during the celebration of mass. Conceive all these shattered walls, with here and there an arched door, or the great arched vacancy of a window; these broken stones and monuments scattered about; these rows of pillars up and down the nave; these arches, through which a giant might have stepped, and not needed to bow his head, unless in reverence to the sanctity of the place,—conceive it all, with such verdure and embroidery of flowers as the gentle, kindly moisture of the English climate procreates on all old things, making them more beautiful than new,—conceive it with the grass for sole pavement of the long and spacious aisle, and the sky above for the only roof. The sky, to be sure, is more majestic than the tallest of those arches; and yet these latter, perhaps, make the stronger impression of sublimity, because they translate the sweep of the sky to our finite comprehension. It was a most beautiful, warm, sunny day, and the ruins had all the pictorial advantage of bright light and deep shadows. I must not forget that birds flew in and out among the recesses, and chirped and warbled, and made themselves at home there. Doubtless the birds of the present generation are the posterity of those who first settled in the ruins, after the Reformation; and perhaps the old monks of a still earlier day may have watched them building about the abbey, before it was a ruin at all.

We had an old description of the place with us, aided by which we traced out the principal part of the edifice, such as the church, as already mentioned, and, contiguous to this, the chapter-house, which is better preserved than the church; also the kitchen, and the room where the monks met to talk; and the range of wall where their cells probably were. I never before had given myself the trouble to form any distinct idea of what an abbey or monastery was,—a place where holy rites were daily and continually to be performed, with places to eat and sleep contiguous and convenient, in order that the monks might always be at hand to perform those rites. They lived only to worship, and therefore lived under the same roof with their place of worship, which, of course, was the principal object in the edifice, and hallowed the whole of it. We found, too, at one end of the ruins, what is supposed to have been a school-house for the children of the tenantry or villeins of the abbey. All round this room is a bench of stone against the wall, and the pedestal also of the master's seat. There are, likewise, the ruins of the mill; and the mill-stream, which is just as new as ever it was, still goes murmuring and babbling, and passes under two or three old bridges, consisting of a low grey arch overgrown with grass and shrubbery. That stream was the most fleeting and vanishing thing about the ponderous and high-piled abbey; and yet it has outlasted everything else, and might still outlast another such edifice, and be none the worse for wear.

There is not a great deal of ivy upon the walls, and though an ivied wall is a beautiful object, yet it is better not to have too much,—else it is but one wall of unbroken verdure, on which you can see none of the sculptural ornaments, nor any of the hieroglyphics of Time. A sweep of ivy here and there, with the grey wall everywhere showing through, makes the better picture; and I think that nothing is so effective as the little bunches of flowers, a mere handful, that grow in spots where the seeds have been carried by the wind ages ago.

I have made a miserable botch of this description; it is no description, but merely an attempt to preserve something of the impression it made on me, and in this I do not seem to have succeeded at all. I liked the contrast between the sombreness of the old walls, and the sunshine falling through them, and gladdening the grass that floored the aisles; also, I liked the effect of so many idle and cheerful people, strolling into the haunts of the dead monks, and going babbling about, and peering into the dark nooks; and listening to catch some idea of what the building was from a clerical-looking personage, who was explaining it to a party of his friends. I don't know how well acquainted this gentleman might be with the subject; but he seemed anxious not to impart his knowledge too extensively, and gave a pretty direct rebuff to an honest man who ventured an inquiry of him. I think that the railway, and the hotel within the abbey grounds, add to the charm of the place. A moonlight, solitary visit might be very good, too, in its way; but I believe that one great charm and beauty of antiquity is, that we view it out of the midst of quite another mode of life; and the more perfectly this can be done, the better. It can never be done more perfectly than at Furness Abbey, which is in itself a very sombre scene, and stands, moreover, in the midst of a melancholy valley, the Saxon name of which means the Vale of the Deadly Nightshade.

The entrance to the stable-yard of the hotel is beneath a pointed arch of Saxon architecture, and on one side of this stands an old building, looking like a chapel, but which may have been a porter's lodge. The Abbot's residence was in this quarter; and the clerical personage, before alluded to, spoke of those as the oldest part of the ruins.

About half a mile on the hither side of the abbey stands the village of Dalton, in which is a castle built on a Roman foundation, and which was afterwards used by the abbots (in their capacity of feudal lords) as a prison. The abbey was founded about 1027 by King Stephen, before he came to the throne; and the faces of himself and of his queen are still to be seen on one of the walls.

We had a very agreeable drive home (our drive

hither had been uncomfortably sunny and hot), and we stopped at Ulverston to buy a pair of shoes for J. and some drawing books and stationery. As we passed through the little town in the morning, it was all alive with the bustle and throng of the weekly market; and though this had ceased on our return, the streets still looked animated, because the heat of the day drew most of the population, I should imagine, out of doors. Old men look very antiquated here in their old-fashioned coats and breeches, sunning themselves by the wayside.

We reached home somewhere about eight o'clock, —home I see I have called it; and it seems as home-like a spot as any we have found in England,—the old inn, close by the bridge, beside the clear river, pleasantly overshadowed by trees. It is entirely English, and like nothing that one sees in America; and yet I feel as if I might have lived here a long while ago, and had now come back because I retained pleasant recollections of it. The children, too, make themselves at home. J. spends his time from morning to night fishing for minnows or trout, and catching nothing at all, and U. and R. have been riding between fields and barn in a hay-cart. The roads give us beautiful walks along the river-side, or wind away among the gentle hills; and if we had nothing else to look at in these walks, the hedges and stone fences would afford interest enough, so many and pretty are the flowers, roses, honeysuckles, and other sweet things, and so abundantly does the moss and ivy grow among the old stones of the fences, which would never have a single shoot of vegetation on them in America till the very end of time. But here, no sooner is a stone fence built, than Nature sets to work to make it a part of herself. She adopts it and adorns it, as if it were her own child. A little sprig of ivy may be seen creeping up the side, and clinging fast with its many feet; a tuft of grass roots itself between two of the stones, where a little dust from the road has been moistened into soil for it: a small bunch of fern grows in another such crevice; a deep, soft, green moss spreads itself over the top and all along the sides of the fence; and wherever nothing else will grow, lichens adhere to the stones and variegate their hues. Finally, a great deal of shrubbery is sure to cluster along its extent, and take away all hardness from the outline; and so the whole stone fence looks as if God had had at least as much to do with it as man. The trunks of the trees, too, exhibit a similar parasitical vegetation. Parasitical is an unkind phrase to bestow on this beautiful love and kindness which seems to exist here between one plant and another; the strong thing being always ready to give support and sustenance, and the weak thing to repay with beauty, so that both are the richer,—as in the case of ivy and woodbine, clustering up the trunk of a tall tree, and adding Corinthian grace to its lofty beauty.

Mr. W., our landlord, has lent us a splendid work with engravings, illustrating the antiquities of Furness Abbey. I gather from it that the hotel must have been rebuilt or repaired from an old manor-house, which was itself erected by a family of Prestons, after the Reformation, and was a renewal from the Abbot's residence. Much of the edifice probably, as it exists now, may have been part of the original one; and there are bas-reliefs of Scripture subjects, sculptured in stone, and fixed in the wall of the dining-room, which have been there since the Abbot's time. This author thinks that

what we had supposed to be the school-house (on the
authority of an old book) was really the building for
the reception of guests, with its chapel. He says that
the tall arches in the church are sixty feet high. The
Earl of Burlington, I believe, is the present proprietor
of the abbey.

THE LAKES.

July 16*th.*—On Saturday, we left Newby Bridge,
and came by steamboat up Windermere Lake to Lowwood Hotel, where we now are. The foot of the lake
is just above Newby Bridge, and it widens from that
point, but never to such a breadth that objects are not
pretty distinctly visible from shore to shore. The
steamer stops at two or three places in the course of
its voyage, the principal one being Bowness, which
has a little bustle and air of business about it proper
to the principal port of the lake. There are several
small yachts, and many skiffs rowing about. The
banks are everywhere beautiful, and the water, in one
portion, is strewn with islands; few of which are large
enough to be inhabitable, but they all seem to be appropriated, and kept in the neatest order. As yet, I
have seen no wildness; everything is perfectly subdued
and polished and imbued with human taste, except, indeed, the outlines of the hills, which continue very
much the same as God made them. As we approached
the head of the lake, the congregation of great hills in
the distance became very striking. The shapes of these
English mountains are certainly far more picturesque
than those which I have seen in Eastern America,
where their summits are almost invariably rounded, as

I remember them. They are great hillocks, great bunches of earth, similar to one another in their developments. Here they have variety of shape, rising into peaks, falling in abrupt precipices, stretching along in zigzag outlines, and thus making the most of their not very gigantic masses, and producing a remarkable effect.

We arrived at the Lowwood Hotel, which is very near the head of the lake, not long after two o'clock. It stands almost on the shore of Windermere, with only a green lawn between,—an extensive hotel, covering a good deal of ground; but low, and rather village-inn-like than lofty. We found the house so crowded as to afford us no very comfortable accommodation, either as to parlour or sleeping-rooms, and we find nothing like the home-feeling into which we at once settled down at Newby Bridge. There is a very pretty vicinity, and a fine view of mountains to the north-west, sitting together in a family group, sometimes in full sunshine, sometimes with only a golden gleam on one or two of them, sometimes all in a veil of cloud, from which here and there a great, dusky head raises itself, while you are looking at a dim obscurity. Nearer, there are high, green slopes, well wooded, but with such decent and well-behaved wood as you perceive has grown up under the care of man; still no wildness, no ruggedness,—as how should there be, when, every half mile or so, a porter's lodge or a gentleman's gateway indicates that the whole region is used up for villas. On the opposite shore of the lake there is a mimic castle, which I suppose I might have mistaken for a real one two years ago. It is a great, foolish toy of grey stone.

A steamboat comes to the pier as many as six

times a day, and stage-coaches and omnibuses stop at the door still oftener, communicating with Ambleside and the town of Windermere, and with the railway, which opens London and all the world to us. We get no knowledge of our fellow-guests, all of whom, like ourselves, live in their own circles, and are just as remote from us as if the lake lay between. The only words I have spoken since arriving here have been to my own family or to a waiter, save to one or two young pedestrians who met me on a walk, and asked me the distance to Lowwood Hotel. "Just beyond here," said I, and I might stay for months without occasion to speak again.

Yesterday forenoon J. and I walked to Ambleside,—distant barely two miles. It is a little town, chiefly of modern aspect, built on a very uneven hillside, and with very irregular streets and lanes, which bewilder the stranger as much as those of a larger city. Many of the houses look old, and are probably the cottages and farm-houses which composed the rude village a century ago; but there are stuccoed shops and dwellings, such as may have been built within a year or two; and three hotels, one of which has the look of a good old village inn; and the others are fashionable or commercial establishments. Through the midst of the village comes tumbling and rumbling a mountain streamlet, rushing through a deep, rocky dell, gliding under an old stone arch, and turning, when occasion calls, the great block of a water-mill. This is the only very striking feature of the village,—the stream taking its rough pathway to the lake as it used to do before the poets had made this region fashionable.

In the evening, just before eight o'clock, I took a walk alone, by a road which goes up the hill, back of our hotel, and which I supposed might be the road to the town of Windermere. But it went up higher and higher, and for the mile or two that it led me along, winding up, I saw no traces of a town; but at last it turned into a valley between two high ridges, leading quite away from the lake, within view of which the town of Windermere is situated. It was a very lonely road, though as smooth, hard, and well kept as any thoroughfare in the suburbs of a city; hardly a dwelling on either side, except one, half barn, half farm-house, and one gentleman's gateway, near the beginning of the road, and another more than a mile above. At two or three points there were stone barns, which are here built with great solidity. At one place there was a painted board, announcing that a field of five acres was to be sold, and referring those desirous of purchasing to a solicitor in London. The lake country is but a London suburb. Nevertheless, the walk was lonely and lovely; the copses and the broad hillside, the glimpses of the lake, the great misty company of pikes and fells, beguiled me into a sense of something like solitude; and the bleating of the sheep, remote and near, had a like tendency. Gaining the summit of the hill, I had the best view of Windermere which I have yet attained,—the best, I should think, that can be had, though, being towards the south, it brings the softer instead of the more striking features of the landscape into view. But it shows nearly the whole extent of the lake, all the way from Lowwood, beyond Newby Bridge, and I think there can hardly be anything more beautiful in the world. The water

was like a strip and gleam of sky, fitly set among
lovely slopes of earth. It was no broader than many
a river, and yet you saw at once that it could be no
river, its outline being so different from that of a
running stream, not straight nor winding, but stretching to one side or the other, as the shores made room
for it.

This morning it is raining, and we are not very
comfortable nor contented, being all confined to our
little parlour, which has a broken window, against
which I have pinned the *Times* to keep out the chill
damp air. U. has been ill, in consequence of having
been overheated at Newby Bridge. We have no
books, except guide-books, no means of amusement,
nothing to do. There are no newspapers, and I shall
remember Lowwood not very agreeably. As far as
we are concerned, it is a scrambling, ill-ordered hotel,
with insufficient attendance, wretched sleeping accommodations, a pretty fair table, but German-silver forks
and spoons; our food does not taste very good, and
yet there is really no definite fault to be found with it.

Since writing the above, I have found the first
volume of Sir Charles Grandison, and two of G. P. R.
James's works, in the coffee-room. The days pass
heavily here, and leave behind them a sense of having
answered no very good purpose. They are long
enough, at all events, for the sun does not set till
after eight o'clock, and rises I know not when. One
of the most remarkable distinctions between England
and the United States is the ignorance into which we
fall of whatever is going on in the world the moment
we get away from the great thoroughfares and centres
of life. In Leamington we heard no news from week's

end to week's end, and knew not where to find a newspaper; and here the case is neither better nor worse. The rural people really seem to take no interest in public affairs; at all events, they have no intelligence on such subjects. It is possible that the cheap newspapers may, in time, find their way into the cottages, or, at least, into the country taverns; but it is not at all so now. If they generally know that Sebastopol is besieged, it is the extent of their knowledge. The public life of America is lived through the mind and heart of every man in it; here the people feel that they have nothing to do with what is going forward, and, I suspect, care little or nothing about it. Such things they permit to be the exclusive concern of the higher classes.

In front of our hotel, on the lawn between us and the lake, there are two trees, which we have hitherto taken to be yews; but on examining them more closely, I find that they are pine-trees, and quite dead and dry, although they have the aspect of dark rich life. But this is caused by the verdure of two great ivy vines, which have twisted round them like gigantic snakes, and, clambering up and throttling the life out of them, have put out branches, and made crowns of thick green leaves, so that, at a little distance, it is quite impossible not to take them for genuine trees. The trunks of the ivy vines must be more than a foot in circumference, and one feels they have stolen the life that belonged to the pines. The dead branches of one of the pines stick out horizontally through the ivy boughs. The other shows nothing but the ivy, and in shape a good deal resembles a poplar. When the pine trunks shall have quite crumbled away, the ivy stems will doubtless have gained sufficient strength to sustain themselves independently.

July 19*th*.—Yesterday S. went down the lake in the steamboat to take U., baby, and nurse to Newby Bridge, while the three rest of us should make a tour through the lake region. After mamma's departure, and when I had finished some letters, J. and I set out on a walk, which finally brought us to Bowness, through much delightful shade of woods, and past beautiful rivulets or brooklets, and up and down many hills. This chief harbour of the lakes seemed alive and bustling with tourists, it being a sunny and pleasant day, so that they were all abroad, like summer insects. The town is a confused and irregular little place, of very uneven surface. There is an old church in it, and two or three large hotels. We stayed there perhaps half an hour, and then went to the pier, where shortly a steamer arrived, with music sounding,—on the deck of which, with her back to us, sat a lady in a grey travelling dress. J. cried out, "Mamma! mamma!" to which the lady deigned no notice, but, he repeating it, she turned round, and was as much surprised, no doubt, to see her husband and son, as if this little lake had been the great ocean, and we meeting each other from opposite shores of it. We soon steamed back to Lowwood, and took a car thence for Rydal and Grasmere, after a cold luncheon. At Bowness I met Miss Charlotte Cushman, who has been staying at the Lowwood Hotel with us since Monday, without either party being aware of it.

Our road to Rydal lay through Ambleside, which is certainly a very pretty town, and looks cheerfully in a sunny day. We saw Miss Martineau's residence, called

"The Knoll," standing high up on a hillock, and having at its foot a Methodist chapel, for which, or whatever place of Christian worship, this good lady can have no occasion. We stopped a moment in the street below her house, and deliberated a little whether to call on her; but concluded we would not.

After leaving Ambleside, the road winds in and out among the hills, and soon brings us to a sheet (or napkin, rather than a sheet) of water, which the driver tells us is Rydal Lake! We had already heard that it was but three quarters of a mile long, and one quarter broad; still, it being an idea of considerable size in our minds, we had inevitably drawn its ideal physical proportions on a somewhat corresponding scale. It certainly did look very small; and I said, in my American scorn, that I could carry it away easily in a porringer; for it is nothing more than a grassy-bordered pool among the surrounding hills which ascend directly from its margin; so that one might fancy it, not a permanent body of water, but a rather extensive accumulation of recent rain. Moreover, it was rippled with a breeze, and so, as I remember it, though the sun shone, it looked dull and sulky, like a child out of humour. Now, the best thing these small ponds can do is to keep perfectly calm and smooth, and not attempt to show off any airs of their own, but content themselves with serving as a mirror for whatever of beautiful or picturesque there may be in the scenery around them. The hills about Rydal Water are not very lofty, but are sufficiently so as objects of every-day view,—objects to live with; and they are craggier than those we have hitherto seen, and bare of wood, which indeed would hardly grow on some of their precipitous sides.

On the roadside, as we reach the foot of the lake, stands a spruce and rather large house of modern aspect, but with several gables and much overgrown with ivy—a very pretty and comfortable house, built, adorned, and cared for with commendable taste. We inquired whose it was, and the coachman said it was "Mr. Wordsworth's," and that "Mrs. Wordsworth was still residing there." So we were much delighted to have seen his abode, and as we were to stay the night at Grasmere, about two miles farther on, we determined to come back and inspect it as particularly as should be allowable. Accordingly, after taking rooms at Brown's Hotel, we drove back in our return car, and, reaching the head of Rydal Water, alighted to walk through this familiar scene of so many years of Wordsworth's life. We ought to have seen De Quincey's former residence and Hartley Coleridge's cottage, I believe, on our way, but were not aware of it at the time. Near the lake there is a stone-quarry, and a cavern of some extent, artificially formed, probably by taking out the stone. Above the shore of the lake, not a great way from Wordsworth's residence, there is a flight of steps hewn in a rock and ascending to a rock seat where a good view of the lake may be attained; and, as Wordsworth has doubtless sat there hundreds of times, so did we ascend and sit down, and look at the hills and at the flags on the lake's shore.

Reaching the house that had been pointed out to us as Wordsworth's residence, we began to peer about at its front and gables, and over the garden wall, on both sides of the road, quickening our enthusiasm as much as we could, and meditating to pilfer some flower or ivy-leaf from the house or its vicinity, to be kept as

sacred memorials. At this juncture a man approached,
who announced himself as the gardener of the place,
and said, too, that this was not Wordsworth's house at
all, but the residence of Mr. Ball, a Quaker gentleman;
but that his ground adjoined Wordsworth's, and that
he had liberty to take visitors through the latter. How
absurd it would have been if we had carried away ivy-
leaves and tender recollections from this domicile of a
respectable Quaker! The gardener was an intelligent
man, of pleasant, sociable, and respectful address; and
as we went along he talked about the poet, whom he
had known, and who, he said, was very familiar with
the country people. He led us through Mr. Ball's
grounds, up a steep hillside, by winding, gravelled
walks, with summer-houses at points favourable for
them. It was a very shady and pleasant spot, containing about an acre of ground, and all turned to good
account by the manner of laying it out; so that it
seemed more than it really is. In one place, on a small,
smooth slab of slate, let into the rock, there is an inscription by Wordsworth, which I think I have read in
his works, claiming kindly regards from those who visit
the spot after his departure, because many trees had
been spared at his intercession. His own grounds, or
rather his ornamental garden, is separated from Mr.
Ball's only by a wire fence, or some such barrier, and
the gates have no fastening, so that the whole appears
like one possession, and doubtless was so as regarded
the poet's walks and enjoyments. We approached by
paths so winding that I hardly know how the house
stands in relation to the road; but, after much circuity,
we really did see Wordsworth's residence,—an old
house with an uneven ridge-pole, built of stone, no

doubt, but plastered over with some neutral tint,—a house that would not have been remarkably pretty in itself, but so delightfully situated, so secluded, so hedged about with shrubbery, and adorned with flowers, so ivy-grown on one side, so beautified with the personal care of him who lived in it and loved it, that it seemed the very place for a poet's residence; and as if, while he lived so long in it, his poetry had manifested itself in flowers, shrubbery, and ivy. I never smelt such a delightful fragrance of flowers as there was all through the garden. In front of the house there is a circular terrace of two ascents, in raising which Wordsworth had himself performed much of the labour; and here there are seats, from which we obtained a fine view down the valley of the Rothay, with Windermere in the distance,—a view of several miles, and which we did not suppose could be seen, after winding among the hills so far from the lake. It is very beautiful and picture-like. While we sat here, S. happened to refer to the ballad of little Barbara Lewthwaite, and J. began to repeat the poem concerning her, and the gardener said that "little Barbara" had died not a great while ago, an elderly woman, leaving grown-up children behind her. Her marriage-name was Thompson, and the gardener believed there was nothing remarkable in her character.

'There is a summer-house at one extremity of the grounds, in deepest shadow, but with glimpses of mountain views through trees which shut it in, and which have spread intercepting boughs since Wordsworth died. It is lined with pine-cones, in a pretty way enough, but of doubtful taste. I rather wonder that people of real taste should help nature out, and beautify her, or perhaps rather *prettify* her so much as they do,—opening vistas, showing one thing, hiding another, making a scene picturesque, whether or no. I cannot rid myself of the feeling that there is something false—a kind of humbug—in all this. At any rate, the traces of it do not contribute to my enjoyment, and, indeed, it ought to be done so exquisitely as to leave no trace. But I ought not to criticise in any way a spot which gave me so much pleasure, and where it is good to think of Wordsworth in quiet, past days, walking in his home-shadow of trees which he knew, and training flowers, and trimming shrubs, and chanting in an undertone his own verses up and down the winding walks.

The gardener gave J. a cone from the summer-house, which had fallen on the seat, and S. got some mignonette, and leaves of laurel and ivy, and we wended our way back to the hotel. Wordsworth was not the owner of this house; it being the property of Lady Fleming. Mrs. Wordsworth still lives there, and is now at home.

Five 'o'clock.—All day it has been cloudy and showery, with thunder now and then; the mists hang low on the surrounding hills, adown which, at various points, we can see the snow-white fall of little streamlets ("forces" they call them here) swollen by the rain. An overcast day is not so gloomy in the hill-country as in the lowlands; there are more breaks, more transfusion of skylight through the gloom, as has been the case to-day, and as I found in Lenox; we get better acquainted with clouds by seeing at what height they lie on the hillsides, and find that the difference betwixt a fair day and a cloudy and rainy one is very superficial, after all. Nevertheless, rain is rain, and wets a man just as much among the mountains as anywhere else; so we have been kept within doors all day, till an hour or so ago, when J. and I went down to the village in quest of the post-office.

We took a path that leads from the hotel across the fields, and, coming into a wood, crosses the Rothay by a one-arched bridge and passes the village-church. The Rothay is very swift and turbulent to-day, and hurries along with foam-specks on its surface, filling its banks from brim to brim,—a stream perhaps twenty feet wide, perhaps more; for I am willing that the good little river should have all it can fairly claim. It is the St. Lawrence of several of these English lakes, through which it flows, and carries off their superfluous waters. In its haste, and with its rushing sound, it was pleasant both to see and hear; and it sweeps by one side of the old churchyard where Wordsworth lies buried,—the side where his grave is made. The church of Grasmere is a very plain structure, with a low body, on one side of which is a small porch with a pointed arch. The tower is square, and looks ancient; but the whole is overlaid with plaster of a buff or pale yellow hue. It was originally built, I suppose, of rough shingly stones, as many of the houses hereabouts are now, and, like many of them, the plaster is used to give a finish. We found the gate of the churchyard wide open; and the grass was lying on the graves, having probably been mowed yesterday. It is but a small churchyard, and with few monuments of any pretension in it, most of them being slate headstones, standing erect. From the gate at which we entered, a distinct foot-track leads to the corner nearest the riverside, and I turned into it by a sort of instinct, the more readily as I saw a tourist-looking man approaching from that point, and a woman looking among the gravestones. Both of these persons had gone by the time I came up, so that J. and I were left to find Wordsworth's grave all by ourselves.

At this corner of the churchyard there is a hawthorn bush or tree, the extremest branches of which stretch as far as where Wordsworth lies. This whole corner seems to be devoted to himself and his family and friends; and they all lie very closely together, side by side, and head to foot, as room could conveniently be found. Hartley Coleridge lies a little behind, in the direction of the church, his feet being towards Wordsworth's head, who lies in the row of those of his own blood. I found out Hartley Coleridge's grave sooner than Wordsworth's; for it is of marble, and, though simple enough, has more of sculptured device about it, having been erected, as I think the inscription states, by his brother and sister. Wordsworth has only the very simplest slab of slate, with "William Wordsworth" and nothing else upon it. As I recollect it, it is the midmost grave of the row. It is or has been well grass-grown, but the grass is quite worn away from the top, though sufficiently luxuriant at the sides. It looks as if people had stood upon it, and so does the grave next to it, which I believe is of one of his children. I plucked some grass and weeds from it, and as he was buried within so few years they may fairly be supposed to have drawn their nutriment from his mortal remains, and I gathered them from just above his head. There is no fault to be found with his grave,—within view of the hills, within sound of the river, murmuring near by,—no fault except that he is crowded so closely with his kindred; and, more-

over, that, being so old a churchyard, the earth over
him must all have been human once. He might have
had fresh earth to himself; but he chose this grave deliberately. No very stately and broad-based monument
can ever be erected over it without infringing upon,
covering, and overshadowing the graves, not only of
his family, but of individuals who probably were quite
disconnected with him. But it is pleasant to think
and know—were it but on the evidence of this choice
of a resting-place—that he did not care for a stately
monument.

After leaving the churchyard, we wandered about
in quest of the post-office, and for a long time without
success. This little town of Grasmere seems to me as
pretty a place as ever I met with in my life. It is
quite shut in by hills that rise up immediately around
it, like a neighbourhood of kindly giants. These hills
descend steeply to the verge of the level on which the
village stands, and there they terminate at once, the
whole site of the little town being as even as a floor.
I call it a village; but it is no village at all,—all the
dwellings standing apart, each in its own little domain,
and each, I believe, with its own little lane leading to
it, independently of the rest. Most of these are old
cottages, plastered white, with antique porches, and
roses and other vines trained against them, and shrubbery growing about them; and some are covered with
ivy. There are a few edifices of more pretension and
of modern build, but not so strikingly so as to put the
rest out of countenance. The post-office, when we
found it, proved to be an ivied cottage, with a good
deal of shrubbery round it, having its own pathway,
like the other cottages. The whole looks like a real

seclusion, shut out from the great world by these encircling hills, on the sides of which, whenever they are not too steep, you see the division lines of property, and tokens of cultivation,—taking from them their pretensions to savage majesty, but bringing them nearer to the heart of man.

Since writing the above, I have been again with S. to see Wordsworth's grave, and, finding the door of the church open, we went in. A woman and little girl were sweeping at the farther end, and the woman came towards us out of the cloud of dust which she had raised. We were surprised at the extremely antique appearance of the church. It is paved with bluish-grey flagstones, over which uncounted generations have trodden, leaving the floor as well laid as ever. The walls are very thick, and the arched windows open through them at a considerable distance above the floor. There is no middle aisle; but first a row of pews next either wall, and then an aisle on each side of the pews, occupying the centre of the church,—then, two side aisles, but no middle one. And down through the centre of the church runs a row of five arches, very rude and round-headed, all of rough stone, supported by rough and massive pillars, or rather square, stone blocks, which stand in the pews, and stood in the same places, probably, long before the wood of those pews began to grow. Above this row of arches is another row, built upon the same mass of stone, and almost as broad, but lower; and on this upper row rests the framework, the oaken beams, the black skeleton of the roof. It is a very clumsy contrivance for supporting the roof, and if it were modern, we certainly should condemn it as very ugly; but being the relic of a simple age, it comes in well with the antique simplicity of the whole structure. The roof goes up, barn-like, into its natural angle, and all the rafters and crossbeams are visible. There is an old font; and in the chancel is a niche, where (judging from a similar one in Furness Abbey) the holy water used to be placed for the priest's use while celebrating mass. Around the inside of the porch is a stone bench, against the wall, narrow and uneasy, but where a great many people had sat, who now have found quieter resting-places.

The woman was a very intelligent-looking person, not of the usual English ruddiness, but rather thin and somewhat pale, though bright of aspect. Her way of talking was very agreeable. She inquired if we wished to see Wordsworth's monument, and at once showed it to us,—a slab of white marble fixed against the upper end of the central row of stone arches, with a pretty long inscription, and a profile bust, in bas-relief, of his aged countenance. The monument is placed directly over Wordsworth's pew, and could best be seen and read from the very corner seat where he used to sit. The pew is one of those occupying the centre of the church, and is just across the aisle from the pulpit, and is the best of all for the purpose of seeing and hearing the clergyman, and likewise as convenient as any, from its neighbourhood to the altar. On the other side of the aisle, beneath the pulpit, is Lady Fleming's pew. This and one or two others are curtained, Wordsworth's was not. I think I can bring up his image in that corner seat of his pew—a white-headed, tall, spare man, plain in aspect—better than in any other situation. The woman said that she had known him very well, and that he had made some verses on a sister of hers. She repeated the first lines, something about a lamb, but neither S. nor I remembered them.

On the walls of the chancel there are monuments to the Flemings, and painted escutcheons of their arms; and along the side walls also, and on the square pillars of the row of arches, there are other monuments, generally of white marble, with the letters of the inscription blackened. On these pillars, likewise, and in many places in the walls, were hung verses from Scripture, painted on boards. At one of the doors was a poor-box,—an elaborately carved little box, of oak, with the date 1648, and the name of the church—St. Oswald's—upon it. The whole interior of the edifice was plain, simple, almost to grimness,—or would have been so, only that the foolish churchwardens, or other authority, have washed it over with the same buff colour with which they have overlaid the exterior. It is a pity; it lightens it up, and desecrates it greatly, especially as the woman says that there were formerly paintings on the walls, now obliterated for ever. I could have stayed in the old church much longer, and could write much more about it, but there must be an end to everything. Pacing it from the farther end to the elevation before the altar, I found that it was twenty-five paces long.

On looking again at the Rothay, I find I did it some injustice: for at the bridge, in its present swollen state, it is nearer twenty yards than twenty feet across. Its waters are very clear, and it rushes along with a speed which is delightful to see, after an acquaintance with the muddy and sluggish Avon and Leam.

Since tea I have taken a stroll from the hotel in a different direction from heretofore, and passed the Swan

Inn, where Scott used to go daily to get a draught of liquor, when he was visiting Wordsworth, who had no wine nor other inspiriting fluid in his house. It stands directly on the wayside,—a small whitewashed house, with an addition in the rear that seems to have been built since Scott's time. On the door is the painted sign of a swan, and the name, "Scott's Swan Hotel." I walked a considerable distance beyond it, but, a shower coming up, I turned back, entered the inn, and, following the mistress into a snug little room, was served with a glass of bitter ale. It is a very plain and homely inn, and certainly could not have satisfied Scott's wants if he had required anything very farfetched or delicate in his potations. I found two Westmoreland peasants in the room, with ale before them. One went away almost immediately; but the other remained, and, entering into conversation with him, he told me that he was going to New Zealand, and expected to sail in September. I announced myself as an American, and he said that a large party had lately gone from hereabouts to America; but he seemed not to understand that there was any distinction between Canada and the States. These people had gone to Quebec. He was a very civil, well-behaved, kindly sort of person, of a simple character, which I took to belong to the class and locality, rather than to himself individually. I could not very well understand all that he said, owing to his provincial dialect; and when he spoke to his own countrymen, or to the women of the house, I really could but just catch a word here and there. How long it takes to melt English down into a homogeneous mass! He told me that there was a public library in Grasmere, to which he has access in common with the other inhabitants, and a reading-room connected with it, where he reads the *Times* in the evening. There was no American smartness in his mind. When I left the house, it was showering briskly; but the drops quite ceased, and the clouds began to break away before I reached my hotel, and I saw the new moon over my right shoulder.

July 21st.—We left Grasmere yesterday, after breakfast; it being a delightful morning, with some clouds, but the cheerfullest sunshine on great part of the mountain-sides and on ourselves. We returned, in the first place, to Ambleside, along the border of Grasmere Lake, which would be a pretty little piece of water, with its steep and high surrounding hills, were it not that a stubborn and straight-lined stone fence, running along the eastern shore, by the road-side, quite spoils its appearance. Rydal Water, though nothing can make a lake of it, looked prettier and less diminutive than at the first view; and, in fact, I find that it is impossible to know accurately how any prospect or other thing looks, until after at least a second view, which always essentially corrects the first. This, I think, is especially true in regard to objects which we have heard much about, and exercised our imagination upon; the first view being a vain attempt to reconcile our idea with the reality, and at the second we begin to accept the thing for what it really is. Wordsworth's situation is really a beautiful one; and Nab Scaur behind his house rises with a grand, protecting air. We passed Nab's cottage, in which De Quincey formerly lived, and where Hartley Coleridge lived and died. It is a small, buff-tinted, plastered stone cottage, immediately on the roadside, and originally, I should think, of a very humble class; but it now looks as if persons of taste might some time or other have sat down in it, and caused flowers to spring up about it. It is very agreeably situated under the great, precipitous hill, and with Rydal Water close at hand, on the other side of the road. An advertisement of lodgings to let was put up on this cottage.

I question whether any part of the world looks so beautiful as England—this part of England, at least—on a fine summer morning. It makes one think the more cheerfully of human life to see such a bright universal verdure; such sweet, rural, peaceful, flower-bordered cottages,—not cottages of gentility, but dwellings of the labouring poor; such nice villas along the roadside, so tastefully contrived for comfort and beauty, and adorned more and more, year after year, with the care and after-thought of people who mean to live in them a great while, and feel as if their children might live in them also,—and so they plant trees to overshadow their walks, and train ivy and all beautiful vines up against their walls, and thus live for the future in another sense than we Americans do. And the climate helps them out, and makes everything moist, and green, and full of tender life, instead of dry and arid, as human life and vegetable life is so apt to be with us. Certainly, England can present a more attractive face than we can; even in its humbler modes of life, to say nothing of the beautiful lives that might be led, one would think, by the higher classes, whose gateways, with broad, smooth-gravelled drives leading through them, one sees every mile or two along the road, winding into some proud seclusion. All this is passing away, and society must assume new relations; but there is no harm in believing that there has been something very good in English life,—good for all classes while the world was in a state out of which these forms naturally grew.

Passing through Ambleside, our phaeton and pair turned towards Ullswater, which we were to reach through the Pass of Kirkstone. This is some three or four miles from Ambleside, and as we approached it the road kept ascending higher and higher, the hills grew more bare, and the country lost its soft and delightful verdure. At last the road became so steep that J. and I alighted to walk. This is the aspiring road that Wordsworth speaks of in his ode; it passes through the gorge of precipitous hills,—or almost precipitous, —too much so for even the grass to grow on many portions, which are covered with grey shingly stones; and I think this pass, in its middle part, must have looked just the same when the Romans marched through it as it looks now. No trees could ever have grown on the steep hillsides, whereon even the English climate can generate no available soil. I do not know that I have seen anything more impressive than the stern grey sweep of these naked mountains, with nothing whatever to soften or adorn them. The notch of the White Mountains, as I remember it in my youthful days, is more wonderful and richly picturesque, but of quite a different character.

About the centre and at the highest point of the pass stands an old stone building of mean appearance, with the usual sign of an ale-house, "Licensed to retail foreign spirits, ale, and tobacco," over the door, and another small sign, designating it as the highest inhabitable house in England. It is a chill and desolate place for a residence. They keep a visitors' book here, and we recorded our names in it, and were not too sorry to leave the mean little hovel, smelling as it did of tobacco smoke, and possessing all other characteristics of the humblest ale-house on the level earth.

The Kirkstone, which gives the pass its name, is not seen in approaching from Ambleside, until some time after you begin to descend towards Brothers' Water. When the driver first pointed it out, a little way up the hill on our left, it looked no more than a boulder of a ton or two in weight, among a hundred others nearly as big; and I saw hardly any resemblance to a church or church spire, to which the fancies of past generations have likened it. As we descended the pass, however, and left the stone farther and farther behind, it continued to show itself, and assumed a more striking and prominent aspect, standing out clearly relieved against the sky, so that no traveller would fail to observe it, where there are so few defined objects to attract notice, amid the naked monotony of the stern hills; though, indeed, if I had taken it for any sort of an edifice, it would rather have been for a wayside inn or a shepherd's hut than for a church. We lost sight of it, and again beheld it more and more brought out against the sky, by the turns of the road, several times in the course of our descent. There is a very fine view of Brothers' Water, shut in by steep hills, as we go down Kirkstone Pass.

At about half-past twelve we reached Patterdale, at the foot of Ullswater, and here took luncheon. The hotels are mostly very good all through this region, and this deserved that character. A black-coated waiter,

of more gentlemanly appearance than most Englishmen,
yet taking a sixpence with as little scruple as a lawyer
would take his fee; the mistress, in ladylike attire,
receiving us at the door, and waiting upon us to the
carriage steps; clean, comely housemaids everywhere
at hand,—all appliances, in short, for being comfortable,
and comfortable, too, within one's own circle. And,
on taking leave, everybody who has done anything for
you, or who might by possibility have done anything,
is to be feed. You pay the landlord enough, in all
conscience; and then you pay all his servants, who
have been your servants for the time. But, to say the
truth, there is a degree of the same kind of annoyance
in an American hotel, although it is not so much an
acknowledged custom. Here, in the houses where attendance is not charged in the bill, no wages are paid
by the host to those servants—chambermaid, waiter,
and boots—who come into immediate contact with
travellers. The drivers of the cars, phaetons, and flys
are likewise unpaid, except by their passengers, and
claim threepence a mile with the same sense of right
as their masters in charging for the vehicles and horses.
When you come to understand this claim, not as an
appeal to your generosity, but as an actual and necessary part of the cost of the journey, it is yielded to
with a more comfortable feeling; and the traveller has
really option enough, as to the amount which he will
give, to insure civility and good behaviour on the
driver's part.

Ullswater is a beautiful lake, with steep hills wall-
ing it about,—so steep, on the eastern side, that there
seems hardly room for a road to run along the base.
We passed up the western shore, and turned off from

it about midway, to take the road towards Keswick. We stopped, however, at Lyulph's Tower, while our chariot went on up a hill, and took a guide to show us the way to Airey Force,—a small cataract, which is claimed as private property, and out of which, no doubt, a pretty little revenue is raised. I do not think that there can be any rightful appropriation, as private property, of objects of natural beauty. The fruits of the land, and whatever human labour can produce from it, belong fairly enough to the person who has a deed or a lease; but the beautiful is the property of him who can hive it and enjoy it. It is very unsatisfactory to think of a cataract under lock and key. However, we were shown to Airey Force by a tall and graceful mountain-maid, with a healthy cheek, and a step that had no possibility of weariness in it. The cascade is an irregular streak of foamy water, pouring adown a rude shadowy glen. I liked well enough to see it; but it is wearisome, on the whole, to go the rounds of what everybody thinks it necessary to see. It makes me a little ashamed. It is somewhat as if we were drinking out of the same glass, and eating from the same dish, as a multitude of other people.

Within a few miles of Keswick, we passed along at the foot of Saddleback, and by the entrance of the Vale of St. John, and down the valley, on one of the slopes, we saw the Enchanted Castle. Thence we drove along by the course of the Greta, and soon arrived at Keswick, which lies at the base of Skiddaw, and among a brotherhood of picturesque eminences, and is itself a compact little town, with a market-house, built of the old stones of the Earl of Derwentwater's ruined castle, standing in the centre,—the principal street forking into two as it passes it. We alighted at the King's Arms, and went in search of Southey's residence, which we found easily enough, as it lies just on the outskirts of the town. We inquired of a group of people, two of whom, I thought, did not seem to know much about the matter; but the third, an elderly man, pointed it out at once,—a house surrounded by trees, so as to be seen only partially, and standing on a little eminence, a hundred yards or so from the road.

We went up a private lane that led to the rear of the place, and so penetrated quite into the back yard without meeting anybody,—passing a small kennel, in which were two hounds, who gazed at us, but neither growled nor wagged their tails. The house is three stories high, and seems to have a great deal of room in it, so as not to discredit its name, "Greta Hall,"— a very spacious dwelling for a poet. The windows were nearly all closed; there were no signs of occupancy, but a general air of neglect. S., who is bolder than I in these matters, ventured through what seemed a back garden gate, and I soon heard her in conversation with some man, who now presented himself, and proved to be a gardener. He said he had formerly acted in that capacity for Southey, although a gardener had not been kept by him as a regular part of his establishment. This was an old man with an odd crookedness of legs, and strange, disjointed limp. S. had told him that we were Americans, and he took the idea that we had come this long distance, over sea and land, with the sole purpose of seeing Southey's residence, so that he was inclined to do what he could towards exhibiting it. This was but little; the present occupant (a Mr.

Radday, I believe the gardener called him) being away, and the house shut up.

But he showed us about the grounds, and allowed us to peep into the windows of what had been Southey's library, and into those of another of the front apartments, and showed us the window of the chamber in the rear, in which Southey died. The apartments into which we peeped looked rather small and low,—not particularly so, but enough to indicate an old building. They are now handsomely furnished, and we saw over one of the fireplaces an inscription about Southey; and in the corner of the same room stood a suit of bright armour. The house is taller than the country-houses of English gentlemen usually are, and is even stately. All about, in front, beside it and behind, there is a great profusion of trees, most of which were planted by Southey, who came to live here more than fifty years ago, and they have, of course, grown much more shady now than he ever beheld them; for he died about fourteen years since. The grounds are well laid out, and neatly kept, with the usual lawn and gravelled walks, and quaint little devices in the ornamental way. These may be of later date than Southey's time. The gardener spoke respectfully of Southey, and of his first wife, and observed that "it was a great loss to the neighbourhood when that family went down."

The house stands directly above the Greta, the murmur of which is audible all about it; for the Greta is a swift little river, and goes on its way with a continual sound, which has both depth and breadth. The gardener led us to a walk along its banks, close by the Hall, where he said Southey used to walk for hours and hours together. He might, indeed, get

there from his study in a moment. There are two
paths, one above the other, well laid out on the steep
declivity of the high bank; and there is such a very
thick shade of oaks and elms, planted by Southey
himself over the bank, that all the ground and grass
were moist, although it had been a sunny day. It is
a very sombre walk; not many glimpses of the sky
through those dense boughs. The Greta is here, perhaps, twenty yards across, and very dark of hue, and
its voice is melancholy and very suggestive of musings
and reveries; but I should question whether it were
favourable to any settled scheme of thought. The
gardener told us that there used to be a pebbly beach
on the margin of the river, and that it was Southey's
habit to sit and write there, using a tree of peculiar
shape for a table. An alteration in the current of the
river has swept away the beach, and the tree, too,
has fallen. All these things were interesting to me,
although Southey was not, I think, a picturesque man,
—not one whose personal character takes a strong hold
on the imagination. In these walks he used to wear
a pair of shoes heavily clamped with iron; very ponderous they must have been, from the particularity with
which the gardener mentioned them.

The gardener took leave of us at the front entrance
of the grounds, and, returning to the King's Arms,
we ordered a one-horse fly for the fall of Lodore. Our
drive thither was along the banks of Derwentwater,
and it is as beautiful a road, I imagine, as can be
found in England or anywhere else. I like Derwentwater the best of all the lakes, so far as I have yet
seen them. Skiddaw lies at the head of a long even
ridge of mountains, rising into several peaks, and one

higher than the rest. On the eastern side there are
many noble eminences, and on the west, along which
we drove, there is a part of the way a lovely wood,
and nearly the whole distance a precipitous range of
lofty cliffs, descending sheer down without any slope,
except what has been formed in the lapse of ages by
the fall of fragments, and the washing down of smaller
stones.. The declivity thus formed along the base of
the cliffs is in some places covered with trees or shrubs;
elsewhere it is quite bare and barren. The precipitous
parts of the cliffs are very grand; the whole scene, indeed, might be characterized as one of stern grandeur
with an embroidery of rich beauty, without lauding it
too much. All the sternness of it is softened by
vegetative beauty wherever it can possibly be thrown
in; and there is not here, so strongly as along Windermere, evidence that human art has been helping out
Nature. I wish it were possible to give any idea of
the shapes of the hills; with these, at least, man has
nothing to do, nor ever will have anything to do. As
we approached the bottom of the lake, and of the
beautiful valley in which it lies, we saw one hill that
seemed to crouch down like a Titanic watchdog, with
its rear towards the spectator, guarding the entrance
to the valley. The great superiority of these mountains
over those of New England is their variety and definite-
ness of shape, besides the abundance everywhere of
water prospects, which are wanting among our own
hills. They rise up decidedly, and each is a hill by
itself, while ours mingle into one another, and, besides,
have such large bases that you can tell neither where
they begin nor where they end. Many of these Cum-
berland mountains have a marked vertebral shape, so

that they often look like a group of huge lions, lying down with their backs turned toward each other. They slope down steeply from narrow ridges; hence their picturesque seclusions of valleys and dales, which subdivide the lake region into so many communities. Our hills, like apple-dumplings in a dish, have no such valleys as these.

There is a good inn at Lodore,—a small, primitive country inn, which has latterly been enlarged and otherwise adapted to meet the convenience of the guests brought thither by the fame of the cascade; but it is still a country inn though it takes upon itself the title of hotel.

We found pleasant rooms here, and established ourselves for the night. From this point we have a view of the beautiful lake, and of Skiddaw at the head of it. The cascade is within three or four minutes' walk, through the garden gate, towards the cliff, at the base of which the inn stands. The visitor would need no other guide than its own voice, which is said to be audible sometimes at the distance of four miles. As we were coming from Keswick, we caught glimpses of its white foam high up the precipice; and it is only glimpses that can be caught anywhere, because there is no regular sheet of falling water. Once, I think, it must have fallen abruptly over the edge of the long line of precipice that here extends along parallel with the shore of the lake; but, in the course of time, it has gnawed and sawed its way into the heart of the cliff, —this persistent little stream,—so that now it has formed a rude gorge, adown which it hurries and tumbles in the wildest way, over the roughest imaginable staircase. Standing at the bottom of the fall, you have a far vista sloping upward to the sky, with the water everywhere as white as snow, pouring and pouring down, now on one side of the gorge, now on the other, among immense boulders, which try to choke its passage. It does not attempt to leap over these huge rocks, but finds its way in and out among them, and finally gets to the bottom after a hundred tumbles. It cannot be better described than in Southey's verses, though it is worthy of better poetry than that. After all, I do not know that the cascade is anything more than a beautiful fringe to the grandeur of the scene; for it is very grand,—this fissure through the cliff,—with a steep, lofty precipice on the right hand, sheer up and down, and on the other hand, too, another lofty precipice, with a slope of its own ruin on which trees and shrubbery have grown. The right-hand precipice, however, has shelves affording sufficient hold for small trees, but nowhere does it slant. If it were not for the white little stream falling gently downward, and for the soft verdure upon either precipice, and even along the very pathway of the cascade, it would be a very stern vista up that gorge.

I shall not try to describe any more. It has not been praised too much, though it may have been praised amiss. I went thither again in the morning, and climbed a good way up, through the midst of its rocky descent, and I think I could have reached the top in this way. It is remarkable that the bounds of the water, from one step of its broken staircase to another, give an impression of softness and gentleness; but there are black, turbulent pools among the great boulders, where the stream seems angry at the difficulties which it meets with. Looking upward in the sunshine, I could see a rising mist, and I should not wonder if a speck of rainbow were sometimes visible. I noticed a small oak in the bed of the cascade, and there is a lighter vegetation scattered about.

At noon we took a car for Portinscale, and drove back along the road to Keswick, through which we passed, stopping to get a packet of letters at the post-office, and reached Portinscale, which is a mile from Keswick. After dinner we walked over a bridge, and through a green lane, to the church where Southey is buried. It is a white church, of Norman architecture, with a low, square tower. As we approached, we saw two persons entering the portal, and, following them in, we found the sexton, who was a tall, thin old man, with white hair, and an intelligent, reverent face, showing the edifice to a stout, red-faced, self-important, good-natured John Bull of a gentleman. Without any question on our part, the old sexton immediately led us to Southey's monument, which is placed in a side aisle, where there is not breadth for it to stand free of the wall; neither is it in a very good light. But it seemed to me a good work of art,—a recumbent figure of white marble, on a couch, the drapery of which he has drawn about him,—being quite enveloped in what may be a shroud. The sculptor has not intended to represent death, for the figure lies on its side, and has a book in its hand, and the face is lifelike, and looks full of expression,—a thin, high-featured, poetic face, with a finely proportioned head and abundant hair. It represents Southey rightly, at whatever age he died, in the full maturity of manhood, when he was strongest and richest. I liked the statue, and wished that it lay in a broader aisle, or in the chancel, where there is an old tomb of a knight and lady of the Ratcliffe family, who have held the place of honour long enough to yield it now to a poet. Southey's sculptor was Lough. I must not forget to mention that John Bull, climbing on a bench, to get a better view of the statue, tumbled off with a racket that resounded irreverently through the church.

The old, white-headed, thin sexton was a model man of his class, and appeared to take a loving and cheerful interest in the building, and in those who, from age to age, have worshipped and been buried there. It is a very ancient and interesting church. Within a few years it has been thoroughly repaired as to the interior, and now looks as if it might endure ten more centuries; and I suppose we see little that is really ancient, except the double row of Norman arches, of light freestone, that support the oaken beams and rafters of the roof. All the walls, however, are venerable, and quite preserve the identity of the edifice. There is a stained-glass window of modern manufacture, and in one of the side windows, set amidst plain glass, there is a single piece, five hundred years old, representing St. Anthony, very finely executed, though it looks a little faded. Along the walls, on each side, between the arched windows, there are marble slabs affixed, with inscriptions to the memories of those who used to occupy the seats beneath. I remember none of great antiquity, nor any old monument, except that in the chancel, over the knight and lady of the Ratcliffe family. This consists of a slab of stone, on four small stone pillars, about two feet high. The slab is inlaid with a brass plate, on which is sculptured the knight in armour, and the lady in the costume of Elizabeth's time, exceedingly well done and well preserved, and each figure about eighteen inches in length. The sexton showed us a rubbing of them on paper. Under the slab, which, supported by the low stone pillars, forms a canopy for them, lie two sculptured figures of stone, of life size, and at full length, representing the same persons; but I think the sculptor was hardly equal in his art to the engraver.

The most curious antique relic in the church is the font. The bowl is very capacious, sufficiently so to admit of the complete immersion of a child of two or three months old. On the outside, in several compartments, there are bas-reliefs of scriptural and symbolic subjects,—such as the tree of life, the word proceeding out of God's mouth, the crown of thorns,—all in the quaintest taste, sculptured by some hand of a thousand years ago, and preserving the fancies of monkish brains, in stone. The sexton was very proud of this font and its sculpture, and took a kindly personal interest in showing it; and when we had spent as much time as we could inside, he led us to Southey's grave in the churchyard. He told us that he had known Southey long and well, from early manhood to old age; for he was only twenty-nine when he came to Keswick to reside. He had known Wordsworth too, and Coleridge, and Lovell; and he had seen Southey and Wordsworth walking arm in arm together in that churchyard. He seemed to revere Southey's memory, and said that he had been much lamented, and that as many as a hundred people came to the churchyard when he was buried. He spoke with great praise of Mrs. Southey, his first wife, telling of her charity to the poor, and how she was a blessing to the neighbourhood; but he said nothing in favour of the second Mrs. Southey, and only mentioned her selling the library, and other things, after her husband's death, and going to London. Yet I think she was probably a good woman, and meets with less than justice because she took the place of another good woman, and had not time and opportunity to prove herself as good. As for Southey himself, my idea is, that few better or more blameless men have ever lived; but he seems to lack colour, passion, warmth, or something that should enable me to bring him into close relation with myself. The graveyard where his body lies is not so rural and picturesque as that where Wordsworth is buried, although Skiddaw rises behind it, and the Greta is murmuring at no very great distance away. But the spot itself has a somewhat bare and bold aspect, with no shadow of trees, no shrubbery.

Over his grave there is a ponderous, oblong block of slate, a native mineral of this region, as hard as iron, and which will doubtless last quite as long as Southey's works retain any vitality in English literature. It is not a monument fit for a poet. There is nothing airy or graceful about it,—and, indeed, there cannot be many men so solid and matter-of-fact as to deserve a tomb like that. Wordsworth's grave is much better, with only a simple headstone, and the grass growing over his mortality, which, for a thousand years, at least, it never can over Southey's. Most of the monuments are of this same black slate, and some erect headstones are curiously sculptured, and seem to have been recently erected.

We now returned to the hotel, and took a car for the valley of St. John. The sky seemed to portend rain in no long time, and Skiddaw had put on his cap; but the people of the hotel and the driver said that there would be no rain this afternoon, and their opinion proved correct. After driving a few miles, we again came within sight of the Enchanted Castle. It stands rather more than midway adown the declivity of one of the ridges that form the valley to the left, as you go southward, and its site would have been a good one for a fortress, intended to defend the lower entrance of this mountain defile. At a proper distance, it looks not unlike the grey dilapidation of a Gothic castle, which has been crumbling and crumbling away for ages, until Time might be supposed to have imperceptibly stolen its massive pile from man, and given it back to Nature; its towers and battlements and arched entrances being so much defaced and decayed that all the marks of human labour had nearly been obliterated, and the angles of the hewn stone rounded away, while mosses and weeds and bushes grow over it as freely as over a natural ledge of rocks. It is conceivable that in some lights, and in some states of the atmosphere, a traveller, at the entrance of the valley, might really imagine that he beheld a castle here; but, for myself, I must acknowledge that it required a willing fancy to make me see it. As we drew nearer, the delusion did not immediately grow less strong; but, at length, we found ourselves passing at the foot of the declivity, and, behold! it was nothing but an enormous ledge of rock, coming squarely out of the hillside, with other parts of the ledge cropping out in its vicinity. Looking back, after passing, we saw a knoll or hillock, of which the castled rock is the bare face. There are two or three stone cottages along the roadside, beneath the magic castle, and within the enchanted ground. Scott, in *The Bridal of Triermain*, locates the castle in the middle of the valley, and makes King Arthur ride around it, which any mortal would have great difficulty in doing. This vale of St. John has very striking scenery. Blencathra shuts it in to the northward, lying right across the entrance; and on either side there are lofty crags and declivities, those to the west being more broken and better wooded than the ridge to the eastward, which stretches along for several miles, steep, high, and bare, producing only grass enough for sheep pasture, until it rises into the dark brow of Helvellyn. Adown this ridge, seen afar, like a white ribbon, comes here and there a cascade, sending its voice before it, which distance robs of all its fury, and makes it the quietest sound in the world; and while you see the foamy leap of its upper course a mile or two away, you may see and hear the self-same little brook babbling through a field, and passing under the arch of a rustic bridge beneath your feet. It is a deep seclusion, with mountains and crags on all sides.

About a mile beyond the castle we stopped at a little wayside inn, the King's Head, and put up for the night. This, I believe, is the only inn which I have found in England—the only one where I have eaten and slept—that does not call itself a hotel. It is very primitive in its arrangements,—a long, low, whitewashed, unadorned, and ugly cottage of two stories. At one extremity is a barn and cow-house, and next to these the part devoted to the better class of guests, where we had our parlour and chambers, contiguous to which is the kitchen and common room, paved with flagstones,—and, lastly, another barn and stable; all which departments are not under separate roofs, but under the same long contiguity, and forming the same building. Our parlour opens immediately upon the roadside, without any vestibule. The house appears to be of some antiquity, with beams across the low ceilings; but the people made us pretty comfortable at bed and board, and fed us with ham and eggs, veal steaks, honey, oat-cakes, gooseberry tarts, and such cates and dainties,—making a moderate charge for all. The parlour was adorned with rude engravings. I remember only a plate of the Duke of Wellington, at three stages of his life; and there were minerals, delved, doubtless, out of the hearts of the mountains, upon the mantelpiece. The chairs were of an antiquated fashion, and had very capacious seats. We were waited upon by two women, who looked and acted not unlike the country-folk of New England,—say, of New Hampshire, —except that these may have been more deferential.

While we remained here, I took various walks to get a glimpse of Helvellyn, and a view of Thirlmere, —which is rather two lakes than one, being so narrow at one point as to be crossed by a foot-bridge. Its shores are very picturesque, coming down abruptly upon it, and broken into crags and prominences, which view their shaggy faces in its mirror; and Helvellyn slopes steeply upward, from its southern shore, into the clouds. On its eastern bank, near the foot-bridge, stands Armboth House, which Miss Martineau says is haunted; and I saw a painted board at the entrance of the road which leads to it advertising lodgings there. The ghosts, of course, pay nothing for their accommodations.

At noon, on the day after our arrival, J. and I

went to visit the Enchanted Castle; and we were so venturesome as to turn aside from the road, and ascend the declivity towards its walls, which indeed we hoped to surmount. It proved a very difficult undertaking, the site of the fortress being much higher and steeper than we had supposed; but we did clamber upon what we took for the most elevated portion, when, lo! we found that we had only taken one of the outworks, and that there was a gorge of the hill betwixt us and the main walls; while the citadel rose high above, at more than twice the elevation which we had climbed. J. wished to go on, and I allowed him to climb, till he appeared to have reached so steep and lofty a height that he looked hardly bigger than a monkey, and I should not at all have wondered had he come rolling down to the base of the rock where I sat. But neither did he get actually within the castle, though he might have done so but for a high stone fence, too difficult for him to climb, which runs from the rock along the hillside. The sheep probably go thither much oftener than any other living thing, and to them we left the castle of St. John, with a shrub waving from its battlements, instead of a banner.

After dinner we ordered a car for Ambleside, and while it was getting ready, I went to look at the river of St. John, which, indeed, flows close beside our inn, only just across the road, though it might well be overlooked unless you specially sought for it. It is a brook brawling over the stones, very much as brooks do in New England, only we never think of calling them rivers there. I could easily have made a leap from shore to shore, and J. scrambled across on no better footing than a rail. I believe I have complained of the want of brooks in other parts of England, but there is no want of them here, and they are always interesting, being of what size they may.

We drove down the valley, and gazed at the vast slope of Helvellyn, and at Thirlmere beneath it, and at Eagle's Crag and Raven's Crag, which beheld themselves in it, and we cast many a look behind at Blencathra, and that noble brotherhood of mountains out of the midst of which we came. But, to say the truth, I was weary of fine scenery, and it seemed to me that I had eaten a score of mountains, and quaffed as many lakes, all in the space of two or three days,—and the natural consequence was a surfeit. There was scarcely a single place in all our tour where I should not have been glad to spend a month; but, by flitting so quickly from one point to another, I lost all the more recondite beauties, and had come away without retaining even the surface of much that I had seen. I am slow to feel,—slow, I suppose, to comprehend, and, like the anaconda, I need to lubricate any object a great deal before I can swallow it and actually make it my own. Yet I shall always enjoy having made this journey, and shall wonder the more at England, which comprehends so much, such a rich variety, within its narrow bounds. If England were all the world, it still would have been worth while for the Creator to have made it, and mankind would have had no cause to find fault with their abode; except that there is not room enough for so many as might be happy here.

We left the great inverted arch of the valley behind us, looking back as long as we could at Blencathra, and Skiddaw over its shoulder, and the clouds were gathering over them at our last glimpse. Passing by

Dunmail Raise (which is a mound of stones over an old British king), we entered Westmoreland, and soon had the vale of Grasmere before us, with the church where Wordsworth lies, and Nab Scaur, and Rydal Water farther on. At Ambleside we took another car for Newby Bridge, whither we drove along the eastern shore of Windermere. The superb scenery through which we had been passing made what we now saw look tame, although a week ago we should have thought it more than commonly interesting. Hawkshead is the only village on our road,—a small, whitewashed old town, with a whitewashed old Norman church, low, and with a low tower, on the same pattern with others that we have seen hereabouts. It was between seven and eight o'clock when we reached Newby Bridge, and heard U.'s voice greeting us, and saw her head, crowned with a wreath of flowers, looking down at us, out of the window of our parlour.

And to-day, July 23d, I have written this most incomplete and unsatisfactory record of what we have done and seen since Wednesday last. I am pretty well convinced that all attempts at describing scenery, especially mountain-scenery, are sheer nonsense. For one thing, the point of view being changed, the whole description, which you made up from the previous point of view, is immediately falsified. And when you have done your utmost, such items as those setting forth the scene in a play,—"a mountainous country, in the distance a cascade tumbling over a precipice, and in front a lake; on one side an ivy-covered cottage,"—this dry detail brings the matter before one's mind's eyes more effectually than all the art of word-painting.

July 27th.—We are still at Newby Bridge, and nothing has occurred of remarkable interest, nor have we made any excursions, beyond moderate walks. Two days have been rainy, and to-day there is more rain. We find such weather as tolerable here as it would probably be anywhere; but it passes rather heavily with the children,—and for myself, I should prefer sunshine, though Mr. White's books afford me some entertainment, especially an odd volume of Ben Jonson's plays, containing "Volpone," "The Alchemist," "Bartholomew Fair," and others. "The Alchemist" is certainly a great play. We watch all arrivals and other events from our parlour window,—a stage-coach driving up four times in the twenty-four hours, with its forlorn outsiders, all saturated with rain; the steamer, from the head of the lake, landing a crowd of passengers, who stroll up to the hotel, drink a glass of ale, lean over the parapet of the bridge, gaze at the flat stones which pave the bottom of the river, and then hurry back to the steamer again; cars, phaetons, horsemen, all damped and disconsolate. There are a number of young men staying at the hotel, some of whom go forth in all the rain, fishing, and come back at nightfall, trudging heavily, but with creels on their backs that do not seem very heavy. Yesterday was fair, and enlivened us a good deal. Returning from a walk in the forenoon, I found a troop of yeomanry cavalry in the stable-yard of the hotel. They were the North Lancashire Regiment, and were on their way to Liverpool for the purpose of drill. Not being old campaigners, their uniforms and accoutrements were in so much the finer order, all bright, and looking span-new, and they themselves were a body of handsome and stalwart young men; and it was pleasant to look at their helmets, and red jackets, and carbines, and steel scabbarded swords, and gallant steeds,—all so martial in aspect,—and to know that they were only play-soldiers, after all, and were never likely to do nor suffer any warlike mischief. By-and-by their bugles sounded, and they trotted away, wheeling over the ivy-grown stone bridge, and disappearing behind the trees on the Milnethorpe road. Our host comes forth from the bar with a bill, which he presents to an orderly-sergeant. He, the host, then tells me that he himself once rode many years, a trooper, in this regiment, and that all his comrades were larger men than himself. Yet Mr. Thomas White is a good-sized man, and now, at all events, rather overweight for a dragoon.

Yesterday came one of those bands of music that seem to itinerate everywhere about the country. It consisted of a young woman who played the harp, a bass-viol player, a fiddler, a flutist, and a bugler, besides a little child, of whom, I suppose, the woman was the mother. They sat down on a bench by the roadside, opposite the house, and played several tunes, and by-and-by the waiter brought them a large pitcher of ale, which they quaffed with apparent satisfaction; though they seemed to be foreigners by their mustachios and sallow hue, and would perhaps have preferred a vinous potation. One would like to follow these people through their vagrant life, and see them in their social relations, and overhear their talk with each other. All vagrants are interesting; and there is a much greater variety of them here than in America,—people who cast themselves on Fortune, and take whatever she gives without a certainty of anything. I saw a travelling tinker yesterday,—a man with a leather apron, and a string of skewers hung at his girdle, and a pack over his shoulders, in which, no doubt, were his tools and materials of trade.

It is remarkable what a natural interest everybody feels in fishing. An angler from the bridge immediately attracts a group to watch his luck. It is the same with J., fishing for minnows, on the platform near which the steamer lands its passengers. By-the-bye, U. caught a minnow last evening, and, immediately after, a good-sized perch,—her first fish.

July 30th.—We left Newby Bridge, all of us, on Saturday, at twelve o'clock, and steamed up the lake to Ambleside; a pretty good day as to weather, but with a little tendency to shower. There was nothing new on the lake, and no new impressions, as far as I can remember. At Ambleside, S. and Fanny went shopping, after which we took a carriage for Grasmere, and established ourselves at Brown's Hotel. I find that my impressions from our previous sight of all these scenes do not change on revision. They are very beautiful; but, if I must say it, I am a little weary of them. We soon tire of things which we visit merely by way of spectacle, and with which we have no real and permanent connection. In such cases we very quickly wish the spectacle to be taken away, and another substituted; at all events, I do not care about seeing anything more of the English lakes for at least a year.

Perhaps a part of my weariness is owing to the hotel-life which we lead. At an English hotel the traveller feels as if everybody, from the landlord downward, united in a joint and individual purpose to fleece him, because all the attendants who come in contact with him are to be separately considered. So, after paying, in the first instance, a very heavy bill, for what would seem to cover the whole indebtedness, there remain divers dues still to be paid, to no trifling amount, to the landlord's servants,—dues not to be ascertained, and which you never can know whether you have properly satisfied. You can know, perhaps, when you have less than satisfied them, by the aspect of the waiter, which I wish I could describe,—not disrespectful in the slightest degree, but a look of profound surprise, a gaze at the offered coin (which he nevertheless pockets) as if he either did not see it, or did not know it, or could not believe his eyesight;—all this, however, with the most quiet forbearance, a Christian-like non-recognition of an unmerited wrong and insult; and finally, all in a moment's space indeed, he quits you and goes about his other business. If you have given him too much, you are made sensible of your folly by the extra amount of his gratitude, and the bows with which he salutes you from the door-step. Generally, you cannot very decidedly say whether you have been right or wrong; but, in almost all cases, you decidedly feel that you have been fleeced. Then the living at the best of English hotels, so far as my travels have brought me acquainted with them, deserves but moderate praise, and is especially lacking in variety. Nothing but joints, joints, joints; sometimes, perhaps, a meat-pie, which, if you eat it, weighs upon your conscience, with the idea that you have eaten the scraps of other people's dinners. At the lake hotels, the fare is lamb and mutton and trout,—the latter not always fresh, and soon tired of. We pay like nabobs, and are expected to be content with plain mutton.

We spent the day yesterday at Grasmere, in quiet walks about the hotel; and at a little past six in the afternoon, I took my departure in the stage-coach for Windermere. The coach was greatly overburdened with outside passengers,—fifteen in all, besides the four insiders,—and one of the fifteen formed the apex of an immense pile of luggage on the top. It seems to me miraculous that we did not topple over, the road being so hilly and uneven, and the driver, I suspect, none the steadier for his visits to all the tap-rooms along the route from Cockermouth. There was a tremendous vibration of the coach now and then; and I saw that, in case of our going over, I should be flung headlong against the high stone fence that bordered most of the road. In view of this I determined to muffle my head in the folds of my thick shawl at the moment of overturn, and as I could do no better for myself, I awaited my fate with equanimity. As far as apprehension goes, I had rather travel from Maine to Georgia by rail, than from Grasmere to Windermere by stage-coach.

At Lowwood, the landlady espied me from the window, and sent out a large packet that had arrived by mail; but as it was addressed to some person of the Christian name of William, I did not venture to open it. She said, also, that a gentleman had been there, who very earnestly desired to see me, and I have since had reason to suppose that this was Allingham, the poet. We arrived at Windermere at half-past seven, and waited nearly an hour for the train to start. I took a ticket for Lancaster, and talked there about the war with a gentleman in the coffee-room, who took me for an Englishman, as most people do nowadays, and I heard from him—as you may from all his countrymen—an expression of weariness and dissatisfaction with the whole business. These fickle islanders! How differently they talked a year ago! John Bull sees now that he never was in a worse predicament in his life; and yet it would not take much to make him roar as bellicosely as ever. I went to bed at eleven, and slept unquietly on feathers.

I had purposed to rise betimes, and see the town of Lancaster before breakfast. But here I reckoned without my host; for, in the first place, I had no water for my ablutions, and my boots were not brushed; and so I could not get down-stairs till the hour I named for my coffee and chops; and, secondly, the breakfast was delayed half an hour, though promised every minute. In fine, I had but just time to take a hasty walk round Lancaster Castle, and see what I could of the town on my way,—a not very remarkable town, built of stone, with taller houses than in the middle shires of England, narrow streets up and down an eminence on which the castle is situated, with the town immediately about it. The castle is a satisfactory edifice, but so renovated that the walls look almost entirely modern, with the exception of the fine old front, with the statue of an armed warrior, very likely John of Gaunt himself, in a niche over the Norman arch of the entrance. Close beside the castle stands an old church.

The train left Lancaster at half-past nine, and reached Liverpool at twelve, over as flat and uninteresting a country as I ever travelled. I have betaken myself to the Rock Ferry Hotel, where I am as comfortable as I could be anywhere but at home; but it is rather comfortless to think of home as three years off, and three thousand miles away. With what a sense of utter weariness, not fully realized till then, we shall sink down on our own threshold, when we reach it! The moral effect of being without a settled abode is very wearisome.

Our coachman from Grasmere to Windermere looked like a great beer barrel, oozy with his proper liquor. I suppose such solid soakers never get upset.

THE LAUNCH.

August 2nd.—Mr. —— has urged me very much to go with his father and family to see the launch of a great ship which has been built for their house, and afterwards to partake of a picnic; so, on Tuesday morning I presented myself at the landing-stage, and met the party, to take passage for Chester. It was a showery morning, and looked woefully like a rainy day; but nothing better is to be expected in England; and, after all, there is seldom such a day that you cannot glide about pretty securely between the drops of rain. This, however, did not turn out one of those tolerable days, but grew darker and darker, and worse and worse; and was worst of all when we had passed about six miles beyond Chester, and were just on the borders of Wales, on the hither side of the river Dee, where the ship was to be launched. Here the train stopped, and absolutely deposited our whole party of excursionists, under a heavy shower, in the midst of a muddy potato-field, whence we were to wade through mud and mire to the ship-yard, almost half a mile off. Some kind Christian, I know not whom, gave me half of his umbrella, and half of his cloak, and thereby I got to a shed near the ship, without being entirely soaked through.

The ship had been built on the banks of the Dee, at a spot where it is too narrow for her to be launched directly across, and so she lay lengthwise of the river, and was so arranged as to take water parallel with the stream. She is, for aught I know, the largest ship in the world; at any rate, longer than the Great Britain, —an iron-screw steamer,—and looked immense and magnificent, and was gorgeously dressed out in flags. Had it been a pleasant day, all Chester and half Wales would have been there to see the launch; and, in spite of the rain, there were a good many people on the opposite shore, as well as on our side; and one or two booths, and many of the characteristics of a fair,—that is to say, men and women getting intoxicated without any great noise and confusion.

The ship was expected to go off at about twelve o'clock, and at that juncture all Mr. ——'s friends assembled under the bows of the ship, where we were a little sheltered from the rain by the projection of that part of the vessel over our heads. The bottle of port wine with which she was to be christened was suspended from the bows to the platform where we stood by a blue ribbon; and the ceremony was to be performed by Mrs. ——, who, I could see, was very nervous in anticipation of the ceremony. Mr. —— kept giving her instructions in a whisper, and showing her how to throw the bottle; and as the critical moment approached, he took hold of it along with her. All this time we were waiting in momentary expectation of the ship going off, everything being ready, and only the touch of a spring, as it were, needed to make her slide into the water. But the chief manager kept delaying a little longer, and a little longer; though the pilot on board sent to tell him that it was time she was off. "Yes, yes; but I want as much water as I can get," answered the manager; and so he held on till, I suppose, the tide had raised the river Dee to its very acme of height. At last the word was given; the ship began slowly to move; Mrs. —— threw the bottle against the bow with a spasmodic effort that dashed it into a thousand pieces, and diffused the fragrance of the old port all around, where it lingered several minutes. I did not think that there could have been such a breathless moment in an affair of this kind.

The ship moved majestically down toward the river; and unless it were Niagara, I never saw anything grander and more impressive than the motion of this mighty mass as she departed from us. We on the platform, and everybody along both shores of the Dee, took off our hats in the rain, waved handkerchiefs, cheered, shouted,—"Beautiful!" "What a noble launch!" "Never was so fair a sight!—and, really, it was so grand, that calm, majestic movement, that I felt the tears come into my eyes. The wooden pathway adown which she was gliding began to smoke with the friction; when all at once, when we expected to see her plunge into the Dee, she came to a full stop. Mr. ——, the father of my friend, a gentleman with white hair, a dark, expressive face, bright eyes, and an Oriental cast of features, immediately took the alarm. A moment before his countenance had been kindled with triumph; but now he turned pale as death, and seemed to grow ten years older while I was looking at him. Well he might, for his noble ship was stuck fast in the mud of the Dee, and without deepening the bed of the river, I do not see how her vast iron hulk is ever to be got out.

[This steamer was afterwards successfully floated off on the 29th of the same month.]

There was no help for it. A steamboat was hitched on to the stranded vessel, but broke two or three cables without stirring her an inch. So, after waiting long after we had given up all hope, we went to the office of the ship-yard, and there took a lunch; and still the rain was pouring, pouring, pouring, and I never experienced a blacker affair in all my days. Then we had to wait a great while for a train to take us back, so that it was almost five o'clock before we arrived at Chester, where I spent an hour in rambling about the old town, under the Rows: and on the walls, looking down on the tree-tops, directly under my feet, and through their thick branches at the canal, which creeps at the base, and at the Cathedral; walking under the dark, intertwining arches of the cloisters, and looking up at the great cathedral tower, so wasted away externally by time and weather that it looks, save for the difference of colour between white snow and red freestone, like a structure of snow, half dissolved by several warm days.

At the lunch I met with a graduate of Cambridge (England), tutor of a grandson of Percival (Percival, the assassinated minister, I mean), with his pupil. I should not like this position of tutor to a young Englishman; it certainly has an ugly twang of upper servitude. I observed that the tutor gave his pupil the best seat in the railway carriage, and in all respects provided for his comfort before thinking of his own; and this, not as a father does for his child, out of love, but from a sense of place and duty, which I did not quite see how a gentleman could consent to feel. And yet this Mr. C. was evidently a gentleman, and a quiet, intelligent, agreeable, and, no doubt, learned man. —— being mentioned, Mr. C. observed that he had known him well at college, having been his contemporary there. He did not like him, however,—thought him "a dangerous man," as well as I could gather; he thinks there is some radical defect in ——'s moral nature, a lack of sincerity; and, further-more, he believes him to be a sensualist in his disposition, in support of which view he said Mr. —— had made drawings such as no pure man could have made, or could allow himself to show or look at. This was the only fact which Mr. C. adduced, bearing on his opinion of ——; otherwise, it seemed to be one of those early impressions which a collegian gets of his fellow-students, and which he never gets rid of, whatever the character of the person may turn out to be in after years. I have judged several persons in this way, and still judge them so, though the world has come to very different conclusions. Which is right?—the world, which has the man's whole mature life on its side; or his early companion, who has nothing for it but some idle passages of his youth?

Mr. M. remarked of newspaper reporters, that they may be known at all celebrations, and on any public occasion, by the enormous quantity of luncheon they eat.

August 12*th.*—Mr. B. dined with us at the Rock Ferry Hotel the day before yesterday. Speaking of Helvellyn, and the death of Charles Gough, about whom Wordsworth and Scott have both sung, Mr. B. mentioned a version of that story which rather detracts from the character of the faithful dog.

But somehow it lowers one's opinion of human nature itself, to be compelled so to lower one's standard of a dog's nature. I don't intend to believe the disparaging story, but it reminds me of the story of the New-Zealander who was asked whether he loved a missionary who had been labouring for his soul and those of his countrymen. "To be sure I loved him. Why, I ate a piece of him for my breakfast this morning."

For the last week or two I have passed my time between the hotel and the Consulate, and a weary life it is, and one that leaves little of profit behind it. I am sick to death of my office,—brutal captains and brutal sailors; continual complaints of mutual wrong, which I have no power to set right, and which, indeed, seem to have no right on either side; calls of idleness or ceremony from my travelling countrymen, who seldom know what they are in search of at the commencement of their tour, and never have attained any desirable end at the close of it; beggars, cheats, simpletons, unfortunates, so mixed up that it is impossible to distinguish one from another, and so, in self-defence, the Consul distrusts them all. . . . .

At the hotel, yesterday, there was a large company of factory people from Preston, who marched up from the pier with a band of military music playing before them. They spent the day in the gardens and ball-

room of the hotel, dancing and otherwise merry-making;
but I saw little of them, being at the Consulate. Towards evening it drizzled, and the assemblage melted
away gradually; and when the band marched down to
the pier, there were few to follow, although one man
went dancing before the musicians, flinging out his
arms, and footing it with great energy and gesticula-
tion. Some young women along the road likewise began to dance as the music approached.

Thackeray has a dread of servants, insomuch that
he hates to address them, or to ask them for anything.
His morbid sensibility, in this regard, has perhaps led
him to study and muse upon them, so that he may be
presumed to have a more intimate knowledge of this
class than any other man.

C. dresses so badly, and wears such a rough outside, that the flunkeys are rude to him at gentlemen's
doors.

In the afternoon J. and I took a walk towards
Tranmere Hall, and beyond, as far as Oxton. This
part of the country, being so near Liverpool and
Birkenhead, is all sprinkled over with what they call
"Terraces," "Bellevues," and other pretty names for
semi-detached villas ("Recluse Cottage" was one) for
a somewhat higher class. But the old, whitewashed
stone cottage is still frequent, with its roof of slate or
thatch, which perhaps is green with weeds or grass.
Through its open door, you see that it has a pavement
of flagstones, or perhaps of red freestone; and hogs
and donkeys are familiar with the threshold. The

door always opens directly into the kitchen, without any vestibule; and, glimpsing in, you see that a cottager's life must be the very plainest and homeliest that ever was lived by men and women. Yet the flowers about the door often indicate a native capacity for the beautiful; but often there is only a pavement of round stones or of flagstones, like those within. At one point, where there was a little bay, as it were, in the hedge fence, we saw something like a small tent or wigwam,—an arch of canvas three or four feet high, and open in front, under which sat a dark-complexioned woman and some children. The woman was sewing, and I took them for gypsies.

August 17th.—Yesterday afternoon J. and I went to Birkenhead Park, which I have already described. .... It so happened that there was a large school spending its holiday there; a school of girls of the lower classes, to the number of a hundred and fifty, who disported themselves on the green, under the direction of the schoolmistresses and of an old gentleman. It struck me, as it always has, to observe how the lower orders of this country indicate their birth and station by their aspect and features. In America there would be a good deal of grace and beauty among a hundred and fifty children and budding girls, belonging to whatever rank of life. But here they had universally a most plebeian look,—stubbed, sturdy figures, round, coarse faces, snub-noses,—the most evident specimens of the brown bread of human nature. They looked wholesome and good enough, and fit to sustain their rough share of life; but it would have been impossible to make a lady out of any one of them. Climate, no doubt, has much to do with diffusing a slender elegance over American young-womanhood; but something, perhaps, is also due to the circumstance of classes not being kept apart there as they are here: they interfuse, amid the continual ups and downs of our social life; and so, in the lowest stations of life, you may see the refining influence of gentle blood. At all events, it is only necessary to look at such an assemblage of children as I saw yesterday, to be convinced that birth and blood do produce certain characteristics. To be sure, I have seen no similar evidence in England or elsewhere of old gentility refining and elevating the race.

These girls were all dressed in black gowns, with white aprons and neckerchiefs, and white linen caps on their heads,— a very dowdyish attire, and well suited to their figures. I saw only two of their games, —in one, they stood in a circle, while two of their number chased one another within and without the ring of girls, which opened to let the fugitive pass, but closed again to impede the passage of the pursuer. The other was blind-man's-buff on a new plan: several of the girls, sometimes as many as twenty, being blinded at once, and pursuing a single one, who rang a hand-bell to indicate her whereabouts. This was very funny; the bell-girl keeping just beyond their reach, and drawing them after her in a huddled group, so that they sometimes tumbled over one another and lay sprawling. I think I have read of this game in Strutt's "English Sports and Pastimes."

We walked from the Park home to Rock Ferry, a distance of three or four miles,—a part of which was made delightful by a foot-path, leading us through fields where the grass had just been mown, and others where the wheat harvest was commenced. The path led us into the very midst of the rural labour that was going forward; and the labourers rested a moment to look at us; in fact, they seemed to be more willing to rest than American labourers would have been. Children were loitering along this path, or sitting down beside it; and we met one little maid, passing from village to village, intent on some errand. Reaching Tranmere, I went into an ale-house, nearly opposite the Hall, and called for a glass of ale. The door-step before the house, and the flagstone floor of the entry and tap-room, were chalked all over in corkscrew lines, —an adornment that gave an impression of care and neatness, the chalked lines being evidently freshly made. It was a low, old-fashioned room, ornamented with a couple of sea-shells, and an earthenware figure on the mantelpiece; also with advertisements of Allsopp's ale, and other drinks, and with a pasteboard handbill of "The Ancient Order of Foresters;" any member of which, paying sixpence weekly, is entitled to ten shillings per week, and the attendance of a firstrate physician, in sickness, and twelve pounds to be paid to his friends in case of death. Any member of this order, when travelling, is sure (says the handbill) to meet with a brother member to lend him a helping hand, there being nearly three thousand districts of this order, and more than a hundred and nine thousand members in Great Britain, whence it has extended to Australia, America, and other countries.

Looking up at the gateway of Tranmere Hall, J. discovered an inscription on the red freestone lintel, and, though much time-worn, I succeeded in reading it. "Labor omnia vincit. 1614." There were likewise some initials which I could not satisfactorily make out. The sense of this motto would rather befit the present agricultural occupants of the house than the idle gentlefolks who built and formerly inhabited it.

SMITHELL'S HALL.

August 25*th*.—On Thursday I went by invitation to Smithell's Hall in Bolton-le-Moors to dine and spend the night. The Hall is two or three miles from the town of Bolton, where I arrived by railway from Liverpool, and which seems to be a pretty large town, though the houses are generally modern, or with modernized fronts of brick or stucco. It is a manufacturing town, and the tall brick chimneys rise numerously in the neighbourhood, and are so near Smithell's Hall that I suspect the atmosphere is somewhat impregnated with their breath. Mr. ——— can comfort himself with the rent which he receives from the factories erected upon his own grounds; and I suppose the value of his estate has greatly increased by the growth of manufactories; although, unless he wish to sell it, I do not see what good this can do him.

Smithell's Hall is one of the oldest residences of England, and still retains very much the aspect that it must have had several centuries ago. The house formerly stood around all four sides of a quadrangle, enclosing a court, and with an entrance through an archway. One side of this quadrangle was removed in the time of the present Mr. ———'s father, and the front is now formed by the remaining three sides. They look exceedingly ancient and venerable, with their range of gables and lesser peaks. The house is probably timber-framed throughout, and is overlaid with plaster, and its generally light hue is painted with a row of trefoils in black, producing a very quaint effect. The wing, forming one side of the quadrangle, is a chapel, and has been so from time immemorial; and Mr. —— told me that he had a clergyman, and even a bishop, in his own diocese. The drawing-room is on the opposite side of the quadrangle; and through an arched door, in the central portion, there is a passage to the rear of the house. It is impossible to describe such an old rambling edifice as this, or to get any clear idea of its plan, even by going over it, without the aid of a map. Mr. —— has added some portions, and altered others, but with due regard to harmony with the original structure, and the great body of it is still mediæval.

The entrance hall opens upon the quadrangular court; and is a large, low room, with a settle of carved old oak, and other old oaken furniture,—a centre-table with periodicals and newspapers on it,—some family pictures on the walls,—and a large, bright coal fire in the spacious grate. The fire is always kept up, throughout summer and winter, and it seemed to me an excellent plan, and rich with cheerful effects; insuring one comfortable place, and that the most central in the house, whatever may be the inclemency of the weather. It was a cloudy, moist, showery day, when I arrived; and this fire gave me the brightest and most hospitable smile, and took away my shivery feeling by its mere presence. The servant showed me thence into a low-studded dining-room, where soon Mrs. —— made her appearance, and, after some talk, brought me into the billiard-room, opening from the hall, where Mr. —— and a young gentleman were playing billiards, and two ladies looking on. After the game was finished, Mr. —— took me round to see the house and grounds.

The peculiarity of this house is what is called "'The Bloody Footstep." In the time of Bloody Mary, a Protestant clergyman—George Marsh by name—was examined before the then proprietor of the Hall, Sir Roger Barton, I think, and committed to prison for his herotical opinions, and was ultimately burned at the stake. As his guards were conducting him from the justice-room, through the stone-paved passage that leads from front to rear of Smithell's Hall, he stamped his foot upon one of the flagstones in earnest protestation against the wrong which he was undergoing. The foot, as some say, left a bloody mark in the stone; others have it, that the stone yielded like wax under his foot, and that there has been a shallow cavity ever since. This miraculous footprint is still extant; and Mrs. —— showed it to me before her husband took me round the estate. It is almost at the threshold of the door opening from the rear of the house, a stone two or three feet square, set among similar ones, that seem to have been worn by the tread of many generations. The footprint is a dark brown stain in the smooth grey surface of the flagstone; and, looking sidelong at it, there is a shallow cavity perceptible, which Mrs. —— accounted for as having been worn by people setting their feet just on this place, so as to tread the very spot where the martyr wrought the miracle. The mark is longer than any mortal foot, as if caused by sliding along the stone, rather than sinking into it; and it might be supposed to have been made by a pointed shoe, being blunt at the heel, and decreasing towards the toe. The blood-stained version of the story is more consistent with the appearance of the mark than the imprint would be; for if the martyr's blood oozed out through his shoe and stocking, it might have made his foot slide along the stone, and thus have lengthened the shape. Of course it is all a humbug,—a darker vein cropping up through the grey flagstone; but it is probably a fact, and, for aught I know, may be found in Fox's Book of Martyrs, that George Marsh underwent an examination in this house; and the tradition may have connected itself with the stone within a short time after the martyrdom;[*] or, perhaps, when the old persecuting knight departed this life, and Bloody Mary was also dead, people who had stood at a little distance from the Hall door, and had seen George Marsh lift his hand and stamp his foot just at this spot,—perhaps they remembered this action and gesture, and really believed that Providence had thus made an indelible record of it on the stone; although the very stone and the very mark might have lain there at the threshold hundreds of years before. But, even if it had been always there, the footprint might, after the fact, be looked upon as a prophecy, from the time when the foundation of the old house was laid, that a holy and persecuted man should one day set his foot here, on the way that was to lead him to the stake. At any rate, the legend is a good one.

[*] There is a full and pathetic account of the examination and martyrdom of George Marsh in the eleventh section of "Fox's Book of Martyrs," as I have just found (June 9, 1867). He went to Smithell's Hall, among other places, to be questioned by Mr. Barton.—ED.

Mrs. —— tells me that the miraculous stone was once taken up from the pavement, and flung out of doors, where it remained many years; and in proof of this, it is cracked quite across at one end. This is a pity, and rather interferes with the authenticity, if not of the stone itself, yet of its position in the pavement. It is not far from the foot of the staircase, leading up to Sir Roger Barton's examination-room, whither we ascended, after examining the footprint. This room now opens sideways on the chapel, into which it looks down, and which is spacious enough to accommodate a pretty large congregation. On one of the walls of the chapel there is a marble tablet to the memory of one of the present family,—Mr. ——'s father, I suppose; he being the first of the name who possessed the estate. The present owners, however, seem to feel pretty much the same pride in the antiquity and legends of the house as if it had come down to them in an unbroken succession of their own forefathers. It has, in reality, passed several times from one family to another, since the Conquest.

Mr. —— led me through a spacious old room, which was formerly panelled with carved oak, but which is converted into a brewhouse, up a pair of stairs, into the garret of one of the gables, in order to show me the ancient framework of the house. It is of oak, and preposterously ponderous,—immense beams and rafters, which no modern walls could support,—a gigantic old skeleton, which architects say must have stood a thousand years; and, indeed, it is impossible to ascertain the date of the original foundation, though it is known to have been repaired and restored between five and six centuries ago. Of course; in the lapse of ages, it must continually have been undergoing minor changes, but without at all losing its identity. Mr. —— says that this old oak wood, though it looks as strong and as solid as ever, has really lost its strength, and that it would snap short off, on application of any force.

After this we took our walk through the grounds, which are well wooded, though the trees will bear no comparison with those which I have seen in the midland parts of England. It takes, I suspect, a much longer time for trees to attain a good size here than in America; and these trees, I think Mr. —— told me, were principally set out by himself. He is upwards of sixty,—a good specimen of the old English country-gentleman, sensible, loving his land and his trees and his dogs and his game, doing a little justice-business, and showing a fitness for his position; so that you feel satisfied to have him keep it. He was formerly a member of Parliament. I had met him before at dinner at Mrs. H.'s. . . . . He took pleasure in showing me his grounds, through which he has laid out a walk, winding up and down through dells and over hillocks, and now and then crossing a rustic bridge; so that you have an idea of quite an extensive domain.

Beneath the trees there is a thick growth of ferns, serving as cover for the game. A little terrier dog, who had hitherto kept us company, all at once disappeared; and soon afterwards we heard the squeak of some poor victim in the cover, whereupon Mr. —— set out with agility, and ran to the rescue. By-and-by the terrier came back with a very guilty look. From the wood we passed into the open park, whence we had a distant view of the house; and, returning thither, we viewed it in other aspects, and on all sides. One portion of it is occupied by Mr. ——'s gardener, and seems not to have been repaired, at least as to its exterior, for a great many years,—showing the old wooden frame, painted black, with plaster in the interstices; and broad windows, extending across the whole breadth of the rooms, with hundreds of little diamond-shaped panes of glass. Before dinner I was shown to my room, which opens from an ancient gallery, lined with oak, and lighted by a row of windows along one side of the quadrangle. Along this gallery are the doors of several sleeping-chambers, one of which—I think it is here—is called "The Dead Man's Chamber." It is supposed to have been the room where the corpses of persons connected with the household used to be laid out. My own room was called "The Beam Chamber," from an immense cross-beam that projects from the ceiling, and seems to be an entire tree, laid across, and left rough-hewn, though at present it is whitewashed. The butt of the tree (for it diminishes from one end of the chamber to the other) is nearly two feet square, in its visible part.

We dined, at seven o'clock, in a room some thirty-five or forty feet long, and proportionably broad, all panelled with the old carved oak which Mr. —— took from the room which he had converted into a brew-house. The oak is now of a very dark-brown hue, and, being highly polished, it produces a sombre but rich effect. It is supposed to be of the era of Henry VII., and when I examined it the next morning, I found it very delicately and curiously wrought. There are carved profiles of persons in the costume of the times, done with great skill; also foliage, intricate puzzles of inter-secting lines, sacred devices, anagrams, and, among others, the device of a bar across a tun, indicating the name of Barton. Most of the carving, however, is less elaborate and intricate than these specimens, being in a perpendicular style, and on one pattern. Before the wood grew so very dark, the beauty of the work must have been much more easily seen than now, as to particulars, though I hardly think that the general effect could have been better; at least the sombre richness that overspreads the entire square of the room is suitable to such an antique house. An elaborate Gothic cornice runs round the whole apartment. The sideboard and other furniture are of Gothic patterns, and very likely of genuine antiquity; but the fireplace is perhaps rather out of keeping, being of white marble, with the arms of this family sculptured on it.

Though hardly sunset when we sat down to dinner, yet, it being an overcast day, and the oaken room so sombre, we had candles burning on the table; and, long before dinner was over, the candle-light was all the light we had. It is always pleasanter to dine by artificial light. Mrs. ——'s dinner was a good one, and Mr. ——'s wines were very good.

. . . .

After dinner there were two card-parties formed in the dining-room, at one of which there was a game of Vingt-et-un, and at the other a game of whist, at which Mrs. —— and I lost several shillings to a Mrs. Halton and Mr. Gaskell. . . . . After finishing our games at cards, Mrs. Halton drove off in a pony-chaise to her own house; the other ladies retired, and the gentlemen sat down to chat awhile over the hall fire, occasionally sipping a glass of wine and water, and finally we all went off to our rooms. It was past twelve o'clock when I composed myself to sleep, and I could not have slept long, when a tremendous clap of thunder woke me just in time to see a vivid flash of lightning. I saw no ghosts, though Mrs. —— tells me there is one, which makes a disturbance, unless religious services are regularly kept up in the chapel.

In the morning, before breakfast, we had prayers, read by Mr. ——, in the oak dining-room, all the servants coming in, and everybody kneeling down. I should like to know how much true religious feeling is indicated by this regular observance of religious rites in English families. In America, if people kneel down to pray, it is pretty certain that they feel a genuine interest in the matter, and their daily life is supposed to be in accordance with their devotions. If an American is an infidel, he knows it; but an Englishman is often so without suspecting it,—being kept from that knowledge by this formality of family prayer, and his other regularities of external worship. . . .

There was a parrot in a corner of the dining-room, and, when prayers were over, Mrs. —— praised it very highly for having been so silent; it being Poll's habit, probably, to break in upon the sacred exercises with unseemly interjections and remarks. While we were at breakfast, Poll began to whistle and talk very vociferously, and in a tone and with expressions that surprised me, till I learnt that the bird is usually kept in the kitchen and servants' hall, and is only brought into the dining-room at prayer-time and breakfast. Thus its mouth is full of kitchen talk, which flows out before the gentlefolks with the queerest effect.

After breakfast I examined the carvings of the room. Mr. —— has added to its decorations the coats of arms of all the successive possessors of the house, with those of the families into which they married, including the Ratcliffes, Stanleys, and others. From the dining-room I passed into the library, which contains books enough to make a rainy day pass pleasantly. I remember nothing else that I need to record; and as I sat by the hall fire, talking with Mr. Gaskell, at about eleven o'clock, the butler brought me word that a fly, which I had bespoken, was ready to convey me to the railway. I took leave of Mrs. ——, her last request being that I would write a ghost-story for her house,— and drove off.

SHREWSBURY.

September 5th.—Yesterday we all of us set forth from Rock Ferry at half-past twelve, and reached Shrewsbury between three and four o'clock, and took up our quarters at the Lion Hotel. We found Shrewsbury situated on an eminence, around which the Severn winds, making a peninsula of it, quite densely covered by the town. The streets ascend, and curve about, and intersect each other with the customary irregularity of these old English towns, so that it is quite impossible to go directly to any given point, or for a stranger to find his way to a place which he wishes to reach, though, by what seems a singular good fortune, the sought-for place is always offering itself when least expected. On this account I never knew such pleasant walking as in old streets like those of Shrewsbury. And there are passages opening under archways, and winding up between high edifices, very tempting to the explorer, and generally leading to some court, or some queer old range of buildings or piece of architecture, which it would be the greatest pity to miss seeing. There was a delightful want of plan in the laying out of these ancient towns. In fact, they never were laid out at all, nor were restrained by any plan whatever, but grew naturally, with streets as eccentric as the pathway of a young child toddling about the floor.

The first curious thing we particularly noticed, when we strolled out after dinner, was the old market-house, which stands in the midst of an oblong square; a grey edifice, elevated on pillars and arches, and with the statue of an armed knight, Richard Plantagenet, Duke of York, in a central niche, in its front. The statue is older than the market-house, having been moved thither from one of the demolished towers of the city wall in 1795. The market-house was erected in 1595. There are other curious sculptures and carvings and quirks of architecture about this building; and the houses that stand about the square are, many of them, very striking specimens of what dwelling-houses used to be in Elizabeth's time, and earlier. I have seen no such stately houses, in that style, as we found here in Shrewsbury. There were no such fine ones in Coventry, Stratford, Warwick, Chester, nor anywhere else where we have been. Their stately height and spaciousness seem to have been owing to the fact that Shrewsbury was a sort of metropolis of the country round about, and therefore the neighbouring gentry had their town-houses there, when London was several days' journey off, instead of a very few hours; and, besides, it was once much the resort of kings, and the centre-point of great schemes of war and policy. One such house formerly belonging to a now extinct family, that of Ireland, rises to the height of four stories, and has a

front consisting of what look like four projecting towers.
There are ranges of embowered windows, one above
another, to the full height of the house, and these are
surmounted by peaked gables. The people of those
times certainly did not deny themselves light; and
while window-glass was an article of no very remote
introduction, it was probably a point of magnificence
and wealthy display to have enough of it. One whole
side of the room must often have been formed by the
window. This Ireland mansion, as well as all the rest
of the old houses in Shrewsbury, is a timber house,—
that is, a skeleton of oak, filled up with brick, plaster,
or other material, and with the beams of the timber
marked out with black paint; besides which, in houses
of any pretension, there are generally trefoils, and other
Gothic-looking ornaments, likewise painted black. They
have an indescribable charm for me,—the more, I think,
because they are wooden; but, indeed, I cannot tell
why it is that I like them so well, and am never tired
of looking at them. A street was a development of
human life, in the days when these houses were built,
whereas a modern street is but the cold plan of an
architect, without individuality or character, and without the human emotion which a man kneads into the
walls which he builds on a scheme of his own.

We strolled to a pleasant walk under a range of
trees, along the shore of the Severn. It is called the
Quarry Walk. The Severn is a pretty river, the
largest, I think (unless it be such an estuary as the
Mersey), that I have met with in England; that is to
say, about a fair stone's-throw across. It is very gentle
in its course, and winds along between grassy and
sedgy banks, with a good growth of weeds in some

part of its current. It has one stately bridge, called the English Bridge, of several arches, and, as we sauntered along the Quarry Walk, we saw a ferry where the boat seemed to be navigated across by means of a rope, stretched from bank to bank of the river. After leaving the Quarry Walk, we passed an old tower of red freestone, the only one remaining of those formerly standing at intervals along the whole course of the town wall; and we also went along what little is now left of the wall itself. And thence, through the irregular streets, which gave no account of themselves, we found our way, I know not how, back to our hotel. It is an uncheerful old hotel, which takes upon itself to be in the best class of English country hotels, and charges the best price; very dark in the lower apartments, pervaded with a musty odour, but provided with a white-neckclothed waiter, who spares no ceremony in serving the joints of mutton.

J. and I afterwards walked forth again, and went this time to the castle, which stands exactly above the railway station. A path, from its breadth quite a street, leads up to the arched gateway; but we found a board, giving notice that these are private grounds, and no strangers admitted; so that we only passed through the gate a few steps, and looked about us, and retired, on perceiving a man approaching us through the trees and shrubbery. A private individual, it seems, has burrowed in this old warlike den, and turned the keep, and any other available apartment, into a modern dwelling, and laid out his pleasure-grounds within the precincts of the castle wall, which allows verge enough for the purpose. The ruins have been considerably repaired. This castle was built at various times, the keep by Edward I., and other portions at an earlier period, and it stands on the isthmus left by the Severn in its wandering course about the town. The Duke of Cleveland now owns it. I do not know who occupies it.

In the course of this walk, we passed St. Mary's church,—a very old church indeed, no matter how old, but say, eight hundred or a thousand years. It has a very tall spire, and the spire is now undergoing repairs; and, seeing the door open, I went into the porch, but found no admission further. Then, walking around it, through the churchyard, we saw that all the venerable Gothic windows—one of them grand in size—were set with stained glass, representing coats of arms and ancient armour, and kingly robes, and saints with glories about their heads, and scriptural people; but all of these, as far as our actual perception was concerned, quite colourless, and with only a cold outline, dimly filled up. Yet, had we been within the church, and had the sunlight been streaming through, what a warm, rich, gorgeous, roseate, golden life would these figures have showed!

In the churchyard, close upon the street, so that its dust must be continually scattered over the spot, I saw a heavy grey tombstone, with a Latin inscription, purporting that Bishop Butler, the author of the Analogy, in his lifetime had chosen this as a burial-place for himself and his family. There is a statue of him within the church. From the top of the spire a man, above a hundred years ago, attempted to descend, by means of a rope, to the other side of the Severn; but the rope broke, and he fell in his midway flight, and was killed. It was an undertaking worthy of Sam Patch. There is a record of the fact on the outside of the tower.

I remember nothing more that we saw yesterday; but before breakfast, J. and I sallied forth again, and inspected the gateway and interior court of the Council House,—a very interesting place, both in itself and for the circumstances connected with it, it having been the place where the councillors for the Welsh marches used to reside during their annual meetings; and Charles I. also lived here for six weeks in 1642. James II. likewise held his court here in 1687. The house was originally built in 1501,—that is, the Council House itself,—the gateway, and the house through which it passes, being of as late date as 1620. This latter is a fine old house, in the usual style of timber architecture, with the timber lines marked out, and quaint adornments in black paint; and the pillars of the gateway which passes beneath the front chamber are of curiously carved oak, which has probably stood the action of English atmosphere better than marble would have done. Passing through this gateway, we entered a court, and saw some old buildings more or less modernized, but without destroying their aged stateliness, standing round three sides of it, with arched entrances and bow-windows, and windows in the roofs, and peaked gables, and all the delightful irregularity and variety that these houses have, and which make them always so fresh,—and with so much detail that every minute you see something heretofore unseen. It must have been no unfit residence for a king and his court, when those three sides of the square, all composing one great fantastic house, were in their splendour. The square itself, too, must have been a busy and cheerful scene, thronged with attendants, guests, horses, &c.

After breakfast, we all walked out, and, crossing the English Bridge, looked at the Severn over its parapet. The river is here broader than elsewhere, and very shallow, and has an island covered with bushes, about midway across. Just over the bridge we saw a church, of red freestone, and evidently very ancient. This is the Church of the Holy Cross, and is a portion of the Abbey of St. Peter and St. John, which formerly covered ten acres of ground. We did not have time to go into the church; but the windows and other points of architecture, so far as we could discern them, and knew how to admire them, were exceedingly venerable and beautiful. On the other side of the street, over a wide space, there are other remains of the old abbey; and the most interesting was a stone pulpit, now standing in the open air, seemingly in a garden, but which originally stood in the refectory of the abbey, and was the station whence one of the monks read to his brethren at their meals. The pulpit is much overgrown with ivy. We should have made further researches among these remains, though they seem now to be in private grounds; but a large mastiff came out of his kennel, and, approaching us to the length of his iron chain, began barking very fiercely. Nor had we time to see half that we would gladly have seen and studied here and elsewhere about Shrewsbury. It would have been very interesting to have visited Hotspur's and Falstaff's battle-field, which is four miles from the town; too distant, certainly, for Falstaff to have measured the length of the fight by Shrewsbury clock. There is now a church, built there by Henry IV., and said to cover the bones of those slain in the battle.

Returning into the town, we penetrated some narrow lanes, where, as the old story goes, people might almost shake hands across from the top windows of the opposite houses, impending towards each other. Emerging into a wider street, at a spot somewhat more elevated than other parts of the town, we went into a shop to buy some Royal Shrewsbury cakes, which we had seen advertised at several shop windows. They are a very rich cake, with plenty of eggs, sugar, and butter, and very little flour.

A small public building of stone, of modern date, was close by; and asking the shopwoman what it was, she said it was the Butter Cross, or market for butter, eggs, and poultry. It is a remarkable site, for here, in ancient times, stood a stone cross, where heralds used to make proclamation, and where criminals of state used to be executed. David, the last of the Welsh princes, was here cruelly put to death by Edward I., and many noblemen were beheaded on this spot, after being taken prisoners in the battle of Shrewsbury.

I can only notice one other memorable place in Shrewsbury, and that is the Raven Inn, where Farquhar wrote his comedy of "The Recruiting Officer" in 1701. The window of the room in which he wrote is said to look into the inn yard, and I went through the arched entrance to see if I could distinguish it. The hostlers were currying horses in the yard, and so stared at me that I gave but the merest glance. The Shrewsbury inns have not only the customary names of English inns,—as the Lion, the Stag,—but they have also the carved wooden figures of the object named, whereas, in all other towns, the name alone remains.

We left Shrewsbury at half-past ten, and arrived in London at about four in the afternoon.

LONDON.

September 7th.—On Wednesday, just before dusk, J. and I walked forth, for the first time, in London. Our lodgings are in George Street, Hanover Square, No. 24; and St. George's church, where so many marriages in romance and in fashionable life have been celebrated, is a short distance below our house, in the same street. The edifice seems to be of white marble, now much blackened with London smoke, and has a Grecian pillared portico. In the square, just above us, is a statue of William Pitt. We went down Bond Street, and part of Regent Street, just estraying a little way from our temporary nest, and taking good account of landmarks and corners, so as to find our way readily back again. It is long since I have had such a childish feeling; but all that I had heard and felt about the vastness of London made it seem like swimming in a boundless ocean, to venture one step beyond the only spot I knew. My first actual impression of London was of stately and spacious streets, and by no means so dusky and grimy as I had expected,—not merely in the streets about this quarter of the town, which is the aristocratic quarter, but in all the streets through which we had passed from the railway station. If I had not first been so imbued with the smoke and dinginess of Liverpool, I should doubtless have seen a stronger contrast betwixt dusky London and the cheerful glare of our American cities. There are no red bricks here; all are of a dark hue, and whatever of stone or stucco has been white soon clothes itself in mourning.

Yesterday forenoon I went out alone, and plunged headlong into London, and wandered about all day, without any particular object in view, but only to lose myself for the sake of finding myself unexpectedly among things that I had always read and dreamed about. The plan was perfectly successful, for, besides vague and unprofitable wanderings, I saw, in the course of the day, Hyde Park, Regent's Park, Whitehall, the two new Houses of Parliament, Charing Cross, St. Paul's, the Strand, Fleet Street, Cheapside, Whitechapel, Leadenhall Street, the Haymarket, and a great many other places, the names of which were classic in my memory. I think what interests me most here, is the London of the writers of Queen Anne's age,—whatever Pope, the *Spectator*, De Foe, and down as late as Johnson and Goldsmith, have mentioned. The Monument, for instance, which is of no great height nor beauty compared with that on Bunker Hill, charmed me prodigiously. St. Paul's appeared to me unspeakably grand and noble, and the more so from the throng and bustle continually going on around its base, without in the least disturbing the sublime repose of its great dome, and, indeed, of all its massive height and breadth. Other edifices may crowd close to its foundation, and people may tramp as they like about it; but still the great cathedral is as quiet and serene as if it stood in the middle of Salisbury Plain. There cannot be anything else in its way so good in the world as just this effect of St. Paul's in the very heart and densest tumult of London. I do not know whether the church is built of marble, or of whatever other white or nearly white material; but in the time that it has been standing there, it has grown black with the smoke of ages, through which there are nevertheless gleams of white, that make a most picturesque impression on the whole. It is much better than staring white; the edifice would not be nearly so grand without this drapery of black.

I did not find these streets of the old city so narrow and irregular as I expected. All the principal ones are sufficiently broad, and there are few houses that look antique, being, I suppose, generally modern-fronted, when not actually of modern substance. There is little or no show or pretension in this part of London; it has a plain, business air,—an air of homely, actual life, as of a metropolis of tradesmen, who have been carrying on their traffic here, in sober earnest, for hundreds of years. You observe on the sign-boards, "Established ninety years in Threadneedle Street," "Established in 1709,"—denoting long pedigrees of silk-mercers and hosiers,—De Foe's contemporaries still represented by their posterity, who handle the hereditary yard-stick on the same spot.

I must not forget to say that I crossed the Thames over a bridge which, I think, is near Charing Cross. Afterwards, I found my way to London Bridge, where there was a delightful density of throng. The Thames is not so wide and majestic as I had imagined,—nothing like the Mersey, for example. As a picturesque object, however, flowing through the midst of a city, it would lose by any increase of width. . . . .

Omnibuses are a most important aid to wanderers about London. I reached home, well wearied, about

six o'clock. In the course of the day, I had seen one
person whom I knew,—Mr. Clarke, to whom Henry
B. introduced me, when we went to see the great ship
launched on the Dee. This, I believe, was in Regent
Street. In that street, too, I saw a company of dra-
goons, beautifully mounted, and defensively armed, in
brass helmets and steel cuirasses, polished to the utmost excess of splendour. It was a pretty sight. At
one of the public edifices, on each side of the portal,
sat a mounted trooper similarly armed, and with his
carbine resting on his knee, just as motionless as a
statue. This, too, as a picturesque circumstance, was
very good, and really made an impression on me with
respect to the power and stability of the government,
though I could not help smiling at myself for it. But
then the thought, that for generations an armed warrior
has always sat just there, on his war-steed, and with
his weapon in his hand, is pleasant to the imagination,
—although it is questionable whether his carbine be
loaded; and, no doubt, if the authorities had any message to send, they would choose some other messenger
than this heavy dragoon,—the electric wire, for instance.
Still, if he and his horse were to be withdrawn from
their post, night or day (for I suppose the sentinels are
on duty all night), it seems as if the monarchy would
be subverted, and the English constitution crumble into
rubbish; and in honest fact, it will signify something
like that, when guard is relieved there for the last time.

September 8th.—Yesterday forenoon, S., the two
eldest children, and I went forth into London streets,
and proceeded down Regent Street, and thence to St.
James's Park, at the entrance of which is a statue of

somebody,—I forget whom. On the very spacious gravel walks, covering several acres, in the rear of the Horse Guards, some soldiers were going through their exercise; and, after looking at them awhile, we strolled through the Park, alongside of a sheet of water, in which various kinds of ducks, geese, and rare specimens of water-fowl were swimming. There was one swan of immense size, which moved about among the lesser fowls like a stately, full-rigged ship among gunboats. By-and-by we found ourselves near what we since have discovered to be Buckingham Palace,—a long building in the Italian style, but of no impressiveness, and which one soon wearies of looking at. The Queen having gone to Scotland the day before, the palace now seemed deserted, although there was a one-horse cab, of shabby aspect, standing at the principal front, where doubtless the carriages of princes and the nobility draw up. There is a fountain playing before the palace, and waterfowl love to swim under its perpetual showers. These ducks and geese are very tame, and swim to the margin of the pond to be fed by visitors, looking up at you with great intelligence.

S. asked a man in a sober suit of livery (of whom we saw several about the Park), whose were some of the large mansions which we saw, and he pointed out Stafford House, the residence of the Duke of Sutherland,—a very noble edifice, much more beautiful than the palace, though not so large; also the house of the Earl of Ellesmere, and residences of other noblemen. This range of mansions, along the Park, from the spot whence we viewed them, looks very much like Beacon Street, in Boston, bordering on the common, allowing for a considerable enlargement of scale in favour of the Park residences. The Park, however, has not the beautiful elms that overshadow Boston Common, nor such a pleasant undulation of surface, nor the fine off-view of the country, like that across Charles River. I doubt whether London can show so delightful a spot as that Common, always excepting the superiority of English lawns, which, however, is not so evident in the London parks, there being less care bestowed on the grass than I should have expected.

From this place we wandered into what I believe to be Hyde Park, attracted by a gigantic figure on horseback, which loomed up in the distance. The effect of this enormous steed and his rider is very grand, seen in the misty atmosphere. I do not understand why we did not see St. James's Palace, which is situated, I believe, at the extremity of the same range of mansions of which Stafford House is the opposite end. From the entrance of Hyde Park, we seem to have gone along Piccadilly, and, making two or three turns, and getting bewildered, I put S. and the children into a cab, and sent them home. Continuing my wanderings, I went astray among squares of large aristocratic-looking edifices, all apparently new, with no shops among them, some yet unfurnished, and the whole seeming like a city built for a colony of gentlefolks, who might be expected to emigrate thither in a body. It was a dreary business to wander there, turning corner after corner, and finding no way of getting into a less stately and more genial region. At last, however, I passed in front of the Queen's Mews, where sentinels were on guard, and where a jolly-looking man, in a splendidly laced scarlet coat and white-topped boots, was lounging at the entrance. He looked like the prince of grooms or coachmen. . . . .

The corner of Hyde Park was within a short distance, and I took a Hansom at the cab-stand there, and drove to the American Despatch Agency, 26, Henrietta Street, Covent Garden, having some documents of State to be sent by to-day's steamer. The business of forwarding despatches to America, and distributing them to the various legations and consulates in Europe, must be a pretty extensive one; for Mr. Miller has a large office, and two clerks in attendance.

From this point I went through Covent Garden Market, and got astray in the City, so that I can give no clear account of my afternoon's wanderings. I passed through Holborn, however, and I think it was from that street that I passed through an archway (which I almost invariably do when I see one), and found myself in a very spacious, gravelled square, surrounded on the four sides by a continuous edifice of dark brick, very plain, and of cold and stern aspect. This was Gray's Inn, all tenanted by a multitude of lawyers. Passing thence, I saw "Furnival's Inn" over another archway, but, being on the opposite side of the street, I did not go thither. In Holborn, still, I went through another arched entrance, over which was "Staples Inn," and here likewise seemed to be offices; but, in a court opening inwards from this, there was a surrounding seclusion of quiet dwelling-houses, with beautiful green shrubbery and grassplots in the court, and a great many sunflowers in full bloom. The windows were open; it was a lovely summer afternoon, and I have a sense that bees were humming in the court, though this may have been suggested by my fancy, because the sound would have been so well suited to the scene. A boy was reading at one of the windows. There was

not a quieter spot in England than this, and it was
very strange to have drifted into it so suddenly out of
the bustle and rumble of Holborn; and to lose all this
repose as suddenly, on passing through the arch of
the outer court. In all the hundreds of years since
London was built, it has not been able to sweep its
roaring tide over that little island of quiet. In Holborn I saw the most antique-looking houses that I
have yet met with in London, but none of very remarkable aspect.

I think I must have been under a spell of enchantment to-day, connecting me with St. Paul's; for, trying to get away from it by various avenues, I still got
bewildered, and again and again saw its great dome
and pinnacles before me. I observe that the smoke
has chiefly settled on the lower part of the edifice,
leaving its loftier portions and its spires much less be-
grimed. It is very beautiful, very rich. I did not
think that anything but Gothic architecture could so
have interested me. The statues, the niches, the embroidery, as it were, of sculpture traced around it, produced a delightful effect. In front of St. Paul's there
is a statue of Queen Anne, which looks rather more
majestic, I doubt not, than that fat old dame ever did.
St. Paul's churchyard had always been a place of immense interest in my imagination. It is merely the
not very spacious street, running round the base of the
church, — at least this street is included in the churchyard, together with the enclosure immediately about
the church, sowed with tombstones. I meant to look
for the children's book-shop, but forgot it, or neglected
it, from not feeling so much interest in a thing near
at hand as when it seemed unattainable.

  · · · · ·

I watched a man tearing down the brick wall of a house that did not appear very old; but it surprised me to see how crumbly the brick-work was, one stroke of his pick often loosening several bricks in a row. It is my opinion that brick houses, after a moderate term of years, stand more by habit and courtesy than through any adhesive force of the old mortar.

I recommenced my wanderings; but I remember nothing else particularly claiming to be mentioned, unless it be Paternoster Row,—a little, narrow, darksome lane, in which, it being now dusk in that density of the city, I could not very well see what signs were over the doors. In this street, or thereabouts, I got into an omnibus, and, being set down near Regent's Circus, reached home well wearied.

September 9th. — Yesterday, having some tickets to the Zoological Gardens, we went thither with the two eldest children. It was a most beautiful sunny day, the very perfection of English weather,—which is as much as to say, the best weather in the world, except, perhaps, some few days in an American October. These gardens are at the end of Regent's Park, farthest from London, and they are very extensive; though, I think, not quite worthy of London,—not so good as one would expect them to be,—not so fine and perfect a collection of beasts, birds, and fishes as one might fairly look for, when the greatest metropolis of the world sets out to have such a collection at all. My idea was, that here every living thing was provided for, in the way best suited to its nature and habits, and that the refinement of civilisation had here restored a garden of Eden, where all the animal kingdom had regained a happy home. This is not quite the case; though I believe the creatures are as comfortable as could be expected, and there are certainly a good many strange beasts here. The hippopotamus is the chief treasure of the collection,—an immense, almost misshapen, mass of flesh. At this moment I do not remember anything that interested me except a sick monkey,—a very large monkey, and elderly he seemed to be. His keeper brought him some sweetened apple and water, and some tea; for the monkey had quite lost his appetite, and refused all ordinary diet. He came, however, quite eagerly, and smelt of the tea and apple, the keeper exhorting him very tenderly to eat. But the poor monkey shook his head slowly, and with the most pitiable expression, at the same time extending his hand to take the keeper's, as if claiming his sympathy and friendship. By-and-by the keeper (who is rather a surly fellow) essayed harsher measures, and insisted that the monkey should eat what had been brought for him, and hereupon ensued somewhat of a struggle, and the tea was overturned upon the straw of the bed. Then the keeper scolded him, and, seizing him by one arm, drew him out of his little bedroom into the larger cage, upon which the wronged monkey began a loud, dissonant, reproachful chatter, more expressive of a sense of injury than any words could be.

Observing the spectators in front of the cage, he seemed to appeal to them, and addressed his chatter thitherward, and stretched out his long, lean arm and black hand between the bars, as if claiming the grasp of any one friend he might have in the whole world. He was placable, however; for when the keeper called him in a gentler tone, he hobbled towards him with a very stiff and rusty movement, and the scene closed with their affectionately hugging one another. But I fear the poor monkey will die. In a future state of being, I think it will be one of my inquiries, in reference to the mysteries of the present state, why monkeys were made. The Creator could not surely have meant to ridicule his own work. It might rather be fancied that Satan had perpetrated monkeys, with a malicious purpose of parodying the masterpiece of creation!

The Aquarium, containing, in some of its compartments, specimens of the animal and vegetable life of the sea, and, in others, those of the fresh water, was richly worth inspecting; but not nearly so perfect as it might be. Now I think we have a right to claim, in a metropolitan establishment of this kind, in all its departments, a degree of perfection that shall quite outdo the unpractised thought of any man on that particular subject.

There were a good many well-dressed people and children in the garden, Saturday being a fashionable day for visiting them. One great amusement was feeding some bears with biscuits and cakes, of which they seemed exceedingly fond. One of the three bears clambered to the top of a high pole, whence he invited the spectators to hand him bits of cake on the end of a stick, or to toss them into his mouth, which he opened widely for that purpose. Another, apparently an elderly bear, not having skill nor agility for these gymnastics, sat on the ground, on his hinder end, groaning most pitifully. The third took what stray bits he could get, without earning them by any antics.

At four o'clock there was some music from the

band of the First Life-Guards, a great multitude of chairs being set on the greensward in the sunshine and shade, for the accommodation of the auditors. Here we had the usual exhibition of English beauty, neither superior nor otherwise to what I have seen in other parts of England. Before the music was over, we walked slowly homeward, along beside Regent's Park, which is very prettily laid out, but lacks some last touch of richness and beauty; though, after all, I do not well see what more could be done with grass, trees, and gravel walks. The children, especially J., who had raced from one thing to another all day long, grew tired; so we put them into a cab, and walked slowly through Portland Place, where are a great many noble mansions, yet no very admirable architecture; none that possessed, nor that ever can possess, the indefinable charm of some 'of those poor old timber houses in Shrewsbury. The art of domestic architecture is lost. We can rear stately and beautiful dwellings (though we seldom do), but they do not seem proper to the life of man, in the same way that his shell is proper to the lobster; nor, indeed, is the mansion of the nobleman proper to him, in the same kind and degree, that a hut is proper to a peasant.

From Portland Place we passed into Regent Street, and soon reached home.

September 10*th*.—Yesterday forenoon we walked out with the children, intending for Charing Cross; but, missing our way, as usual, we went down a rather wide and stately street, and saw before us an old brick edifice with a pretty extensive front, over which rose a clock-tower,—the whole dingy, and looking both gloomy and mean. There was an arched entrance beneath the clock-tower, at which two Guardsmen, in their bearskin caps, were stationed as sentinels; and from this circumstance, and our having some guess at the locality, we concluded the old brick building to be St. James's Palace. Otherwise we might have taken it for a prison, or for a hospital, which, in truth, it was at first intended for. But, certainly, there are many paupers in England who live in edifices of far more architectural pretension externally than this principal palace of the English sovereigns.

Seeing other people go through the archway, we also went, meeting no impediment from the sentinels, and found ourselves in a large paved court, in the centre of which a banner was stuck down, with a few soldiers standing near it. This flag was the banner of the regiment of Guards on duty. The aspect of the interior court was as naked and dismal as the outside, the brick being of that dark hue almost universal in England. On one side of the court there was a door which seemed to give admission to a chapel, into which several persons went, and probably we might have gone too, had we liked. From this court, we penetrated into at least two or three others; for the palace is very extensive, and all of it, so far as I could see, on the same pattern,—large, enclosed courts, paved, and quite bare of grass, shrubbery, or any beautiful thing,—dark, stern, brick walls, without the slightest show of architectural beauty, or even an ornament over the square, commonplace windows, looking down on those forlorn courts. A carriage drive passes through it, if I remember aright, from the principal front, emerging by one of the sides; and I suppose that the carriages roll

through the palace at the levees and drawing-rooms.
There was nothing to detain us here any long time, so
we went from court to court, and came out through a
side opening. The edifice is battlemented all round, and
this, with somewhat of fantastic in the shape of the clock-
tower, is the only attempt at ornament in the whole.

Then we skirted along St. James's Park, passing
Marlborough House,—a red brick building,—and a very
long range of stone edifices, which, whether they were
public or private, one house or twenty, we knew not.
We ascended the steps of the York column, and soon
reached Charing Cross and Trafalgar Square, where
there are more architectural monuments than in any
other one place in London; besides two fountains, playing in large reservoirs of water, and various edifices of
note and interest.

Northumberland House, now, and for a long while,
the town residence of the Percys, stands on the Strand
side,—over the entrance a lion, very spiritedly sculptured, flinging out his long tail. On another side of
the square is Morley's Hotel, exceedingly spacious, and
looking more American than anything else in the hotel
line that I have seen here.

The Nelson monument, with Lord Nelson, in a
cocked hat, on its top, is very grand in its effect. All
about the square there were sundry loungers, people
looking at the bas-reliefs on Nelson's Column, children
paddling in the reservoirs of the fountains; and, it
being a sunny day, it was a cheerful and lightsome, as
well as an impressive, scene. On second thoughts, I
do not know but that London should have a far better
display of architecture and sculpture than this, on its
finest site, and in its very centre; for, after all, there

is nothing of the very best. But I missed nothing at the time.

In the afternoon S. and I set out to attend divine service in Westminster Abbey. On our way thither we passed through Pall Mall, which is full of club-houses, and we were much struck with the beauty of the one lately erected for the Carlton Club. It is built of a buff-coloured or yellowish stone, with pillars or pilasters of polished Aberdeen granite, wonderfully rich and beautiful; and there is a running border of sculptured figures all round the upper part of the building, besides other ornament and embroidery, wherever there is room or occasion for it. It being an oblong square, the smooth and polished aspect in this union of two rich colours in it—this delicacy and minuteness of finish, this lavish ornament—made me think of a lady's jewel-box; and if it could be reduced to the size of about a foot square, or less, it would make the very prettiest one that ever was seen. I question whether it have any right to be larger than a jewel-box; but it is certainly a most beautiful edifice. We turned down Whitehall, at the head of which, over the very spot where the Regicides were executed, stands the bronze equestrian statue of Charles I.,—the statue that was buried under the earth during the whole of Cromwell's time, and emerged after the Restoration. We saw the Admiralty and the Horse-Guards, and, in front of the latter, the two mounted sentinels, one of whom was flirting and laughing with some girls. On the other side of the street stands the Banqueting-House, built by Inigo Jones; from a window of which King Charles stepped forth, wearing a kingly head, which, within a few minutes afterwards, fell with a dead thump on the scaffold. It was nobly done,—and nobly suffered. How rich is history in the little space around this spot!

I find that the day after I reached London, I entirely passed by Westminster Abbey without knowing it, partly because my eyes were attracted by the gaudier show of the new Houses of Parliament, and partly because this part of the Abbey has been so much repaired and renewed that it has not the marks of age. Looking at its front, I now found it very grand and venerable; but it is useless to attempt a description: these things are not to be translated into words; they can be known only by seeing them, and, until seen, it is well to shape out no idea of them. Impressions, states of mind, produced by noble spectacles of whatever kind, are all that it seems worth while to attempt reproducing with the pen.

After coming out of the Abbey, we looked at the two Houses of Parliament, directly across the way—an immense structure, and certainly most splendid, built of a beautiful warm-coloured stone. The building has a very elaborate finish, and delighted me at first; but by-and-by I began to be sensible of a weariness in the effect, a lack of variety in the plan and ornament, a deficiency of invention; so that, instead of being more and more interested the longer one looks, as is the case with an old Gothic edifice, and continually reading deeper into it, one finds that one has seen all in seeing a little piece, and that the magnificent palace has nothing better to show one or to do for one. It is wonderful how the old weather-stained, and smoke-blackened Abbey shames down this brand-newness; not that the Parliament houses are not fine objects to look at, too.

Yesterday morning we walked to Charing Cross,

with U. and J., and there took a cab to the Tower, driving thither through the Strand, Fleet Street, past St. Paul's, and amid all the thickest throng of the City. I have not a very distinct idea of the Tower, but remember that our cab drove within an outer gate, where we alighted at a ticket-office; the old royal fortress being now a regular show-place, at sixpence a head, including the sight of armoury and crown-jewels. We saw about the gate several warders or yeomen of the guard, or beef-eaters, dressed in scarlet coats of antique fashion, richly embroidered with golden crowns, both on the breast and back, and other royal devices and insignia; so that they looked very much like the kings on a pack of cards, or regular trumps, at all events. I believe they are old soldiers, promoted to this position for good conduct. One of them took charge of us, and when a sufficient number of visitors had collected with us, he led us to see what very small portion of the Tower is shown.

There is a great deal of ground within the outer precincts; and it has streets and houses and inhabitants and a church within it; and, going up and down behind the warder, without any freedom to get acquainted with the place by strolling about, I know little more about it than when I went in,—only recollecting a mean and disagreeable confusion of brick walls, barracks, paved courts, with here and there a low bulky turret, of rather antique aspect, and, in front of one of the edifices, a range of curious old cannon, lying on the ground, some of them immensely large and long, and beautifully wrought in brass. I observe by a plan, however, that the White Tower, containing the armoury, stands about in the centre of the fortress, and that it is a square, battlemented structure, having a turret at each angle. We followed the warder into the White Tower, and there saw, in the first place, a long gallery of mounted knights and men-at-arms, which has been so often described that when I wish to recall it to memory I shall turn to some other person's account of it. I was much struck, however, with the beautiful execution of a good many of the suits of armour, and the exquisite detail with which they were engraved. The artists of those days attained very great skill in this kind of manufacture. The figures of the knights, too, in full array, undoubtedly may have shown a combination of stateliness and grace which heretofore I have not believed in,—not seeing how it could be compatible with iron garments. But it is quite incomprehensible how, in the time of the heaviest armour, they could strike a blow, or possess any freedom of movement, except such as a turtle is capable of; and, in truth, they are said not to have been able to rise up when overthrown. They probably stuck out their lances, and rode straight at the enemy, depending upon upsetting him by their mass and weight. In the row of knights is Henry VIII.; also Charles Brandon, Duke of Suffolk, who must have been an immensely bulky man; also a splendid suit of armour, gilded all over, presented by the City of London to Charles I.; also, two or three suits of boys' armour, for the little princes of the House of Stuart. They began to wear these burdens betimes, in order that their manhood might be the more tolerant of them. We went through this gallery so hastily that it would have been about as well not to have seen it at all.

Then we went up a winding stair to another room, containing armour and weapons, and beautiful brass

cannon, that appeared to have been for ornament rather
than use, some of them being quite covered with em-
bossed sculpture, marvellously well wrought. In this
room was John of Gaunt's suit, indicating a man seven
feet high, and the armour seems to bear the marks of
much wear; but this may be owing to great scrubbing,
throughout the centuries since John of Gaunt died.
There, too, we saw the cloak in which Wolfe fell, on
the Plains of Abraham,—a coarse, faded, threadbare,
light-coloured garment, folded up under a glass case.
Many other things we might have seen, worthy of
being attended to, had there been time to look at them.

Following into still another room, we were told
that this was Sir Walter Raleigh's apartment, while
confined in the Tower, so that it was within these walls
that he wrote the History of the World. The room
was formerly lighted by lancet windows, and must have
been very gloomy; but, if he had the whole length of
it to himself, it was a good space to walk and meditate
in. On one side of the apartment is a low door, giving
admittance, we were told, to the cell where Raleigh
slept; so we went in, and found it destitute of any
window, and so dark that we could not estimate its
small extent except by feeling about. At the threshold
of this sleeping-kennel, there were one or two inscriptions, scratched in the wall, but not, I believe, by Raleigh.

In this apartment, among a great many other
curious things, are shown the devilish instruments of
torture which the Spaniards were bringing to England
in their Armada; and, at the end of the room, sits
Queen Elizabeth on horseback, in her high ruff and
faded finery. Very likely none of these clothes were
ever on her actual person. Here, too, we saw a heads-

man's block,—not that on which Raleigh was beheaded, which I would have given gold to see, but the one which was used for the Scotch Lords Kilmarnock, Lovat, and others, executed on account of the Rebellion of 1745. It is a block of oak, about two feet high, with a large knot in it, so that it would not easily be split by a blow of the axe; hewn and smoothed in a very workmanlike way, and with a hollow to accommodate the head and shoulders on each side. There were two or three very strong marks of the axe in the part over which the neck lay, and several smaller cuts; as if the first stroke nearly severed the head, and then the chopping off was finished by smaller blows, as we see a butcher cutting meat with his cleaver. A headsman's axe was likewise shown us,—its date unknown.

In the White Tower we were shown the Regalia, under a glass, and within an iron cage. Edward the Confessor's golden staff was very finely wrought; and there were a great many pretty things; but I have a suspicion, I know not why, that these are not the real jewels,—at least, that such inestimable ones as the Koh-i-noor (or however it is spelt) are less freely exhibited.

The warder then led us into a paved court, which he said was the place of execution of all royal personages and others, who, from motives of fear or favour, were beheaded privately. Raleigh was among these, and so was Anne Boleyn. We then followed to the Beauchamp Tower, where many state prisoners of note were confined, and where, on the walls of one of the chambers, there are several inscriptions and sculptures of various devices, done by the prisoners,—and very skilfully done, too, though perhaps with no better in-

strument than an old nail. These poor wretches had
time and leisure enough to spend upon their work. This
chamber is lighted by small lancet windows, pierced at
equal intervals round the circle of the Beauchamp
Tower; and it contains a large, square fireplace, in
which is now placed a small modern stove. We were
hurried away, before we could even glance at the inscriptions, and we saw nothing else, except the low,
obscure doorway in the Bloody Tower, leading to the
staircase, under which were found the supposed bones
of the little princes; and lastly, the round, Norman
arch, opening to the water passage, called the Traitors'
Gate. Finally, we ate some cakes and buns in the
refreshment-room connected with the ticket-office, and
then left the fortress. The ancient moat, by the way,
has been drained within a few years, and now forms a
great hollow space, with grassy banks, round about the
citadel.

We now wished to see the Thames, and therefore
threaded our way along Thames Street, towards London Bridge, passing through a fish-market, which I suppose to be the actual Billingsgate, whence originated
all the foul language in England. Under London
Bridge there is a station for steamers running to Greenwich and Woolwich. We got on board one of these,
not very well knowing, nor much caring, whither it
might take us, and steamed down the river, which is
bordered with the shabbiest, blackest, ugliest, meanest
buildings: it is the back side of the town; and, in truth,
the muddy tide of the Thames deserves to see no better.
There was a great deal of shipping in the river, and
many steamers, and it was much more crowded than
the Mersey, where all the ships go into docks; but

the vessels were not so fine. By-and-by we reached Greenwich, and went ashore there, proceeding up from the quay, past beer-shops and eating-houses in great numbers and variety. Greenwich Hospital is here a very prominent object, and after passing along its extensive front, facing towards the river, we entered one of the principal gates, as we found ourselves free to do.

. . . . .

We now left the hospital, and steamed back to London Bridge, whence we went up into the City, and, to finish the labours of the day, ascended the Monument. This seems to be still a favourite adventure with the cockneys; for we heard one woman, who went up with us, saying that she had been thinking of going up all her life, and another said that she had gone up thirty years ago. There is an iron railing, or rather a cage, round the top, through which it would be impossible for people to force their way, in order to precipitate themselves, as six persons have heretofore done. There was a mist over London, so that we did not gain a very clear view, except of the swarms of people running about, like ants, in the streets at the foot of the Monument.

Descending, I put S. and the children into a cab, and I myself wandered about the City. Passing along Fleet Street, I turned in through an archway, which I rightly guessed to be the entrance to the Temple. It is a very large space, containing many large, solemn, and serious edifices of dark brick, and no sooner do you pass under the arch than all the rumble and bustle of London dies away at once; and it seems as if a person might live there in perfect quiet, without suspecting that it was not always a Sabbath. People appear to have their separate residences here; but I do not understand what is the economy of their lives. Quite in the deepest interior of this region, there is a large garden, bordering on the Thames, along which it has a gravel walk, and benches where it would be pleasant to sit. On one edge of the garden, there is some scanty shrubbery, and flowers of no great brilliancy; and the greensward, with which the garden is mostly covered, is not particularly rich nor verdant.

Emerging from the Temple, I stopped at a tavern in the Strand, the waiter of which observed to me, "They say Sebastopol is taken, sir!" It was only such an interesting event that could have induced an English waiter to make a remark to a stranger, not called for in the way of business.

The best view we had of the Tower—in fact, the only external view, and the only time we really saw the White Tower—was from the river, as we steamed past it. Here the high, square, battlemented White Tower, with the four turrets at its corners, rises prominently above all other parts of the fortress.

. . . .

September 13th.—Mr. ——, the American Minister, called on me on Tuesday, and left his card; an intimation that I ought sooner to have paid my respects to him; so yesterday forenoon I set out to find his residence, 56, Harley Street. It is a street out of Cavendish Square, in a fashionable quarter, although fashion is said to be ebbing away from it. The Ambassador seems to intend some little state in his arrangements; but, no doubt, the establishment compares shabbily enough with those of the legations of other great countries, and with the houses of the English aristocracy.

A servant, not in livery, or in a very unrecognisable one, opened the door for me, and gave my card to a sort of upper attendant, who took it in to Mr. ——. He had three gentlemen with him, so desired that I should be ushered into the office of the legation, until he should be able to receive me. Here I found a clerk or *attaché*, Mr. M., who has been two or three years on this side of the water; an intelligent person, who seems to be in correspondence with the New York *Courier and Inquirer*. By-and-by came in another American to get a passport for the Continent, and soon the three gentlemen took leave of the Ambassador, and I was invited to his presence.

The tall, large figure of Mr. —— has a certain air of state and dignity; he carries his head in a very awkward way, but still looks like a man of long and high authority, and, with his white hair, is now quite venerable. There is certainly a lack of polish, a kind of rusticity, notwithstanding which you feel him to be a man of the world. I should think he might succeed very tolerably in English society, being heavy and sensible, cool, kindly, and good-humoured, with a great deal of experience of life. We talked about various matters, politics among the rest; and he observed that if the President had taken the advice which he gave him in two long letters, before his inauguration, he would have had a perfectly quiet and successful term of office. The advice was, to form a perfectly homogeneous cabinet of Union men, and to satisfy the extremes of the party by a fair distribution of minor offices; whereas he formed his cabinet of extreme men, on both sides, and gave the minor offices to moderate ones. But the anti-slavery people, surely, had no representative in the cabinet. Mr. —— further observed, that he thought the President had a fair chance of renomination, for that the South could not, in honour, desert him; to which I replied that the South had been guilty of such things heretofore. Mr. —— thinks that the next presidential term will be more important and critical, both as to our foreign relations and internal affairs, than any preceding one,—which I should judge likely enough to be the case, although I heard the same prophecy often made respecting the present term.

The Ambassador dined with us at Rock Park a year or two ago, and I then felt, and always feel, as if he were a man of hearty feeling and simplicity, and certainly it would be unjust to conclude otherwise, merely from the fact (very suspicious, it is true) of his having been a life-long politician. After we had got through a little matter of business (respecting a young American who has enlisted at Liverpool), the Minister rang his bell, and ordered another visitor to be admitted; and so I took my leave. In the other room I found the Secretary of Legation,—a tall, slender man of about forty, with a small head and face,—gentlemanly enough, sensible, and well informed, yet, I should judge, not quite up to his place. There was also a Dr. B. from Michigan present, and I rather fancy the Ambassador is quite as much bored with visitors as the Consul at Liverpool. Before I left the office, Mr. —— came in with Miss Sarah Clarke on his arm. She had come thither to get her passport viséd; and when her business was concluded, we went out together.

She was going farther towards the West End, and I into the City; so we soon parted, and I lost myself among the streets and squares, arriving at last at Oxford

Street, though even then I did not know whether my face were turned cityward or in the opposite direction. Crossing Regent Street, however, I became sure of my whereabout, and went on through Holborn, and sought hither and thither for Gracechurch Street, in order to find the American Consul, General Campbell; for I needed his aid to get a bank post-bill cashed. But I could not find the street, go where I would; so at last I went to No. 65, Cheapside, and introduced myself to Mr. ——, whom I already know by letter, and by a good many of his poems, which he has sent me, and by two excellent watches, which I bought of him. This establishment, though it has the ordinary front of dingy brick, common to buildings in the City, looks like a time-long stand, the old shop of a London tradesman, with a large figure of a watch over the door, a great many watches (and yet no gorgeous show of them) in the window, a low, dark front shop, and a little room behind, where there was a chair or two. Mr. —— is a small, slender young man, quite un-English in aspect, with black, curly hair, a thin, dark, colourless visage, very animated and of quick expression, with a nervous temperament. . . . . He dismounted from a desk when my card was handed to him, and turned to me with a vivid, glad look of recognition.

We talked, in the first place, about poetry and such matters, about England and America, and the nature and depth of their mutual dislike, and, of course, the slavery question came up, as it always does, in one way or another. Anon, I produced my bank post-bill; and Mr. —— kindly engaged to identify me at the bank, being ready to swear to me, he said, on the strength of my resemblance to my engraved portrait.

So we set out for the Bank of England, and, arriving
there, were directed to the proper clerk, after much inquiry; but he told us that the bill was not yet due,
having been drawn at seven days, and having two still
to run,—which was the fact. As I was almost shilling-
less, Mr. —— now offered to cash it for me. He is
very kind and good. . . . . Arriving at his shop again,
he went out to procure the money, and soon returned
with it. At my departure he gave me a copy of a
new poem of his, entitled "Verdicts," somewhat in the
manner of Lowell's satire. . . . . Mr. —— resides now
at Greenwich, whither he hoped I would come and see
him on my return to London. Perhaps I will, for I
like him. It seems strange to see an Englishman with
so little physical ponderosity and obtuseness of nerve.

After parting from him, it being three o'clock or
thereabouts, I resumed my wanderings about the City,
of which I never weary as long as I can put one foot
before the other.

Seeing that the door of St. Paul's, under one of
the semicircular porches, was partially open, I went in,
and found that the afternoon service was about to be
performed; so I remained to hear it, and to see what I
could of the cathedral. What a total and admirable
contrast between this and a Gothic church! the latter
so dim and mysterious, with its various aisles, its intricacy of pointed arches, its dark walls and columns
and pavement, and its painted glass windows, bedim-
ming even what daylight might otherwise get into its
eternal evening. But this cathedral was full of light,
and light was proper to it. There were no painted
windows, no dim recesses, but a wide and airy space
beneath the dome; and even through the long per-

spective of the nave there was no obscurity, but one
lofty and beautifully rounded arch succeeding to another, as far as the eye could reach. The walls were
white, the pavement constructed of squares of grey and
white marble. It is a most grand and stately edifice,
and its characteristic seems to be to continue for ever
fresh and new; whereas such a church as Westminster
Abbey must have been as venerable as it is now from
the first day when it grew to be an edifice at all. How
wonderful man is in his works! How glad I am that
there can be two such admirable churches, in their opposite styles, as St. Paul's and Westminster Abbey!

The organ was played while I was there, and there
was an anthem beautifully chanted by voices that came
from afar off and remotely above, as if out of a sunny
sky. Meanwhile I looked at such monuments as were
near; chiefly those erected to military or naval men,—
Picton, General Ponsonby, Lord St. Vincent, and others;
but against one of the pillars stands a statue of Dr.
Johnson,—a noble and thoughtful figure, with a development of muscle befitting an athlete. I doubt
whether sculptors do not err in point of taste, by making all their statues models of physical perfection, instead of expressing by them the individual character
and habits of the man. The statue in the market-place
at Lichfield has more of the homely truth of Johnson's
actual personality than this.

St. Paul's, as yet, is by no means crowded with
monuments; there is, indeed, plenty of room for a mob
of the illustrious yet to come. But it seems to me that
the character of the edifice would be injured by allowing the monuments to be clustered together so closely
as at Westminster, by incrusting the walls with them,

or letting the statues throng about the pedestals of columns. There must be no confusion in such a cathedral as this, and I question whether the effect will ever be better than it is now, when each monument has its distinct place, and as your eye wanders around, you are not distracted from noting each marble man, in his niche against the wall, or at the base of a marble pillar. Space, distance, light, regualrity, are to be preserved, even if the result should be a degree of nakedness.

I saw Mr. Appleton of the Legation, and Dr. Brown, on the floor of the cathedral. They were about to go over the whole edifice, and had engaged a guide for that purpose; but, as I intend to go thither again with S., I did not accompany them, but went away the quicker that one of the gentlemen put on his hat, and I was ashamed of being seen in company with a man who could wear his hat in a cathedral. Not that he meant any irreverence; but simply felt that he was in a great public building,—as big, nearly, as all out of doors,—and so forgot that it was a consecrated place of worship. The sky is the dome of a greater cathedral than St. Paul's, and built by a greater architect than Sir Christopher Wren, and yet we wear our hats unscrupulously beneath it.

I remember no other event of importance, except that I penetrated into a narrow lane or court, either in the Strand or Fleet Street, where was a tavern, calling itself the "Old Thatched House," and purporting to have been Nell Gwynn's dairy. I met with a great many alleys and obscure archways, in the course of the day's wanderings.

September 14*th.*—Yesterday, in the earlier part of

the day, it poured with rain, and I did not go out till
five o'clock in the afternoon; nor did I then meet with
anything interesting. I walked through Albemarle
Street, for the purpose of looking at Murray's shop,
but missed it entirely at my first inquisition. The
street is one of hotels, principally, with only a few
tradesmen's shops, and has a quiet, aristocratic aspect.
On my return down the other sidewalk, I did discover
the famous publisher's locality; but merely by the
name, "Mr. Murray," engraved on a rather large brass
plate, such as doctors use, on the door. There was no
sign of a book, nor of its being a place of trade in
any way; and I should have taken the house to be, if
not a private mansion, then a lawyer's office.

At seven o'clock S., U., and I went to dine with
Mr. R. S. in Portland Place. . . . . Mr. S.'s house is a
very fine one, and he gave us a very quiet, elegant,
and enjoyable dinner, in much better taste and with
less fuss than some others we have attended elsewhere.
Mr. S. is a friend of Thackeray, and, speaking of the
last number of "The Newcomes,"—so touching that
nobody can read it aloud without breaking down,—he
mentioned that Thackeray himself had read it to James
Russell Lowell and William Story in a cider-cellar! I
read all the preceding numbers of "The Newcomes"
to my wife, but happened not to have an opportunity
to read this last, and was glad of it,—knowing that
my eyes would fill, and my voice quiver. Mr. S. likes
Thackeray, and thinks him a good fellow. Mr. S. has
a—or I don't know but I ought better to say *the*—
beautiful full-length picture of Washington by Stuart,
and I was proud to see that noblest face and figure
here in England. The picture of a man beside whom,

considered physically, any English nobleman whom I have seen would look like common clay.

Speaking of Thackeray, I cannot but wonder at his coolness in respect to his own pathos, and compare it with my emotions, when I read the last scene of "The Scarlet Letter" to my wife, just after writing it,—tried to read it rather, for my voice swelled and heaved, as if I were tossed up and down on an ocean as it subsides after a storm. But I was in a very nervous state then, having gone through a great diversity of emotion, while writing it, for many months. I think I have never overcome my own adamant in any other instance.

Tumblers, hand-organists, puppet-showmen, bag-pipers, and all such vagrant mirth-makers, are very numerous in the streets of London. The other day, passing through Fleet Street, I saw a crowd filling up a narrow court, and high above their heads a tumbler, standing on his head, on the top of a pole, that reached as high as the third story of the neighbouring houses. Sliding down the pole head foremost, he disappeared out of my sight. A multitude of Punches go the rounds continually. Two have passed through Hanover Street, where we reside, this morning. The first asked two shillings for his performance; so we sent him away. The second demanded, in the first place, half a crown; but finally consented to take a shilling, and gave us the show at that price, though much maimed in its proportions. Besides the spectators in our windows, he had a little crowd on the sidewalk, to whom he went round for contributions, but I did not observe that anybody gave him so much as a halfpenny. It is strange to see how many people are aiming at the small change in your pocket. In every square a beggar-woman meets you, and turns back to follow your steps with her miserable murmur. At the street-crossings there are old men or little girls with their brooms; urchins propose to brush your boots; and if you get into a cab, a man runs to open the door for you, and touches his hat for a fee, as he closes it again.

September 15th.—It was raining yesterday, and I kept within doors till after four o'clock, when J. and I took a walk into the City. Seeing the entrance to Clement's Inn, we went through it, and saw the garden, with a kneeling bronze figure in it; and when just in the midst of the Inn, I remembered that Justice Shallow was of old a student there. I do not well understand these Inns of Court, or how they differ from other places. Anybody seems to be free to reside in them, and a residence does not seem to involve any obligation to study law, or to have any connection therewith. Clement's Inn consists of large brick houses, accessible by narrow lanes and passages, but, by some peculiar privilege or enchantment, enjoying a certain quiet and repose, though in close vicinity to the noisiest part of the City. I got bewildered in the neighbourhood of St. Paul's, and, try how I might to escape from it, its huge dusky dome kept showing itself before me, through one street and another. In my endeavours to escape it, I at one time found myself in St. John's Street, and was in hopes to have seen the old St. John's Gate, so familiar for above a century on the cover of the *Gentleman's Magazine*. But I suppose it is taken down, for we went through the entire street,

I think, and saw no trace of it. Either afterwards or before this we came upon Smithfield, a large irregular square, filled up with pens for cattle, of which, however, there were none in the market at that time. I leaned upon a post, at the western end of the square, and told J. how the martyrs had been burnt at Smithfield in Bloody Mary's days. Again we drifted back to St. Paul's; and, at last, in despair of ever getting out of this enchanted region, I took a Hansom cab to Charing Cross, whence we easily made our way home.

LIVERPOOL.

September 16th.—I took the ten-o'clock train yesterday morning from the Euston station, and arrived at Liverpool at about five, passing through the valley of Trent, without touching at Birmingham. English scenery, on the tracks, is the tamest of the tame, hardly a noticeable hill breaking the ordinary gentle undulation of the landscape, but still the verdure and finish of the fields and parks make it worth while to throw out a glance now and then, as you rush by. Few separate houses are seen, as in America; but sometimes a village, with the square, grey, battlemented tower of its Norman church, and rows of thatched cottages, reminding one of the clustered mud nests of swallows, under the eaves of a barn; here and there a lazy little river, like the Trent; perhaps, if you look sharply where the guide-book indicates, the turrets of an old castle in the distance; perhaps the great steeple and spires of a cathedral; perhaps the tall chimney of a manufactory; but, on the whole, the traveller comes to his journey's end unburdened with a single new idea. I observe that the harvest is not all gathered in as yet, and this rainy weather must look very gloomy to the farmer. I saw gleaners, yesterday, in the stubble-fields. There were two gentlemen in the same railway carriage with me, and we did not exchange half a dozen words the whole day.

I am here established at Mrs. Blodgett's boarding-house, which I find quite full; insomuch that she had to send one of her sea-captains to sleep in another house, in order to make room for me. It is exclusively American society; four shipmasters, and a doctor from Pennsylvania, who has been travelling a year on the Continent, and who seems to be a man of very active intelligence, interested in everything, and especially in agriculture. . . . . He asserted that we are fifty years ahead of England in agricultural science, and that he could cultivate English soil to far better advantage than English farmers do, and at vastly less expense. Their tendency to cling to old ideas, which retards them in everything else, keeps them behindhand in this matter too. Really, I do not know any other place in England where a man can be made so sensible that he lives in a progressive world as here in Mrs. Blodgett's boarding-house.

The captains talk together about their voyages, and how they manage with their unruly mates and crews; and how freights are in America, and the prospects of business; and of equinoctial gales, and the qualities of different ships, and their commanders, and how crews, mates, and masters have all deteriorated since their remembrance. . . . . But these men are alive, and talk of real matters, and of matters which they know. The shipmasters who come to Mrs. Blodgett's are favourable specimens of their class; being all respectable men, in the employ of good houses, and raised by their capacity to the command of first-rate ships. In my official intercourse with them, I do not generally see their best side; as they are seldom before me except as complainants, or when summoned to answer to some complaint made by a seaman. But hearing their daily talk, and listening to what is in their minds, and their reminiscences of what they have gone through, one becomes sensible that they are men of energy and ability, fit to be trusted, and retaining a hardy sense of honour, and a loyalty to their own country, the stronger because they have compared it with many others. Most of them are gentlemen, too, to a certain extent,—some more than others, perhaps; and none to a very exquisite point, or, if so, it is none the better for them as sailors or as men.

September 17*th*.—It is singular to feel a sense of my own country returning upon me with the intercourse of the people whom I find here. . . . .

The doctor is much the most talkative of our company, and sometimes bores me thereby; though he seldom says anything that is not either instructive or amusing. He tells a curious story of Prince Albert, and how he avails himself of American sharp-shooting. During the doctor's tour in Scotland, which he has just finished, he became acquainted with one of the Prince's *attachés*, who invited him very earnestly to join his Royal Highness's party, promising him a good gun, and a keeper to load it for him, two good dogs, besides as many cigars as he could smoke and as much wine as he could drink, on the condition that whatever game he shot should be the Prince's. "The Prince," said the *attaché*, "is very fond of having Americans in his shooting-parties, on account of their being such excellent shots; and there was one with him last year who shot so admirably that his Royal Highness himself left off shooting in utter astonishment." The *attaché* offered to introduce the doctor to the Prince, who would be certain to receive him very graciously. . . . .

I think, perhaps, we talk of kings and queens more at our table than people do at other tables in England; not, of course, that we like them better, or admire them more, but that they are curiosities. Yet I would not say that the doctor may not be susceptible on the point of royal attentions; for he told us with great complacency how emphatically, on two or three occasions, Louis Napoleon had returned his bow, and the last time had turned and made some remark (evidently about the doctor) to the Empress. . . . .

I ought not to omit mentioning that he has been told in France that he personally resembles the Emperor, and I suspect he is trying to heighten the resemblance by training his moustache on the pattern of that which adorns the imperial upper lip. He is a genuine American character, though modified by a good deal of travel; a very intelligent man, full of various ability, with eyes all over him for any object of interest,—a little of the bore, sometimes,—quick to appreciate character, with a good deal of tact, gentlemanly in his manners, but yet lacking a deep and delicate refinement. Not but that Americans are as capable of this last quality as other people are; but what with the circumstances amid which we grow up, and the peculiar activity of our minds, we certainly do often miss it. By-the-bye, he advanced a singular proposition the other evening, namely, that the English people do not so well understand comfort, or attain it so perfectly in their domestic arrangements, as we do. I thought he hardly supported this opinion so satisfactorily as some of his other new ideas.

I saw in an American paper yesterday, that an opera, still unfinished, had been written on the story of "The Scarlet Letter," and that several scenes of it had been performed successfully in New York. I should think it might possibly succeed as an opera, though it would certainly fail as a play.

LONDON.

September 24*th.*—On Saturday, at half-past three o'clock, I left Liverpool by the London and North-West Railway for London. Mrs. Blodgett's table had been thinned by several departures during the week. . . . . My mind had been considerably enlivened, and my sense of American superiority renewed by intercourse with these people; and there is no danger of one's intellect becoming a standing pool in such society. I think better of American shipmasters, too, than I did from merely meeting them in my office. They keep up a continual discussion of professional matters, and of all things having any reference to their profession; the laws of insurance, the rights of vessels in foreign ports, the authority and customs of vessels of war with regard to merchantmen, &c.,—with stories and casual anecdotes of their sea-adventures, gales, shipwrecks, icebergs, and collisions of vessels, and hair-breadth escapes. Their talk runs very much on the sea, and on the land as connected with the sea; and their interest does not seem to extend very far beyond the wide field of their professional concerns.

Nothing remarkable occurred on the journey to London. The greater part of the way there were only two gentlemen in the same compartment with me; and we occupied each our corner, with little other conversation than in comparing watches at the various stations. I got out of the carriage only once, at Rugby, I think, and for the last seventy or eighty miles the train did not stop. There was a clear moon the latter part of the journey, and the mist lay along the ground looking very much like a surface of water. We reached London at about ten, and I found S. expecting me.

Yesterday the children went with Fanny to the Zoological Gardens; and, after sending them off, S. and I walked to Piccadilly, and there took a cab for Kensington Gardens. It was a delightful day,—the best of all weather, the real English good weather,—more like an Indian summer than anything else within my experience; a mellow sunshine, with great warmth in it, —a soft, balmy air, with a slight haze through it. If the sun made us a little too warm, we had but to go into the shade to be immediately refreshed. The light of these days is very exquisite, so gently bright, without any glare,—a veiled glow. In short, it is the kindliest mood of Nature, and almost enough to compensate for chill and dreamy months. Moreover, there is more of such weather here than the English climate has ever had credit for.

Kensington Gardens form an eminently beautiful

piece of artificial woodland and park scenery. The old palace of Kensington, now inhabited by the Duchess of Inverness, stands at one extremity; an edifice of no great mark, built of brick, covering much ground, and low in proportion to its extent. In front of it, at a considerable distance, there is a sheet of water; and in all directions there are vistas of wide paths among noble trees, standing in groves, or scattered in clumps; everything being laid out with free and generous spaces, so that you can see long streams of sunshine among the trees, and there is a pervading influence of quiet and remoteness. Tree does not interfere with tree; the art of man is seen conspiring with Nature, as if they had consulted together how to make a beautiful scene, and had taken ages of quiet thought and tender care to accomplish it. We strolled slowly along these paths, and sometimes deviated from them to walk beneath the trees, many of the leaves of which lay beneath our feet, yellow and brown, and with a pleasant smell of vegetable decay. These were the leaves of chestnut-trees; the other trees (unless elms) have yet hardly begun to shed their foliage, although you can discern a sober change of hue in the woodland masses; and the trees individualise themselves by assuming each its own tint, though in a very modest way. If they could have undergone the change of an American autumn, it would have been like putting on a regal robe. Autumn often puts one on in America, but it is apt to be very ragged.

There were a good many well-dressed people scattered through the grounds,—young men and girls, husbands with their wives and children, nursery-maids and little babes playing about in the grass. Anybody might have entered the gardens, I suppose; but only well-dressed people were there,—not of the upper classes, but shop-keepers, clerks, apprentices, and respectability of that sort. It is pleasant to think that the people have the freedom, and therefore the property, of parks like this, more beautiful and stately than a nobleman can keep to himself. The extent of Kensington Gardens, when reckoned together with Hyde Park, from which it is separated only by a fence of iron rods, is very great, comprising miles of greensward and woodland. The large artificial sheet of water, called the Serpentine River, lies chiefly in Hyde Park, but comes partly within the precincts of the Gardens. It is entitled to honourable mention among the English lakes, being larger than some that are world-celebrated,—several miles long, and perhaps a stone's-throw across in the widest part. It forms the paradise of a great many ducks of various breeds, which are accustomed to be fed by visitors, and come flying from afar, touching the water with their wings, and quacking loudly when bread or cake is thrown to them. I bought a bun of a little hunchbacked man, who kept a refreshment-stall near the Serpentine, and bestowed it piecemeal on these ducks, as we loitered along the bank. We left the park by another gate, and walked homeward, till we came to Tyburnia, and saw the iron memorial which marks where the gallows used to stand. Thence we turned into Park Lane, then into Upper Grosvenor Street, and reached Hanover Square sooner than we expected.

In the evening I walked forth to Charing Cross, and thence along the Strand and Fleet Street, where I made no new discoveries, unless it were the Mitre Tavern. I mean to go into it some day. The streets

were much thronged, and there seemed to be a good
many young people,—lovers, it is to be hoped,—who
had spent the day together, and were going innocently
home. Perhaps so,—perhaps not.

September 25th.—Yesterday forenoon J. and I walked
out, with no very definite purpose; but, seeing a narrow
passage-way from the Strand down to the river,
we went through it, and gained access to a steamboat,
plying thence to London Bridge. The fare was a halfpenny apiece, and the boat almost too much crowded
for standing-room. This part of the river presents the
water-side of London in a rather pleasanter aspect than
below London Bridge,—the Temple with its garden,
Somerset House,—and generally, a less tumble-down
and neglected look about the buildings; although, after
all, the metropolis does not see a very stately face in
its mirror. I saw Alsatia betwixt the Temple and
Blackfriars Bridge. Its precincts looked very narrow,
and not particularly distinguishable, at this day, from
the portions of the City on either side of it. At London
Bridge we got aboard of a Woolwich steamer, and
went farther down the river, passing the Custom-House
and the Tower, the only prominent objects rising out
of the dreary range of shabbiness which stretches along
close to the water's edge.

From this remote part of London we walked towards
the heart of the City; and, as we went, matters
seemed to civilise themselves by degrees, and the
streets grew crowded with cabs, omnibuses, drays, and
carts. We passed, I think, through Whitechapel, and,
reaching St. Paul's, got into an omnibus, and drove to
Regent Street, whence it was but a step or two home.

In the afternoon, at four o'clock, S. and I went to call on the American Ambassador and Miss L. The lady was not at home, but we went in to see Mr. ——, and were shown into a stately drawing-room, the furniture of which was sufficiently splendid, but rather the worse for wear,—being hired furniture, no doubt. The Ambassador shortly appeared, looking venerable, as usual,—or rather more so than usual,—benign and very pale. His deportment towards ladies is highly agreeable and prepossessing, and he paid very kind attention to S., thereby quite confirming her previous good feeling towards him. She thinks that he is much changed since she saw him last, at dinner, at our house, —more infirm, more aged, and with a singular depression in his manner. I, too, think that age has latterly come upon him with great rapidity. He said that Miss L. was going home on the 6th of October, and that he himself had long purposed going, but had received despatches which obliged him to put off his departure. The President, he said, had just written, requesting him to remain till April, but this he was determined not to do. I rather think that he does really wish to return, and not for any ambitious views concerning the Presidency, but from an old man's natural desire to be at home, and among his own people.

S. spoke to him about an order from the Lord Chamberlain for admission to view the two Houses of Parliament; and the Ambassador drew from his pocket a coloured-silk handkerchief, and made a knot in it, in order to remind himself to ask the Lord Chamberlain. The homeliness of this little incident has a sort of propriety and keeping with much of Mr. ——'s manner, but I would rather not have him do so before English people. He arranged to send a close carriage for us to come and see him socially this evening. After leaving his house we drove round Hyde Park, and thence to to Portland Place, where we left cards for Mrs. Russell Sturgis; thence into Regent's Park, thence home. ..... In the evening I strolled out, and walked as far as St. Paul's,—never getting enough of the bustle of London, which may weary, but can never satisfy me. By night London looks wild and dreamy, and fills me with a sort of pleasant dread. It was a clear evening, with a bright English moon,—that is to say, what we Americans should call rather dim.

September 26th.—Yesterday, at eleven, I walked towards Westminster Abbey, and as I drew near the Abbey bells were clamorous for joy, chiming merrily, musically, and obstreperously,—the most rejoicing sound that can be conceived; and we ought to have a chime of bells in every American town and village, were it only to keep alive the celebration of the Fourth of July. I conjectured that there might have been another victory over the Russians, that perhaps the northern side of Sebastopol had surrendered; but soon I saw the riddle that these merry bells were proclaiming. There were a great many private carriages, and a large concourse of loungers and spectators, near the door of the church that stands close under the eaves of the Abbey. Gentlemen and ladies, gaily dressed, were issuing forth, carriages driving away, and others drawing up to the door in their turn; and, in short, a marriage had just been celebrated in the church, and this was the wedding party. The last time I was there,

Westminster was flinging out its great voice of joy for a national triumph; now, for the happy union of two lovers. What a mighty sympathizer is this old Abbey!

It is pleasant to recognise the mould and fashion of English features through the marble of many of the statues and busts in the Abbey, even though they may be clad in Roman robes. I am inclined to think them, in many cases, faithful likenesses; and it brings them nearer to the mind, to see these original sculptures,— you see the man at but one remove, as if you caught his image in a looking-glass. The bust of Gay seemed to me very good, a thoughtful and humorous sweetness in the face. Goldsmith has as good a position as any poet in the Abbey, his bust and tablet filling the pointed arch over a door that seems to lead towards the cloisters. No doubt he would have liked to be assured of so conspicuous a place. There is one monument to a native American, "Charles Wragg, Esq., of South Carolina,"—the only one, I suspect, in Westminster Abbey, and he acquired this memorial by the most un-American of qualities, his loyalty to his king. He was one of the refugees leaving America in 1777, being shipwrecked on his passage, and the monument was put up by his sister. It is a small tablet with a representation of Mr. Wragg's shipwreck at the base. Next to it is the large monument of Sir Cloudesley Shovel, which I think Addison ridicules,—the Admiral, in a full-bottomed wig and Roman dress, but with a broad English face, reclining with his head on his hand, and looking at you with great placidity. I stood at either end of the nave, and endeavoured to take in the full beauty and majesty of the edifice; but apparently was not in a proper state of mind, for nothing came of it. It is singular how like an avenue of overarching trees are these lofty aisles of a cathedral.

Leaving the Abbey about one o'clock, I walked into the City as far as Gracechurch Street, and there called on the American Consul, General ——, who had been warmly introduced to me last year by a letter from the President. I like the General; a kindly and honourable man, of simple manners and large experience of life. Afterwards I called on Mr. Oakford, an American connected in business with Mr. Crosby, from whom I wanted some information as to the sailing of steamers from Southampton to Lisbon. Mr. Crosby was not in town.....

At eight o'clock Mr. —— sent his carriage, according to previous arrangement, to take us to spend the evening socially. Miss L. received us with proper cordiality, and looked quite becomingly,—more sweet and simple in aspect than when I have seen her in full dress. Shortly the Ambassador appeared, and made himself highly agreeable; not that he is a brilliant conversationist, but his excellent sense and good-humour, and all that he has seen and been a part of, are sufficient resources to draw upon. We talked of the Queen, whom he spoke of with high respect; . . . . of the late Czar, whom he knew intimately while minister to Russia,—and he quite confirms all that has been said about the awful beauty of his person. Mr. ——'s characterisation of him was quite favourable; he thought better of his heart than most people, and adduced his sports with a school of children,—twenty of whom, perhaps, he made to stand rigidly in a row, like so many bricks,—then, giving one a push, would laugh obstreperously to see the whole row tumble down. He would lie on his back, and allow the little things to

scramble over him. His Majesty admitted Mr. ——
to great closeness of intercourse, and informed him of
a conspiracy which was then on foot for the Czar's
murder. On the evening when the assassination was
to take place, the Czar did not refrain from going to
the public place where it was to be perpetrated, although, indeed, great precautions had been taken to
frustrate the schemes of the conspirators. Mr. —— said,
that, in case the plot had succeeded, all the foreigners,
including himself, would likewise have been murdered,
the native Russians having a bitter hatred against foreigners. He observed that he had been much attached
to the Czar, and had never joined in the English
abuse of him. His sympathies, however, are evidently
rather English than Russian, in this war. Speaking
of the present Emperor, he said that Lord Heytesbury,
formerly English Ambassador in Russia, lately told
him that he complimented the Czar Nicholas on the
good qualities of his son, saying that he was acknowledged by all to be one of the most amiable youths in the
world. "Too amiable, I fear, for his position," answered
the Czar. "He has too much of his mother in him."

September 27th.—Yesterday, much earlier than English people ever do such things, General —— made us
a call on his way to the Consulate, and sat talking a
stricken hour or thereabouts. Scarcely had he gone
when Mrs. O. and her daughter came. After sitting a
long while, they took U. to their house, near St. John's
Wood, to spend the night. I had been writing my
journal and official correspondence during such intervals
as these calls left me; and now, concluding these businesses, S., J., and I went out and took a cab for the

terminus of the Crystal Palace Railway, whither we proceeded over Waterloo Bridge, and reached the palace not far from three o'clock. It was a beautifully bright day, such as we have in wonderful succession this month. The Crystal Palace gleamed in the sunshine; but I do not think a very impressive edifice can be built of glass,—light and airy, to be sure, but still it will be no other than an overgrown conservatory. It is unlike anything else in England; uncongenial with the English character, without privacy, destitute of mass, weight, and shadow, unsusceptible of ivy, lichens, or any mellowness from age.

The train of carriages stops within the domain of the palace, where there is a long ascending corridor up into the edifice. There was a very pleasant odour of heliotrope diffused through the air; and, indeed, the whole atmosphere of the Crystal Palace is sweet with various flower-scents, and mild and balmy, though sufficiently fresh and cool. It would be a delightful climate for invalids to spend the winter in; and if all England could be roofed over with glass, it would be a great improvement on its present condition.

The first thing we did, before fairly getting into the palace, was to sit down in a large ante-hall, and get some bread and butter and a pint of Bass's pale ale, together with a cup of coffee for S. This was the best refreshment we could find at that spot; but farther within we found abundance of refreshment-rooms, and John Bull and his wife and family at fifty little round tables, busily engaged with cold fowl, cold beef, ham, tongue, and bottles of ale and stout, and half-pint decanters of sherry. The English probably eat with more simple enjoyment than any other people; not ravenously, as we often do, and not exquisitely and artificially, like the French, but deliberately and vigorously, and with due absorption in the business, so that nothing good is lost upon them. . . . . It is remarkable how large a feature the refreshment-rooms make in the arrangements of the Crystal Palace.

The Crystal Palace is a gigantic toy for the English people to play with. The design seems to be to reproduce all past ages, by representing the features of their interior architecture, costume, religion, domestic life, and everything that can be expressed by paint and plaster; and, likewise, to bring all climates and regions of the earth within these enchanted precincts, with their inhabitants and animals in living semblance, and their vegetable productions, as far as possible, alive and real. Some part of the design is already accomplished to a wonderful degree. The Indian, the Egyptian, and especially the Arabian, courts are admirably executed. I never saw or conceived anything so gorgeous as the Alhambra. There are Byzantine and mediæval representations, too,—reproductions of ancient apartments, decorations, statues from tombs, monuments, religious and funereal,—that gave me new ideas of what antiquity has been. It takes down one's overweening opinion of the present time, to see how many kinds of beauty and magnificence have heretofore existed, and are now quite passed away and forgotten; and to find that we, who suppose that, in all matters of taste, our age is the very flower-season of the time,—that we are poor and meagre as to many things in which they were rich. There is nothing gorgeous now. We live a very naked life. This was the only reflection I remember making, as we passed

from century to century, through the succession of
classic, Oriental, and mediæval courts, adown the lapse
of time,—seeing all these ages in as brief a space as
the Wandering Jew might glance along them in his
memory. I suppose a Pompeian house with its courts
and interior apartments was as faithfully shown as it
was possible to do it. I doubt whether I ever should feel
at home in such a house.

In the pool of a fountain, of which there are several
beautiful ones within the palace, besides larger ones in
the garden before it, we saw tropical plants growing,
—large water-lilies of various colours, some white, like
our Concord pond-lily, only larger, and more numerously
leafed. There were great circular green leaves, lying
flat on the water, with a circumference equal to that of
a centre-table. Tropical trees, too, varieties of palm
and others, grew in immense pots or tubs, but seemed
not to enjoy themselves much. The atmosphere must,
after all, be far too cool to bring out their native
luxuriance; and this difficulty can never be got over
at a less expense than that of absolutely stewing the
visitors and attendants. Otherwise, it would be very
practicable to have all the vegetable world, at least,
within these precincts.

The palace is very large, and our time was short,
it being desirable to get home early; so, after a stay
of little more than two hours, we took the rail back
again, and reached Hanover Square at about six. After
tea I wandered forth, with some thought of going to
the theatre, and, passing the entrance of one, in the
Strand, I went in, and found a farce in progress. It
was one of the minor theatres, very minor indeed; but
the pieces, so far as I saw them, were sufficiently

laughable. There were some Spanish dances, too, very graceful and pretty. Between the plays a girl from the neighbouring saloon came to the doors of the boxes, offering lemonade and ginger-beer to the occupants. A person in my box took a glass of lemonade, and shared it with a young lady by his side, both sipping out of the same glass. The audience seemed rather heavy,— not briskly responsive to the efforts of the performers, but good-natured, and willing to be pleased, especially with some patriotic dances, in which much waving and intermingling of the French and English flags was introduced. Theatrical performances soon weary me of late years; and I came away before the curtain rose on the concluding piece.

September 28th.—S. and I walked to Charing Cross yesterday forenoon, and there took a Hansom cab to St. Paul's Cathedral. It had been a thick, foggy morning, but had warmed and brightened into one of the balmiest and sunniest of noons. As we entered the cathedral, the long bars of sunshine were falling from its upper windows through the great interior atmosphere, and were made visible by the dust, or mist, floating about in it. It is a grand edifice, and I liked it quite as much as on my first view of it, although a sense of coldness and nakedness is felt when we compare it with Gothic churches. It is more an external work than the Gothic churches are, and is not so made out of the dim, awful, mysterious, grotesque, intricate nature of man. But it is beautiful and grand. I love its remote distances, and wide, clear spaces, its airy massiveness; its noble arches, its sky-like dome, which,

I think, should be all over light, with ground glass, instead of being dark, with only diminutive windows.

We walked round, looking at the monuments, which are so arranged, at the bases of columns and in niches, as to coincide with the regularity of the cathedral, and be each an additional ornament to the whole, however defective individually as works of art. We thought that many of these monuments were striking and impressive, though there was a pervading sameness of idea,—a great many Victorys and Valours and Britannias, and a great expenditure of wreaths, which must have cost Victory a considerable sum at any florist's whom she patronizes. A very great majority of the memorials are to naval and military men, slain in Bonaparte's wars; men in whom one feels little or no interest (except Picton, Abercrombie, Moore, Nelson, of course, and a few others really historic), they having done nothing remarkable, save having been shot, nor shown any more brains than the cannon-balls that killed them. All the statues have the dust of years upon them, strewn thickly in the folds of their marble garments, and on any limb stretched horizontally, and on their noses, so that the expression is much obscured. I think the nation might employ people to brush away the dust from the statues of its heroes. But, on the whole, it is very fine to look through the broad arches of the cathedral, and see, at the foot of some distant pillar, a group of sculptured figures, commemorating some man and deed that (whether worth remembering or no) the nation is so happy as to reverence. In Westminster Abbey, the monuments are so crowded, and so oddly patched together upon the walls, that they are ornamental only in a mural point of view;

and, moreover, the quaint and grotesque taste of many of them might well make the spectator laugh,—an effect not likely to be produced by the monuments in St. Paul's. But, after all, a man might read the walls of the Abbey day after day with ever-fresh interest, whereas the cold propriety of the Cathedral would weary him in due time.

We did not ascend to the galleries and other points of interest aloft, nor go down into the vaults, where Nelson's sarcophagus is shown, and many monuments of the old Gothic cathedral, which stood on this site, before the great fire. They say that these lower regions are comfortably warm and dry; but as we walked round in front, within the iron railing of the churchyard, we passed an open door, giving access to the crypt, and it breathed out a chill like death upon us.

It is pleasant to stand in the centre of the cathedral, and hear the noise of London, loudest all round this spot,—how it is calmed into a sound as proper to be heard through the aisles as the tones of its own organ. If St. Paul's were to be burnt again (having already been burnt and risen three or four times since the sixth century), I wonder whether it would ever be rebuilt in the same spot! I doubt whether the City and the nation are so religious as to consecrate their midmost heart for the site of a church, where land would be so valuable by the square inch.

Coming from the cathedral, we went through Paternoster Row, and saw Ave Maria Lane; all this locality appearing to have got its nomenclature from monkish personages. We now took a cab for the British Museum, but found this to be one of the days on which strangers are not admitted; so we slowly walked into Oxford

Street, and then strolled homeward, till, coming to a sort of bazaar, we went in and found a gallery of pictures. This bazaar proved to be the Pantheon, and the first picture we saw in the gallery was Haydon's Resurrection of Lazarus,—a great height and breadth of canvas, right before you as you ascend the stairs. The face of Lazarus is very awful and not to be forgotten; it is as true as if the painter had seen it, or had been himself the resurrected man and felt it; but the rest of the picture signified nothing, and is vulgar and disagreeable besides. There are several other pictures by Haydon in this collection,—the Banishment of Aristides, Nero with his Harp, and the Conflagration of Rome; but the last is perfectly ridiculous, and all of them are exceedingly unpleasant. I should be sorry to live in a house that contained one of them. The best thing of Haydon was a hasty dash of a sketch for a small, full-length portrait of Wordsworth,* sitting on the crag of a mountain. I doubt whether Wordsworth's likeness has ever been so poetically brought out. This gallery is altogether of modern painters, and it seems to be a receptacle for pictures by artists who can obtain places nowhere else,—at least, I never heard of their names before. They were very uninteresting, almost without exception, and yet some of the pictures were done cleverly enough. There is very little talent in this world, and what there is, it seems to me, is pretty well known and acknowledged. We don't often stumble upon geniuses in obscure corners.

Leaving the gallery, we wandered through the rest of the bazaar, which is devoted to the sale of ladies' finery, jewels, perfumes, children's toys, and all manner

* Now in the possession of Mr. Bennoch.

of small and pretty rubbish. .... In the evening I
again sallied forth, and lost myself for an hour or
two; at last recognising my whereabouts in Tottenham
Court Road. In such quarters of London it seems to
be the habit of people to take their suppers in the
open air. You see old women at the corners, with
kettles of hot water for tea or coffee; and as I passed
a butcher's open shop, he was just taking out large
quantities of boiled beef, smoking hot. Butchers'
stands are remarkable for their profuse expenditure of
gas; it belches forth from the pipes in great flaring
jets of flame, uncovered by any glass, and broadly
illuminating the neighbourhood. I have not observed
that London ever goes to bed.

September 29*th*.—Yesterday we walked to the British
Museum. A sentinel or two kept guard before the
gateway of this extensive edifice in Great Russell
Street, and there was a porter at the lodge, and one
or two policemen lounging about, but entrance was
free, and we walked in without question. Officials
and policemen were likewise scattered about the great
entrance-hall, none of whom, however, interfered with
us; so we took whatever way we chose, and wandered
about at will. It is a hopeless, and to me, generally,
a depressing business to go through an immense multi-
farious show like this, glancing at a thousand things,
and conscious of some little titillation of mind from
them, but really taking in nothing, and getting no
good from anything. One need not go beyond the
limits of the British Museum to be profoundly accomplished in all branches of science, art, and literature;
only it would take a lifetime to exhaust it in any one

department; but to see it as we did, and with no prospect of ever seeing it more at leisure, only impressed me with the truth of the old apophthegm, "Life is short, and Art is long." The fact is, the world is accumulating too many materials for knowledge. We do not recognise for rubbish what is really rubbish; and under this head might be reckoned very many things one sees in the British Museum; and, as each generation leaves its fragments and potsherds behind it, such will finally be the desperate conclusion of the learned.

We went first among some antique marbles,— busts, statues, terminal gods, with several of the Roman emperors among them. We saw here the bust whence Haydon took his ugly and ridiculous likeness of Nero, —a foolish thing to do. Julius Cæsar was there, too, looking more like a modern old man than any other bust in the series. Perhaps there may be a universality in his face, that gives it this independence of race and epoch. We glimpsed along among the old marbles,— Elgin and others, which are esteemed such treasures of art;—the oddest fragments, many of them smashed by their fall from high places, or by being pounded to pieces by barbarians, or gnawed away by time; the surface roughened by being rained upon for thousands of years; almost always a nose knocked off; sometimes a headless form; a great deficiency of feet and hands, —poor, maimed veterans in this hospital of incurables. The beauty of the most perfect of them must be rather guessed at, and seen by faith, than with the bodily eye; to look at the corroded faces and forms is like trying to see angels through mist and cloud. I suppose nine-tenths of those who seem to be in raptures about these fragments do not really care about them; neither do I. And if I were actually moved, I should doubt whether it were by the statues or by my own fancy.

We passed, too, through Assyrian saloons and Egyptian saloons,—all full of monstrosities and horrible uglinesses, especially the Egyptian, and all the innumerable relics that I saw of them in these saloons and among the mummies, instead of bringing me closer to them, removed me farther and farther; there being no common ground of sympathy between them and us. Their gigantic statues are certainly very curious. I saw a hand and arm up to the shoulder fifteen feet in length, and made of some stone that seemed harder and heavier than granite, not having lost its polish in all the rough usage that it has undergone. There was a fist on a still larger scale, almost as big as a hogshead. Hideous, blubber-lipped faces of giants, and human shapes, with beasts' heads on them. The Egyptian controverted Nature in all things, only using it as a groundwork to depict the unnatural upon. Their mummifying process is a result of this tendency. We saw one very perfect mummy,—a priestess, with apparently only one more fold of linen betwixt us and her antique flesh, and this fitting closely to her person from head to foot, so that we could see the lineaments of her face and the shape of her limbs as perfectly as if quite bare. I judge that she may have been very beautiful in her day,—whenever that was. One or two of the poor thing's toes (her feet were wonderfully small and delicate) protruded from the linen, and, perhaps, not having been so perfectly embalmed, the flesh had fallen away, leaving only some little bones. I don't think this

young woman has gained much by not turning to dust
in the time of the Pharaohs. We also saw some bones
of a king that had been taken out of a pyramid; a
very fragmentary skeleton. Among the classic marbles
I peeped into an urn that once contained the ashes of
dead people, and the bottom still had an ashy hue.
I like this mode of disposing of dead bodies; but it
would be still better to burn them and scatter the
ashes, instead of hoarding them up,—to scatter them
over wheat-fields or flower-beds.

Besides these antique halls, we wandered through
saloons of antediluvian animals, some set up in skeletons, others imprisoned in solid stone; also specimens
of still extant animals, birds, reptiles, shells, minerals,
—the whole circle of human knowledge and guesswork,—till I wished that the whole Past might be
swept away, and each generation compelled to bury
and destroy whatever it had produced, before being
permitted to leave the stage. When we quit a house,
we are expected to make it clean for the next occupant; why ought we not to leave a clean world for
the next generation? We did not see the library of
above half a million of volumes; else I suppose I
should have found full occasion to wish that burnt
and buried likewise. In truth, a greater part of it is
as good as buried, so far as any readers are concerned.
Leaving the Museum, we sauntered home. After a
little rest, I set out for St. John's Wood, and arrived
thither by dint of repeated inquiries. It is a pretty
suburb, inhabited by people of the middling class.
U. met me joyfully, but seemed to have had a good
time with Mrs. O. and her daughter; and, being
pressed to stay to tea, I could not well help it. Before

tea I sat talking with Mrs. O. and a friend of hers, Miss C., about the Americans and the English, especially dwelling on the defects of the latter,—among which we reckoned a wretched meanness in money transactions, a lack of any embroidery of honour and liberality in their dealings, so that they require close watching, or they will be sure to take you at advantage. I hear this character of them from Americans on all hands, and my own experience confirms it, as far as it goes, not merely among tradespeople, but among persons who call themselves gentlefolks. The cause, no doubt, or one cause, lies in the fewer chances of getting money here, the closer and sharper regulation of all the modes of life; nothing being left to liberal and gentlemanly feelings, except fees to servants. They are not gamblers in England, as we to some extent are; and getting their money painfully, or living within an accurately known income, they are disinclined to give up so much as a sixpence that they can possibly get. But the result is, they are mean in petty things.

By-and-by Mr. O. came in, well soaked with the heaviest shower that I ever knew in England, which had been rattling on the roof of the little side-room where we sat, and had caught him on the outside of the omnibus. At a little before eight o'clock I came home with U. in a cab,—the gas-light glittering on the wet streets through which we drove, though the sky was clear overhead.

September 30th.—Yesterday, a little before twelve, we took a cab, and went to the two Houses of Parliament,—the most immense building, methinks, that

ever was built; and not yet finished, though it has
now been occupied for years. Its exterior lies hugely
along the ground, and its great unfinished tower is
still climbing towards the sky; but the result (unless
it be the river front, which I have not yet seen) seems
not very impressive. The interior is much more successful. Nothing can be more magnificent and gravely
gorgeous than the Chamber of Peers,—a large oblong
hall, panelled with oak, elaborately carved, to the
height of perhaps twenty feet. Then the balustrade of
the gallery runs around the hall, and above the gallery
are six arched windows on each side, richly painted
with historic subjects. The roof is ornamented and
gilded, and everywhere throughout there is embellish-
ment of colour and carving on the broadest scale, and,
at the same time, most minute and elaborate; statues
of full size in niches aloft; small heads of kings, no
bigger than a doll; and the oak is carved in all parts
of the panelling as faithfully as they used to do it in
Henry VII.'s time,—as faithfully and with as good
workmanship, but with nothing like the variety and
invention which I saw in the dining-room of Smithell's
Hall. There the artist wrought with his heart and
head; but much of this work, I suppose, was done by
machinery. Be that as it may, it is a most noble and
splendid apartment, and, though so fine, there is not a
touch of finery; it glistens and glows with even a
sombre magnificence, owing to the rich, deep hues, and
the dim light, bedimmed with rich colours by coming
through the painted windows. In arched recesses, that
serve as frames, at each end of the hall, there are
three pictures by modern artists from English history;
and though it was not possible to see them well as

pictures, they adorned and enriched the walls marvellously as architectural embellishments. The peers' seats are four rows of long sofas on each side, covered with red morocco; comfortable seats enough, but not adapted to any other than a decorously exact position. The woolsack is between these two divisions of sofas, in the middle passage of the floor,—a great square seat, covered with scarlet, and with a scarlet cushion set up perpendicularly for the Chancellor to lean against. In front of the woolsack there is another still larger ottoman, on which he might lie at full length,—for what purpose intended, I know not. I should take the woolsack to be not a very comfortable seat, though I suppose it was originally designed to be the most comfortable one that could be contrived, in view of the Chancellor's much sitting.

The throne is the first object you see on entering the hall, being close to the door; a chair of antique form, with a high, peaked back, and a square canopy above, the whole richly carved and quite covered with burnished gilding, besides being adorned with rows of rock crystals,—which seemed to me of rather questionable taste.

It is less elevated above the floor than one imagines it ought to be. While we were looking at it, I saw two Americans,—Western men, I should judge,—one of them with a true American slouch, talking to the policeman in attendance, and describing our Senate Chamber in contrast with the House of Lords. The policeman smiled and ah-ed, and seemed to make as courteous and liberal responses as he could. There was quite a mixed company of spectators, and, I think, other Americans present besides the above two and ourselves. The Lord Chamberlain's tickets appear to be distributed with great impartiality. There were two or three women of the lower middle class, with children or babies in arms, one of whom lifted up its voice loudly in the House of Peers.

We next, after long contemplating this rich hall, proceeded through passages and corridors to a great central room, very beautiful, which seems to be used for purposes of refreshment, and for electric telegraphs; though I should not suppose this could be its primitive and ultimate design. Thence we went into the House of Commons, which is larger than the Chamber of Peers, and much less richly ornamented, though it would have appeared splendid had it come first in order. The Speaker's chair, if I remember rightly, is loftier and statelier than the throne itself. Both in this hall and in that of the Lords, we were at first surprised by the narrow limits within which the great ideas of the Lords and Commons of England are physically realised; they would seem to require a vaster space. When we hear of members rising on opposite sides of the house, we think of them as but dimly discernible to their opponents, and uplifting their voices so as to be heard afar; whereas they sit closely enough to feel each other's spheres, to note all expression of face, and to give the debate the character of a conversation. In this view a debate seems a much more earnest and real thing than as we read it in a newspaper. Think of the debaters meeting each other's eyes, their faces flushing, their looks interpreting their words, their speech growing into eloquence, without losing the genuineness of talk! Yet, in fact, the Chamber of Peers is ninety feet long and half as broad and high, and the Chamber of Commons is still larger.

Thence we went to Westminster Hall, through a gallery with statues on each side,—beautiful statues too, I thought; seven of them, of which four were from the times of the Civil Wars,—Clarendon, Falkland, Hampden, Selden, Somers, Mansfield, and Walpole. There is room for more in this corridor, and there are niches for hundreds of their marble brotherhood throughout the edifice; but I suppose future ages will have to fill the greater part of them. Yet I cannot help imagining that this rich and noble edifice has more to do with the past than with the future; that it is the glory of a declining empire; and that the perfect bloom of this great stone flower, growing out of the institutions of England, forebodes that they have nearly lived out their life. It sums up all. Its beauty and magnificence are made out of ideas that are gone by.

We entered Westminster Hall (which is incorporated into this new edifice, and forms an integral part of it) through a lofty archway, whence a double flight of broad steps descends to the stone pavement. After the elaborate ornament of the rooms we had just been viewing, this venerable hall looks extremely simple and bare,—a grey stone floor, grey and naked stone walls, but a roof sufficiently elaborate, its vault being filled with carved beams and rafters of chestnut, very much admired and wondered at for the design and arrangement. I think it would have pleased me more to have seen a clear vaulted roof, instead of this intricacy of wooden points, by which so much skylight space is lost. They make (be it not irreverently said) the vast and lofty apartment look like the ideal of an immense barn. But it is a noble space, and all without the support of a single pillar. It is about eighty of my paces from the foot of the steps to the opposite end of the hall, and twenty-seven from side to side; very high, too, though not quite proportionately to its other dimensions. I love it for its simplicity and antique nakedness, and deem it worthy to have been the haunt and home of History through the six centuries since it was built. I wonder it does not occur to modern ingenuity to make a scenic representation, in this very hall, of the ancient trials for life or death, pomps, feasts, coronations, and every great historic incident in the lives of Kings, Parliaments, Protectors, and all illustrious men, that have occurred here. The whole world cannot show another hall such as this, so tapestried with recollections of whatever is most striking in human annals.

Westminster Abbey being just across the street, we went thither from the hall, and sought out the cloisters, which we had not yet visited. They are in excellent preservation,—broad walks, canopied with intermingled arches of grey stone, on which some sort of lichen, or other growth of ages (which seems, however, to have little or nothing vegetable in it), has grown. The pavement is entirely made of flat tombstones, inscribed with half-effaced names of the dead people beneath; and the wall all round bears the marble tablets which give a fuller record of their virtues. I think it was from a meditation in these cloisters that Addison wrote one of his most beautiful pieces in the *Spectator*. It is a pity that this old fashion of a cloistered walk is not retained in our modern edifices; it was so excellent for shelter and for shade during a thoughtful hour,—this sombre corridor beneath an arched stone roof, with the central space of richest grass, on which the sun might shine or the shower fall, while the monk or student paced through the prolonged archway of his meditations.

As we came out from the cloisters, and walked along by the churchyard of the Abbey, a woman came begging behind us very earnestly. "A bit of bread," she said, "and I will give you a thousand blessings! Hunger is hard to bear. A kind gentleman and kind lady, a penny for a bit of bread! It is a hard thing that gentlemen and ladies should see poor people wanting bread, and make no difference whether they are good or bad." And so she followed us almost all round the Abbey, assailing our hearts in most plaintive terms, but with no success; for she did it far too well to be anything but an impostor, and no doubt she had breakfasted better, and was likely to have a better dinner, than ourselves. And yet the natural man cries out against the philosophy that rejects beggars. It is a thousand to one that they are impostors, but yet we do ourselves a wrong by hardening our hearts against them. At last, without turning round, I told her that I should give her nothing,—with some asperity, doubtless, for the effort to refuse creates a bitterer repulse than is necessary. She still followed us a little farther, but at last gave it up, with a deep groan. I could not have performed this act of heroism on my first arrival from America.

Whether the beggar-woman had invoked curses on us, and Heaven saw fit to grant some slight response, I know not, but it now began to rain on my wife's velvet; so I put her and J. into a cab, and hastened

to ensconce myself in Westminster Abbey while the
shower should last. Poets' Corner has never seemed
like a strange place to me; it has been familiar from
the very first; at all events, I cannot now recollect the
previous conception, of which the reality has taken the
place. I seem always to have known that somewhat
dim corner, with the bare brown stone-work of the
old edifice aloft, and a window shedding down its
light on the marble busts and tablets, yellow with
time, that cover the three walls of the nook up to a
height of about twenty feet. Prior's is the largest and
richest monument. It is observable that the bust and
monument of Congreve are in a distant part of the
Abbey. His duchess probably thought it a degrada-
tion to bring a gentleman among the beggarly poets.

I walked round the aisles, and paced the nave, and
came to the conclusion that Westminster Abbey, both
in itself and for the variety and interest of its monuments, is a thousand times preferable to St. Paul's.
There is as much difference as between a snow-bank
and a chimney-corner in their relation to the human
heart. By-the-bye, the monuments and statues in the
Abbey seem all to be carefully dusted.

The shower being over, I walked down into the
City, where I called on Mr. B. and left S.'s watch to
be examined and put in order. He told me that he
and his brother had lately been laying out and letting
a piece of land at Blackheath, that had been left them
by their father, and that the ground-rent would bring
them in two thousand pounds per annum. With such
an independent income, I doubt whether any American
would consent to be anything but a gentleman,—
certainly not an operative watchmaker. How sensible
these Englishmen are in some things!

Thence I went at adventure, and lost myself, of course. At one part of my walk I came upon St. Luke's Hospital, whence I returned to St. Paul's, and thence along Fleet Street and the Strand. Contiguous to the latter is Holywell Street,—a narrow lane, filled up with little bookshops and bookstalls, at some of which I saw sermons and other works of divinity, old editions of classics, and all such serious matters, while at stalls and windows close beside them (and, possibly, at the same stalls) there were books with title-pages displayed, indicating them to be of the most indecent kind.

October 2nd.—Yesterday forenoon I went with J. into the City, to 67, Gracechurch Street, to get a bank post-note cashed by Mr. Oakford, and afterwards to the offices of two lines of steamers, in Moorgate Street and Leadenhall Street. The City was very much thronged. It is a marvel what sets so many people a going at all hours of the day. Then it is to be considered that these are but a small portion of those who are doing the business of the City; much the larger part being occupied in offices at desks, in discussions of plans of enterprise, out of sight of the public, while these earnest hurriers are merely the froth in the pot.

After seeing the steam-officials, we went to London Bridge, which always swarms with more passengers than any of the streets. Descending the steps that lead to the level of the Thames, we took passage in a boat bound up the river to Chelsea, of which there is one starting every ten minutes, the voyage being of forty minutes' duration. It began to sprinkle a little just as we started; but after a slight showeriness, lasting till we had passed Westminster Bridge, the day grew rather pleasant.

* * * * *

At Westminster Bridge we had a good view of the river-front of the two Houses of Parliament, which look very noble from this point,—a long and massive extent, with a delightful promenade for the legislative people exactly above the margin of the river. This is certainly a magnificent edifice, and yet I doubt whether it is so impressive as it might and ought to have been made, considering its immensity. It makes no more impression than you can well account to yourself for, and you rather wonder that it does not make more. The reason must be that the architect has not "builded better than he knew." He felt no power higher and wiser than himself, making him its instrument. He reckoned upon and contrived all his effects with malice aforethought, and therefore missed the crowning glory,—that being a happiness which God, out of his pure grace, mixes up with only the simple-hearted, best efforts of men.

* * * * *

October 3rd.—I again went into the City yesterday forenoon, to settle about the passages to Lisbon, taking J. with me. From Hungerford Bridge we took the steamer to London Bridge, that being an easy and speedy mode of accomplishing distances that take many footsteps through the crowded thoroughfares. After leaving the steamer-office, we went back through the Strand, and, crossing Waterloo Bridge, walked a good way on to the Surrey side of the river; a coarse, dingy, disagreeable suburb, with shops apparently for country produce, for old clothes, second-hand furniture, for iron-ware, and other things bulky and inelegant. How many scenes and sorts of life are comprehended within

London! There was much in the aspect of these streets that reminded me of a busy country village in America on an immensely magnified scale.

Growing rather weary anon, we got into an omnibus, which took us as far as the Surrey Zoological Gardens, which J. wished very much to see. They proved to be a rather poor place of suburban amusement; poor, at least, by daylight,—their chief attraction for the public consisting in out-of-door representations of battles and sieges. The storming of Sebastopol (as likewise at the Cremorne Gardens) was advertised for the evening, and we saw the scenery of Sebastopol painted on a vast scale, in the open air, and really looking like miles and miles of hill and water: with a space for the actual manœuvring of ships on a sheet of real water in front of the scene, on which some ducks were now swimming about, in place of men-of-war. The climate of England must always interfere with this sort of performance; and I can conceive of nothing drearier for spectators or performers than a drizzly evening. Convenient to this central spot of entertainment there were liquor and refreshment rooms, with pies and cakes. The menagerie, though the ostensible staple of the garden, is rather poor and scanty; pretty well provided with lions and lionesses, also one or two giraffes, some camels, a polar bear,—who plunged into a pool of water for bits of cake,—and two black bears, who sat on their haunches or climbed poles; besides a wilderness of monkeys, some parrots and macaws, an ostrich, various ducks, and other animal and ornithological trumpery; some skins of snakes, so well stuffed that I took them for living serpents till J. discovered the deception; and an aquarium, with a good many common fishes swimming among sea-weed.

The garden is shaded with trees, and set out with greensward and gravel walks, from which the people were sweeping the withered autumnal leaves, which now fall every day. Plaster statues stand here and there, one of them without a head, thus disclosing the hollowness of the trunk; there were one or two little drizzly fountains, with the water dripping over the rock-work, of which the English are so fond; and the buildings for the animals and other purposes had a flimsy, pasteboard aspect of pretension. The garden was in its undress; few visitors, I suppose, coming hither at this time of day,—only here and there a lady and children, a young man and girl, or a couple of citizens, loitering about. I take pains to remember these small items, because they suggest the day-life or torpidity of what may look very brilliant at night— these corked-up fountains, slovenly greensward, cracked casts of statues, pasteboard castles, and duck-pond Bay of Balaclava then shining out in magic splendour, and the shabby attendants whom we saw sweeping and shovelling probably transformed into the heroes of Sebastopol.

J. thought it a delightful place; but I soon grew very weary, and came away about four o'clock, and, getting into a City omnibus, we alighted on the hither side of Blackfriars Bridge. Turning into Fleet Street, I looked about for a place to dine at, and chose the Mitre Tavern, in memory of Johnson and Boswell. It stands behind a front of modern shops, through which is an archway, giving admittance into a narrow courtyard, which, I suppose, was formerly open to Fleet Street. The house is of dark brick, and, comparing it with other London edifices, I should take it to have been at least refronted since Johnson's time; but within, the low, sombre coffee-room which we entered might well enough have been of that era or earlier. It seems to be a good, plain, respectable inn; and the waiter gave us each a plate of boiled beef, and, for dessert, a damson tart, which made up a comfortable dinner. After dinner we zigzagged homeward through Clifford's Inn Passage, Holborn, Drury Lane, the Strand, Charing Cross, Pall Mall, and Regent Street; but I remember only an ancient brick gateway as particularly remarkable. I think it was the entrance to Lincoln's Inn. We reached home at about six.

There is a woman who has several times passed through this Hanover Street, in which we live, stopping occasionally to sing songs under the windows; and last evening, between nine and ten o'clock, she came and sang "Kathleen O'More" richly and sweetly. Her voice rose up out of the dim, chill street, and made our hearts throb in unison with it as we sat in our comfortable drawing-room. I never heard a voice that touched me more deeply. Somebody told her to go away, and she stopped like a nightingale suddenly shot; but, finding that S. wished to know something about her, Fanny and one of the maids ran after her, and brought her into the hall. It seems she was educated to sing at the opera, and married an Italian opera-singer, who is now dead; lodging in a model lodging-house at threepence a night, and being a penny short to-night, she tried this method, in hope of getting this penny. She takes in plain sewing when she can get any, and picks up a trifle about the street by means of her voice, which, she says, was once sweet, but has now been injured by the poorness of her living. She is a pale woman, with black eyes, Fanny says, and may have been pretty once, but is not so now. It seems very strange, that with such a gift of Heaven, so cultivated, too, as her voice is, making even an unsusceptible heart vibrate like a harp-string, she should not have had an engagement among the hundred theatres and singing-rooms of London; that she should throw away her melody in the streets for the mere chance of a penny, when sounds not a hundredth part so sweet are worth from other lips purses of gold.

October 5th.—It rained almost all day on Wednesday, so that I did not go out till late in the afternoon, and then only took a stroll along Oxford Street and Holborn, and back through Fleet Street and the Strand. Yesterday, at a little after ten, I went to the Ambassador's to get my wife's passport for Lisbon. While I was talking with the clerk, Mr. —— made his appearance in a dressing-gown, with a morning cheerfulness and alacrity in his manner. He was going to Liverpool with his niece, who returns to America by the steamer of Saturday. She has had a good deal of success in society here; being pretty enough to be remarked among English women, and with cool, self-possessed, frank, and quiet manners, which look very like the highest breeding.

I next went to Westminster Abbey, where I had long promised myself another quiet visit; for I think I never could be weary of it; and when I finally leave England, it will be this spot which I shall feel most unwilling to quit for ever. I found a party going through the seven chapels (or whatever their number may be), and again saw those stately and quaint old tombs,—ladies and knights stretched out on marble slabs, or beneath arches and canopies of stone, let into the walls of the Abbey, reclining on their elbows, in ruff and farthingale or riveted armour, or in robes of state, once

painted in rich colours, of which only a few patches
of scarlet now remain; bearded faces of noble knights,
whose noses, in many cases, had been smitten off; and
Mary, Queen of Scots, had lost two fingers of her
beautiful hands, which she is clasping in prayer. There
must formerly have been very free access to these tombs;
for I observed that all the statues (so far as I examined
them) were scratched with the initials of visitors, some
of the names being dated above a century ago. The
old coronation-chair, too, is quite covered, over the back
and seat, with initials cut into it with pocket-knives,
just as Yankees would do it; only it is not whittled
away, as would have been its fate in our hands. Edward
the Confessor's shrine, which is chiefly of wood, likewise abounds in these inscriptions, although this was
esteemed the holiest shrine in England, so that pilgrims
still come to kneel and kiss it. Our guide, a rubicund
verger of cheerful demeanour, said that this was true
in a few instances.

There is a beautiful statue in memory of Horace
Walpole's mother; and I took it to be really a likeness,
till the verger said that it was a copy of a statue which
her son had admired in Italy, and so had transferred
it to his mother's grave. There is something characteristic in this mode of filial duty and honour. In all
these chapels, full of the tombs and effigies of kings,
dukes, arch-prelates, and whatever is proud and pompous
in mortality, there is nothing that strikes me more than
the colossal statue of plain Mr. Watt, sitting quietly in
a chair, in St. Paul's Chapel, and reading some papers.
He dwarfs the warriors and statesmen; and as to the
kings, we smile at them. Telford is in another of the
chapels. This visit to the chapels was much more satisfactory than my former one; although I in vain strove

to feel it adequately, and to make myself sensible how
rich and venerable was what I saw. This realisation
must come at its own time, like the other happinesses
of life. It is unaccountable that I could not now find
the seat of Sir George Downing's squire, though I
examined particularly every seat on that side of
Henry VII.'s Chapel, where I before found it. I must
try again.....

October 6th.—Yesterday was not an eventful day.
I took J. with me to the City, called on Mr. Sturgis
at the Barings' House, and got his checks for a bank
post-note. The house is at 8, Bishopsgate Street Within.
It has no sign of any kind, but stands back from the
street, behind an iron-grated fence. The firm appears
to occupy the whole edifice, which is spacious, and fit
for princely merchants. Thence I went and paid for
the passage to Lisbon (£ 32) at the Peninsular Steam
Company's office, and thence to call on General ——.
I forgot to mention, that, first of all, I went to Mr. B.'s,
whom I found kind and vivacious as usual. It now
rained heavily, and, being still showery when we came
to Cheapside again, we first stood under an archway
(a usual resort for passengers through London streets),
and then betook ourselves to sanctuary, taking refuge
in St. Paul's Cathedral. The afternoon service was
about to begin, so, after looking at a few of the monuments, we sat down in the choir, the richest and most
ornamented part of the cathedral, with screens and
partitions of oak, cunningly carved. Small white-robed
choristers were flitting noiselessly about, making pre-
parations for the service, which by-and-by began. It
is a beautiful idea, that, several times in the course of
the day, a man can slip out of the thickest throng and

bustle of London into the religious atmosphere, and hear the organ, and the music of young, pure voices; but, after all, the rites are lifeless in our day. We found, on emerging, that we had escaped a very heavy shower, and it still sprinkled and misted as we went homeward through Holborn and Oxford Street.

SOUTHAMPTON.

October 11th.—We all left London on Sunday morning, between ten and eleven, from the Waterloo station, and arrived in Southampton about two, without meeting with anything very remarkable on the way. We put up at Chapple's Castle Hotel, which is one of the class styled "commercial," and, though respectable, not such a one as the nobility and gentry usually frequent. I saw little difference in the accommodation, except that young women attended us instead of men,—a pleasant change. It was a showery day, but J. and I walked out to see the shore and the town and the docks, and, if possible, the ship in which S. was to sail. The most noteworthy object was the remains of an old castle, near the water-side; the square, grey, weed-grown, weird keep of which shows some modern chimney-pots above its battlements, while remaining portions of the fortress are made to seem as one of the walls for coal-depôts, and perhaps for small dwellings. The English characteristically patch new things into old things in this manner, materially, legally, constitutionally, and morally. Walking along the pier, we observed some pieces of ordnance, one of which was a large brass cannon of Henry VIII.'s time, about twelve feet long, and very finely made. The bay of Southampton presents a pleasant prospect, and I believe it is the great rendezvous of the Yacht Club. Old and young seafaring people were strolling about, and lounging at corners, just as they do on Sunday afternoons in the minor seaports of America.

From the shore we went up into the town, which is handsome, and of a cheerful aspect, with streets generally wide and well-paved,—a cleanly town, not smoke-begrimed. The houses, if not modern, are, at least with few exceptions, new fronted. We saw one relic of antiquity,—a fine mediæval gateway across the principal street, much more elevated than the gates of Chester, with battlements at the top, and a spacious apartment over;—the great arch for the passage of carriages, and the smaller one on each side for footpassengers. There were two statues in armour or antique costume on the hither side of the gateway, and two old paintings on the other. This, so far as I know, is the only remnant of the old wall of Southampton.

On Monday the morning was bright, alternating with a little showeriness. U., J., and I went into the town to do some shopping before the steamer should sail; and a little after twelve we drove down to the dock. The *Madeira* is a pleasant-looking ship enough, not very large, but accommodating, I believe, about seventy passengers. We looked at my wife's little state-room, with its three berths for herself and the two children; and then sat down in the saloon, and afterwards on deck, to spend the irksome and dreary hour or two before parting. Many of the passengers seemed to be Portuguese, undersized, dark, mustachioed people, smoking cigars. John Bull was fairly represented too..... U. was cheerful, and R. seemed anxious to get off. Poor Fanny was altogether cast down, and shed tears, either from regret at leaving her native land, or dread of sea-sickness, or general despondency, being a person of no spring of spirits. I waited till the captain came on board,—a middle-aged or rather elderly man, with a sensible expression, but, methought, with a hard, cold eye, to whom I introduced my wife, recommending her to his especial care, as she was unattended by any gentleman; and then we thought it best to cut short the parting scene. So we bade one another farewell; and, leaving them on the deck of the vessel, J. and I returned to the hotel, and, after dining at the *table d'hôte*, drove down to the railway. This is the first great parting that we have ever had.

It was three o'clock when we left Southampton. In order to get to Worcester, where we were to spend the night, we strode, as it were, from one line of railway to another, two or three times, and did not arrive at our journey's end till long after dark.

. . . . . .

At Worcester we put ourselves into the hands of a cabman, who drove us to the Crown Hotel,—one of the old-fashioned hotels, with an entrance through an arched passage, by which vehicles were admitted into the inn yard, which has also an exit, I believe, into another street. On one side of the arch was the coffee-room, where, after looking at our sleeping-chambers on the other side of the arch, we had some cold pigeon-pie for supper, and for myself a pint of ale.

. . . . . .

It should be mentioned, that in the morning, before embarking S. and the children on board the steamer, I saw a fragment of a rainbow among the clouds, and remembered the old adage bidding "sailors take warning." In the afternoon, as J. and I were railing from Southampton, we saw another fragmentary rainbow, which, by the same adage, should be the "sailor's delight." The weather has rather tended to confirm the first omen, but the sea-captains tell me that the steamer must have gone beyond the scope of these winds.

WORCESTER.

October 14th.—In the morning of Tuesday, after breakfast in the coffee-room, J. and I walked about to see the remarkables of Worcester. It is not a particularly interesting city compared with other old English cities; the general material of the houses being red brick, and almost all modernised externally, whatever may be the age of their original framework. We saw a large brick jail in castellated style, with battlements,—a very barren and dreary-looking edifice; likewise, in the more central part of the town, a Guildhall with a handsome front, ornamented with a statue of Queen Anne above the entrance, and statues of Charles I. and Charles II. on either side of the door, with the motto, "Floreat semper civitas fidelis." Worcester seems to pride itself upon its loyalty. We entered the building, and in the large interior hall saw some old armour hanging on the wall at one end,—corselets, helmets, greaves, and a pair of breeches of chain mail. An inscription told us that these suits of armour had been left by Charles II. after the battle of Worcester, and presented to the city, at a much later date, by a gentleman of the neighbourhood. On the stone floor of the hall, under the armour, were two brass cannon, one of which had been taken from the French in a naval battle within the present century; the other was a beautiful piece, bearing, I think, the date of 1632, and manufactured in Brussels for the Count de Burgh, as a Latin inscription testified. This likewise was a relic of the battle of Worcester, where it had been lost by Charles. Many gentlemen—connected with the city government, I suppose—were passing through the hall; and, looking through its interior doors, we saw stately staircases and council-rooms panelled with oak or other dark wood. There seems to be a good deal of state in the government of these old towns.

Worcester Cathedral would have impressed me much had I seen it earlier; though its aspect is less venerable than that of Chester or Lichfield, having been faithfully renewed and repaired, and stone-cutters and masons were even now at work on the exterior. At our first visit, we found no entrance; but coming again at ten o'clock, when the service was to begin, we found the door open, and the chorister-boys, in their white robes, standing in the nave and aisles, with elder people in the same garb, and a few black-robed ecclesiastics and an old verger. The interior of the cathedral has been covered with a light-coloured paint, at some recent period. There is, as I remember, very little stained glass to enrich and bedim the light; and the effect produced is a naked, daylight aspect, unlike what I have seen in any other Gothic cathedral. The plan of the edifice, too, is simple; a nave and side aisles, with great clustered pillars, from which spring the intersecting arches; and, somehow or other, the venerable mystery which I have found in Westminster Abbey and elsewhere does not lurk in these arches and behind these pillars. The choir, no doubt, is richer and more beautiful; but we did not enter it. I remember two tombs, with recumbent figures on them, between the pillars that divide the nave from the side aisles, and there were also mural monuments,—one, well executed, to an officer slain in the Peninsular war, representing him falling from his horse; another, by a young widow to her husband, with an inscription of passionate grief, and a record of her purpose finally to sleep beside him. He died in 1803. I did not see on the monument any record of the consummation of her purpose; and so perhaps she sleeps beside a second husband. There are more antique memorials than these two on the wall, and I should have been interested to examine them; but the service was now about to begin in the choir, and at the far-off end of the nave, the old verger waved his hand to banish us from the cathedral. At the same time he moved towards us, probably to say that he would show it to us after service; but having little time, and being so moderately impressed with what I had already seen, I took my departure, and so disappointed the old man of his expected shilling or half-crown. The tomb of King John is somewhere in this cathedral.

We renewed our rambles through the town, and, passing the Museum of the Worcester Natural History Society, I yielded to J.'s wish to go in. There are three days in the week, I believe, on which it is open to the public; but this being one of the close days, we were admitted on payment of a shilling. It seemed a very good and well-arranged collection in most departments of Natural History, and J., who takes more interest in these matters than I do, was much delighted. We were left to examine the hall and galleries quite at our leisure. Besides the specimens of beasts, birds, shells, fishes, minerals, fossils, insects, and all other natural things before the flood and since, there was a stone bearing a Roman inscription, and various antiquities, coins, and medals, and likewise portraits, some of which were old and curious.

Leaving the museum, we walked down to the stone bridge over the Severn, which is here the largest river I have seen in England, except, of course, the Mersey and the Thames. A flight of steps leads from the bridge down to a walk along the river-side, and this we followed till we reached the spot where an angler was catching chubs and dace, under the walls of the bishop's palace, which here faces the river. It seems to be an old building, but with modern repairs and improvements. The angler had pretty good success while we were looking at him, drawing out two or three silvery fish, and depositing them in his basket, which was already more than half full. The Severn is not a transparent stream, and looks sluggish, but has really movement enough to carry the angler's float along pretty fast. There were two vessels of considerable size (that is, as large as small schooners) lying at the bridge. We now passed under an old stone archway, through a lane that led us from the river-side up past the cathedral, whence a gentleman and lady were just emerging, and the verger was closing the door behind them.

We returned to our hotel, and ordered luncheon,—some cold chicken, cold ham, and ale, and after paying the bill (about fifteen shillings, to which I added five shillings for attendance) we took our departure in a fly for the railway. The waiter (a young woman), chambermaid, and boots, all favoured us with the most benign and deferential looks at parting, whence it was easy to see that I had given them more than they had any claim to receive. Nevertheless, this English system of fees has its good side, and I never travel without finding the advantage of it, especially on railways, where the officials are strictly forbidden to take fees, and where, in consequence, a fee secures twice as much good service as anywhere else. Be it recorded, that I never knew an Englishman to refuse a shilling,—or, for that matter, a halfpenny.

From Worcester we took tickets to Wolverhampton, and thence to Birkenhead. It grew dark before we reached Chester, and began to rain; and when we got to Birkenhead, it was a pitiless, pelting storm, under which, on the deck of the steamboat, we crossed the detestable Mersey, two years' trial of which has made me detest it every day more and more. It being the night of rejoicing for the taking of Sebastopol and the visit of the Duke of Cambridge, we found it very difficult to get a cab on the Liverpool side; but after much waiting in the rain, and afterwards in one of the refreshment-rooms, on the landing stage, we took a Hansom and drove off. The cloudy sky reflected the illuminations, and we saw some gas-lighted stars and other devices, as we passed, very pretty, but much marred by the wind and rain. So we finally arrived at Mrs. Blodgett's, and made a good supper of ham and cold chicken, like our luncheon, after which, wet as we were, and drizzling as the weather was, and though it was two hours beyond his bed-time, I took J. out to see the illuminations. I wonder what his mother would have said. But the boy must now begin to see life and to feel it.

There was a crowd of people in the street; such a crowd that we could hardly make a passage through them, and so many cabs and omnibuses, that it was difficult to cross the ways. Some of the illuminations were very brilliant; but there was a woeful lack of variety and invention in the devices. The Star of the

Garter, which kept flashing out from the continual extinguishment of the wind and rain,—V and A, in capital letters of light,—were repeated a hundred times; as were loyal and patriotic mottoes,—crowns formed by coloured lamps. In some instances a sensible tradesman had illuminated his own sign, thereby at once advertising his loyalty and his business. Innumerable flags were suspended before the houses and across the streets, and the crowd plodded on, silent, heavy and without any demonstration of joy, unless by the discharge of pistols close at one's ear. The rain, to be sure, was quite sufficient to damp any joyous ebullition of feeling; but the next day, when the rain had ceased, and when the streets were still thronged with people, there was the same heavy, purposeless strolling from place to place, with no more alacrity of spirit than while it rained. The English do not know how to rejoice; and, in their present circumstances, to say the truth, have not much to rejoice for. We soon came home; but I believe it was nearly, if not quite eleven.

At Mrs. Blodgett's, Mr. Archer (surgeon to some prison or house of correction here in Liverpool) spoke of an attorney who many years ago committed forgery, and, being apprehended, took a dose of prussic acid. Mr. Archer came with the stomach-pump, and asked the patient how much prussic acid he had taken. "Sir," he replied, attorney-like, "I decline answering that question!" He recovered, and afterwards arrived at great wealth in New South Wales.

November 14th.—At dinner at Mr. Bright's, a week or two ago, Mr. Robertson Gladstone spoke of a magistrate of Liverpool, many years since, Sir John ———.

Of a morning, sitting on the bench in the police court, he would take five shillings out of his pocket and say, "Here, Mr. Clerk, so much for my fine. I was drunk last night!" Mr. Gladstone witnessed this personally.

November 16*th.*—I went to the North Hospital yesterday, to take the deposition of a dying man as to his ill-treatment by the second and third mates of the ship *Assyria*, on the voyage from New Orleans. This hospital is a very gloomy place, with its wide, bleak entries and staircases, which may be very good for summer weather, but which are most ungenial at this bleak November season. I found the physicians of the house laughing and talking very cheerfully with Mr. Wilding, who had preceded me. We went forthwith up two or three pairs of stairs, to the ward where the sick man lay, and where there were six or eight other beds, in almost each of which was a patient,—narrow beds, shabbily furnished. The man whom I came to see was the only one who was not perfectly quiet; neither was he very restless. The doctor, informing him of my presence, intimated that his disease might be fatal, and that I was come to hear what he had to say as to the causes of his death. Afterwards, a Testament was sought for, in order to swear him, and I administered the oath, and made him kiss the book. He then (in response to Mr. Wilding's questions) told how he had been beaten and ill-treated, banged and thwacked, from the moment he came on board, to which usage he ascribed his death. Sometimes his senses seemed to sink away, so that I almost thought him dead; but by-and-by the questions would appear to reach him, and bring him back, and he went on with his evidence, interspersing it, however, with dying groans, and almost death-rattles. In the midst of whatever he was saying, he often recurred to a sum of four dollars and a half, which he said he had put into the hands of the porter of the hospital, and which he wanted to get back. Several times he expressed his wish to return to America (of which he was not a native), and, on the whole, I do not think he had any real sense of his precarious condition, notwithstanding that he assented to the doctor's hint to that effect. He sank away so much at one time, that they brought him wine in a tin cup, with a spout to drink out of, and he mustered strength to raise himself in his bed and drink; then hemmed, with rather a disappointed air, as if it did not stimulate and refresh him as drink ought to do. When he had finished his evidence (which Mr. Wilding took down in writing from his mouth), he marked his cross at the foot of the paper, and we ceased to torment him with farther question. His deposition will probably do no good, so far as the punishment of the persons implicated is concerned; for he appears to have come on board in a sickly state, and never to have been well during the passage. On a pallet, close by his bed, lay another seaman of the same ship, who had likewise been abused by the same men, and bore more ostensible marks of ill-usage than this man did, about the head and face. There is a most dreadful state of things aboard our ships. Hell itself can be no worse than some of them, and I do pray that some New-Englander with the rage of reform in him, may turn his thoughts this way. The first step towards better things — the best practicable step for the present — is to legalise flogging on shipboard; thereby doing away with the miscellaneous assaults and batteries, kickings, fisticuffings, ropes'-endings, marline-spikings, which the ling of rosewood, mahogany, and bird's-eye maple, polished and varnished, and gilded along the cornices and the edges of the panels. It is all a piece of elaborate cabinet-work; and one does not altogether see why it should be given to the gales, and the salt-sea atmosphere, to be tossed upon the waves, and occupied by a rude shipmaster in his dreadnought clothes, when the fairest lady in the land has no such boudoir. A tell-tale compass hung beneath the skylight, and a clock was fastened near it, and ticked loudly. A stewardess, with the aspect of a woman at home, went in and out of the cabin, about her domestic calls. Through the cabin door (it being a house on deck) I could see the arrangement of the ship.

The first sailor that I examined was a black-haired, powerful fellow, in an oil-skin jacket, with a good face enough, though he, too, might have been taken for a pirate. In the affray in which the homicide occurred, he had received a cut across the forehead, and another slantwise across his nose, which had quite cut it in two, on a level with the face, and had thence gone downward to his lower jaw. But neither he nor any one else could give any testimony elucidating the matter into which I had come to inquire. A seaman had been stabbed just before the vessel left New York, and had been sent on shore and died there. Most of these men were in the affray, and all of them were within a few yards of the spot where it occurred; but those actually present all pleaded that they were so drunk that the whole thing was now like a dream, with no distinct images; and, if any had been sober, they took care to know nothing that could inculpate any individual. Perhaps they spoke truth; they certainly had a free and honest-like way of giving their evidence, as if their only object was to tell all the truth they knew. But I rather think, in the forecastle, and during the night-watches, they have whispered to one another a great deal more than they told me, and have come to a pretty accurate conclusion as to the man who gave the stab.

While the examination proceeded, there was a drawing of corks in a side closet; and, at its conclusion, the captain asked us to stay to dinner, but we excused ourselves, and drank only a glass of wine. The captain apologized for not joining us, inasmuch as he had drunk no wine for the last seventeen years. He appears to be a particularly good and trustworthy man, and is the only shipmaster whom I have met with, who says that a crew can best be governed by kindness. In the inner closet there was a cage containing two land-birds, who had come aboard him, tired almost to death, three or four hundred miles from shore; and he had fed them, and been tender of them, from a sense of what was due to hospitality. He means to give them to J.

November 28*th.*—I have grown woefully aristocratic in my tastes, I fear, since coming to England; at all events, I am conscious of a certain disgust at going to dine in a house with a small entrance-hall and a narrow staircase, parlour with chintz curtains, and all other arrangements on a similar scale. This is pitiable. However, I really do not think I should mind these things, were it not for the bustle, the affectation, the intensity, of the mistress of the house. It is certain that a woman in England is either decidedly a lady or decidedly not a lady. There seems to be no respectable medium. Bill of fare: broiled soles, half of a roast pig, a haricot of mutton, stewed oysters, a tart, pears, figs, with sherry and port wine, both good, and the port particularly so. I ate some pig, and could hardly resist the lady's importunities to eat more; though to my fancy it tasted of swill,—had a flavour of the pigsty. On the parlour table were some poor editions of popular books, Longfellow's poems and others. The lady affects a literary taste, and bothered me about my own productions.

A beautiful subject for a romance, or for a sermon, would be the subsequent life of the young man whom Jesus bade to sell all he had and give to the poor; and he went away sorrowful, and is not recorded to have done what he was bid.

December 11*th.*—This has been a foggy morning and forenoon, snowing a little now and then, and disagreeably cold. The sky is of an inexpressibly dreary, dun colour. It is so dark at times that I have to hold my book close to my eyes, and then again it lightens up a little. On the whole, disgustingly gloomy; and thus it has been for a long while past, although the disagreeableness seems to lie very near the earth, and just above the steeples and housetops, very probably there may be a bright, sunshiny day. At about twelve there is a faint glow of sunlight, like the gleaming reflection from a not highly polished copper kettle.

December 26*th.*—On Christmas eve and yesterday, there were little branches of mistletoe hanging in several parts of the house, in the kitchen, the entries, the parlour, and the smoking-room,—suspended from the gas-fittings. The maids of the house did their utmost to entrap the gentlemen boarders, old and young, under the privileged places, and there to kiss them, after which they were expected to pay a shilling. It is very queer, being customarily so respectful, that they should assume this license now, absolutely trying to pull the gentlemen into the kitchen by main force, and kissing the harder and more abundantly the more they were resisted. A little rosy-cheeked Scotch lass—at other times very modest—was the most active in this business. I doubt whether any gentleman but myself escaped. I heard old Mr. S. parleying with the maids last evening, and pleading his age; but he seems to have met with no mercy, for there was a sound of prodigious smacking immediately afterwards. J. was assaulted, and fought most vigorously; but was outrageously kissed,—receiving some scratches, moreover, in the conflict. The mistletoe has white, wax-looking berries, and dull green leaves, with a parasitical stem.

Early in the morning of Christmas day, long before daylight, I heard music in the street, and a woman's voice, powerful and melodious, singing a Christmas hymn. Before bed-time I presume one half of England, at a moderate calculation, was the worse for liquor.

The market-houses, at this season, show the national taste for heavy feeding,—carcasses of prize oxen, immensely fat and bulky; fat sheep, with their woolly heads and tails still on, and stars and other devices ingeniously wrought on the quarters; fat pigs, adorned with flowers, like corpses of virgins; hares, wild-fowl, geese, ducks, turkeys; and green boughs and banners suspended about the stalls,—and a great deal of dirt and griminess on the stone floor of the market-house, and on the persons of the crowd.

There are some Englishmen whom I like,—one or two for whom I might say I have an affection; but still there is not the same union between us as if they were Americans. A cold, thin medium intervenes betwixt our most intimate approaches. It puts me in mind of Alnaschar and his princess, with the cold steel blade of his scimitar between them. Perhaps if I were at home I might feel differently; but in a foreign land I can never forget the distinction between English and American.

January 1st, 1856.—Last night, at Mrs. Blodgett's, we sat up till twelve o'clock to open the front door, and let the New Year in. After the coming guest was fairly in the house, the back door was to be opened, to let the Old Year out; but I was tired, and did not wait for the latter ceremony. When the New Year made its entrance, there was a general shaking of hands, and one of the shipmasters said it was customary to kiss the ladies all round; but to my great satisfaction, we did not proceed to such extremity. There was singing in the streets, and many voices of people passing, and when twelve had struck, all the bells of the town, I believe, rang out together. I went upstairs, sad and lonely, and, stepping into J.'s little room, wished him a Happy New Year, as he slept, and many of them.

To a cool observer, a country does not show to best advantage during a time of war. All its self-conceit is doubly visible, and, indeed, is sedulously kept uppermost by direct appeals to it. The country must be humbugged in order to keep its courage up.

Sentiment seems to me more abundant in middle-aged ladies in England than in the United States. I don't know how it may be with young ladies.

The shipmasters bear testimony to the singular

delicacy of common sailors in their behaviour in the presence of women; and they say that this good trait is still strongly observable even in the present race of seamen, greatly deteriorated as it is. On shipboard, there is never an indecorous word or unseemly act said or done by sailors when a woman can be cognisant of it; and their deportment in this respect differs greatly from that of landsmen of similar position in society. This is remarkable, considering that a sailor's female acquaintances are usually and exclusively of the worst kind, and that his intercourse with them has no relation whatever to morality or decency. For this very reason, I suppose, he regards a modest woman as a creature divine and to be reverenced.

January 16th.—I have suffered woefully from low spirits for some time past; and this has not often been the case since I grew to be a man, even in the least auspicious periods of my life. My desolate bachelor condition, I suppose, is the cause. Really, I have no pleasure in anything, and I feel my tread to be heavier, and my physical movement more sluggish, than in happier times. A weight is always upon me. My appetite is not good. I sleep ill, lying awake till late at night, to think sad thoughts and to imagine sombre things, and awaking before light with the same thoughts and fancies still in my mind. My heart sinks always as I ascend the stairs to my office, from a dim augury of grim news from Lisbon that I may perhaps hear,— of black-sealed letters, or some such horrors. Nothing gives me any joy. I have learned what the bitterness of exile is in these days; and I never should have known it but for the absence of——. "Remote, unfriended, melancholy, slow,"—I can perfectly appreciate

that line of Goldsmith; for it well expresses my own
torpid, unenterprising, joyless state of mind and heart.
I am like an uprooted plant, wilted and drooping. Life
seems so purposeless as not to be worth the trouble of
carrying it on any further.

I was at a dinner, the other evening, at Mr. B.'s,
where the entertainment was almost entirely American,
—New York oysters, raw, stewed, and fried; soup of
American partridges, particularly good; also terrapin
soup, rich, but not to my taste; American pork and
beans, baked in Yankee style; a noble American turkey,
weighing thirty-one pounds; and, at the other end of
the table, an American round of beef, which the
Englishmen present allowed to be delicious, and worth
a guinea an ounce. I forget the other American dishes,
if there were any more,—Oh yes!—canvas-back ducks,
coming on with the sweets, in the usual English fashion.
We ought to have had Catawba wine; but this was
wanting, although there was plenty of hock, champagne, sherry, Madeira, port, and claret. Our host is
a very jolly man, and the dinner was a merrier and
noisier one than any English dinner within my experience.

February 8th.—I read to-day, in the little office-
Bible (greasy with perjuries), St. Luke's account of the
agony, the trial, the crucifixion, and the resurrection;
and how Christ appeared to the two disciples on their
way to Emmaus, and afterwards to a company of disciples. On both these latter occasions he expounded
the Scriptures to them, and showed the application of
the old prophecies to himself; and it is to be supposed
that he made them fully, or at least sufficiently, aware
what his character was,—whether God, or man, or both,

or something between, together with all other essential points of doctrine. But none of these doctrines or of these expositions is recorded, the mere facts being most simply stated, and the conclusion to which he led them, that, whether God himself, or the Son of God, or merely the Son of man, he was, at all events, the Christ foretold in the Jewish Scriptures. This last, therefore, must have been the one essential point.

February 18*th.*—On Saturday there called on me an elderly Robinson-Crusoe sort of man, Mr. H., shipwright, I believe, of Boston, who has lately been travelling in the East. About a year ago he was here, after being shipwrecked on the Dutch coast, and I assisted him to get home. Again I have supplied him with five pounds, and my credit for an outside garment. He is a spare man, with closely-cropped grey, or rather white hair, closely-cropped whiskers fringed round his chin, and a close-cropped white moustache, with his under lip and a portion of his chin bare beneath,—sunburnt and weather-worn. He has been in Syria and Jerusalem, through the Desert, and at Sebastopol; and says he means to get Ticknor to publish his travels, and the story of his whole adventurous life, on his return home. A free-spoken, confiding, hardy, religious, unpolished, simple, yet world-experienced man; very talkative, and boring me with longer visits than I liked. He has brought home, among other curiosities, "a lady's arm," as he calls it, two thousand years old, — a piece of a mummy, of course; also some coins, one of which, a gold coin of Vespasian, he showed me, and said he bought it of an Arab of the desert. The Bedouins possess a good many of these coins, handed down immemorially from father to son, and never sell them unless compelled by want. He had likewise a Hebrew manuscript of the Book of Ruth, on a parchment roll, which was put into his care to be given to Lord Haddo.

He was at Sebastopol during the siege, and nearly got his head knocked off by a cannon-ball. His strangest statement is one in reference to Lord Raglan. He says that an English officer told him that his Lordship shut himself up, desiring not to be disturbed, as he needed sleep. When fifteen hours had gone by, his attendants thought it time to break open the door; and Lord Raglan was found dead, with a bottle of strychnine by the bedside. The affair, so far as the circumstances indicated suicide, was hushed up, and his death represented as a natural one. The English officer seems to have been an unscrupulous fellow, jesting thus with the fresh memory of his dead commander; for it is impossible to believe a word of the story. Even if Lord Raglan had wished for death, he would hardly have taken strychnine, when there were so many chances of being honourably shot. In Wood's "Narrative of the Campaign," it is stated that he died surrounded by the members of his staff, after having been for some time ill. It appears, however, by the same statement, that no serious apprehensions had been entertained, until, one afternoon, he shut himself up, desiring not to be disturbed till evening. After two or three hours he called Lord Burghersh,—"Frank, Frank!" and was found to be almost in a state of collapse, and died that evening. Mr. H.'s story might very well have been a camp rumour.

It seems to me that the British Ministry, in its notion of a life-peerage, shows an entire misunderstanding of what makes people desire the peerage. It is not for the immediate personal distinction; but because it removes the peer and his consanguinity from the common rank of men, and makes a separate order of them, as if they should grow angelic. A life-peer is but a mortal amid the angelic throng.

February 28*th*.—I went yesterday with Mrs. —— and another lady, and Mr. M., to the West Derby workhouse. . . . .

[Here comes in the visit to the West Derby workhouse, which was made the subject of a paper in "Our Old Home," called "Outside Glimpses of English Poverty." As the purpose in publishing these passages from the private note-books is to give to those who ask for a memoir of Mr. Hawthorne every possible incident recorded by himself which shows his character and nature, the editor thinks it proper to disclose the fact that Mr. Hawthorne was himself the gentleman of that party who took up in his arms the little child, so fearfully repulsive in its condition. And it seems better to quote his own words in reference to it, than merely to say it was he.

Under date February 28, 1856—

"After this, we went to the ward where the children were kept, and, on entering this, we saw, in the first place, two or three unlovely and unwholesome little imps, who were lazily playing together. One of them (a child about six years old, but I know not whether girl or boy) immediately took the strangest fancy for me. It was a wretched, pale, half-torpid little thing, with a humour in its eyes which the Governor said was the scurvy. I never saw, till a few moments afterwards, a child that I should feel less inclined to fondle.

But this little, sickly, humour-eaten fright prowled around me, taking hold of my skirts, following at my heels, and at last held up its hands, smiled in my face, and standing directly before me, insisted on my taking it up!. Not that it said a word, for I rather think it was under-witted, and could not talk; but its face expressed such perfect confidence that it was going to be taken up and made much of, that it was impossible not to do it. It was as if God had promised the child this favour on my behalf, and that I must needs fulfil the contract. I held my undesirable burden a little while; and, after setting the child down, it still followed me, holding two of my fingers and playing with them, just as if it were a child of my own. It was a foundling, and out of all human kind it chose me to be its father! We went up-stairs into another ward; and, on coming down again, there was this same child waiting for me, with a sickly smile round its defaced mouth, and in its dim-red eyes..... I never should have forgiven myself if I had repelled its advances."—ED.]

After leaving the workhouse, we drove to Norris Green; and Mrs. —— showed me round the grounds, which are very good and nicely kept. O these English homes, what delightful places they are! I wonder how many people live and die in the workhouse, having no other home, because other people have a great deal more home than enough..... We had a very pleasant dinner, and Mr. M. and I walked back, four miles and a half, to Liverpool, where we arrived just before midnight.

Why did Christ curse the fig-tree? It was not in the least to blame; and it *seems* most unreasonable to have expected it to bear figs out of season. Instead

of withering it away, it would have been as great a
miracle, and far more beautiful,—and, one would think,
of more beneficent influence,—to have made it suddenly
rich with ripe fruit. Then, to be sure, it might have
died joyfully, having answered so good a purpose. I
have been reminded of this miracle by the story of a
man in Heywood, a town in Lancashire, who used
such horribly profane language that a plane-tree in
front of his cottage is said to have withered away from
that hour. I can draw no moral from the incident of
the fig-tree, unless it be that all things perish from the
instant when they cease to answer some divine purpose.

March 6th.—Yesterday I lunched on board Captain
Russell's ship, the *Princeton*. These daily lunches on
shipboard might answer very well the purposes of a
dinner; being, in fact, noontide dinners, with soup,
roast mutton, mutton chops, and a macaroni pudding,
—brandy, port and sherry wines. There were three
elderly Englishmen at table, with white heads,—which,
I think, is oftener the predicament of elderly heads
here than in America. One of these was a retired
Custom-House officer, and the other two were connected
with the shipping in some way. There is a satisfaction
in seeing Englishmen eat and drink, they do it so
heartily, and, on the whole, so wisely,—trusting so
entirely that there is no harm in good beef and mutton,
and a reasonable quantity of good liquor; and these
three hale old men, who had acted on this wholesome
faith so long, were proofs that it is well on earth to
live like earthly creatures. In America, what squeam-
ishness, what delicacy, what stomachic apprehension,
would there not be among three stomachs of sixty or
seventy years' experience! I think this failure of

American stomachs is partly owing to our ill-usage of our digestive powers, and partly to our want of faith in them.

After lunch, we all got into an omnibus, and went to the Mersey Iron Foundry, to see the biggest piece of ordnance in the world, which is almost finished. The overseer of the works received us, and escorted us courteously throughout the establishment; which is very extensive, giving employment to a thousand men, what with night-work and day-work. The big gun is still on the axle, or turning-machine, by means of which it has been bored. It is made entirely of wrought and welded iron, fifty tons of which were originally used; and the gun, in its present state, bored out and smoothed away, weighs nearly twenty-three tons. It has, as yet, no trunnions, and does not look much like a cannon, but only a huge iron cylinder, immensely solid, and with a bore so large that a young man of nineteen shoved himself into it, the whole length, with a light, in order to see whether it were duly smooth and regular. I suppose it will have a better effect, as to the impression of size, when it is finished, polished, mounted, and fully equipped, after the fashion of ordinary cannon. It is to throw a ball of three hundred pounds' weight five miles, and woe be to whatever ship or battlement shall bear the brunt!

After inspecting the gun, we went through other portions of the establishment, and saw iron in various stages of manufacture. I am not usually interested in manufacturing processes, being quite unable to understand them, at least in cotton machinery and the like; but here there were such exhibitions of mighty strength, both of men and machines, that I had a satisfaction in looking on. We saw lumps of iron, intensely white-hot, and in all but a melting state, passed through rollers of various size and pressure, and speedily converted into long bars, which came curling and waving out of the rollers like great red ribbons, or like fiery serpents wriggling out of Tophet; and finally, being straightened out, they were laid to cool in heaps. Trip-hammers are very pleasant things to look at, working so massively as they do, and yet so accurately; chewing up the hot iron, as it were, and fashioning it into shape, with a sort of mighty and gigantic gentleness in their mode of action. What great things man has contrived, and is continually performing? What a noble brute he is!

Also, I found much delight in looking at the molten iron, boiling and bubbling in the furnace, and sometimes slopping over, when stirred by the attendant. There were numberless fires on all sides, blinding us with their intense glow; and continually the pounding strokes of huge hammers, some wielded by machinery and others by human arms. I had a respect for these stalwart workmen, who seemed to be near kindred of the machines amid which they wrought,—mighty men, smiting stoutly, and looking into the fierce eyes of the furnace fearlessly, and handling the iron at a temperature which would have taken the skin off from ordinary fingers. They looked strong, indeed, but pale; for the hot atmosphere in which they live cannot but be deleterious, and I suppose their very strength wears them quickly out. But I would rather live ten years as an iron-smith than fifty as a tailor.

So much heat can be concentrated into a mass of iron, that a lump a foot square heats all the atmosphere about it, and burns the face at a considerable distance. As the trip-hammer strikes the lump, it seems still more to intensify the heat by squeezing it together, and the fluid iron oozes out like sap or juice.

"He was ready for the newest fashions!"—this expression was used by Mrs. Blodgett in reference to Mr. —— on his first arrival in England, and it is a very tender way of signifying that a person is rather poorly off as to apparel.

March 15th.—Mr. ——, our new Ambassador, arrived on Thursday afternoon by the *Atlantic*, and I called at the Adelphi Hotel, after dinner, to pay him my respects. I found him and his family at supper. .... They seem to be plain, affable people..... The Ambassador is a venerable old gentleman, with a full head of perfectly white hair, looking not unlike an old-fashioned wig; and this, together with his collarless white neckcloth and his brown coat, gave him precisely such an aspect as one would expect in a respectable person of pre-revolutionary days. There was a formal simplicity, too, in his manners, that might have belonged to the same era. He must have been a very handsome man in his youthful days, and is now comely, very erect, moderately tall, not overburdened with flesh; of benign and agreeable address, with a pleasant smile; but his eyes, which are not very large, impressed me as sharp and cold. He did not at all stamp himself upon me as a man of much intellectual or characteristic vigour. I found no such matter in his conversation, nor did I feel it in the indefinable way by which strength always makes itself acknowledged. B., though, somehow, plain and uncouth, yet vindicates himself as a large man of the world, able, experienced, fit to handle difficult circumstances of life; dignified, too, and ab!

to hold his own in any society. Mr. —— has a kind
of venerable dignity; but yet, if a person could so little
respect himself as to insult him, I should say that there
was no innate force in Mr. —— to prevent it. It is
very strange that he should have made so considerable
a figure in public life, filling offices that the strongest
men would have thought worthy of their highest ambi-
tion. There must be something shrewd and sly under
his apparent simplicity; narrow, cold, selfish, perhaps.
I fancied these things in his eyes. He has risen in life
by the lack of two powerful qualities, and by a certain
tact, which enables him to take advantage of circumstances and opportunities, and avail himself of his un-
objectionableness, just at the proper time. I suppose
he must be pronounced a humbug, yet almost or quite
an innocent one. Yet he is a queer representative to be
sent from brawling and boisterous America at such a
critical period. It will be funny if England sends him
back again, on hearing the news of ——'s dismissal.
Mr. —— gives me the impression of being a very
amiable man in his own family. He has brought his
son with him, as Secretary of Legation,—a small young
man, with a little moustache. It will be a feeble embassy.

I called again the next morning, and introduced
Mrs. ——, who, I believe, accompanied the ladies about
town. This simplicity in Mr. ——'s manner puzzles
and teases me; for, in spite of it, there was a sort of
self-consciousness, as if he were being looked at,—as
if he were having his portrait taken.

LONDON.

March 22*nd.*—Yesterday,—no, day before yesterday,
—I left Liverpool for London by rail, from the Lime
Street station. The journey was a dull and monotonous

one, as usual. Three passengers were in the same carriage with me at starting; but they dropped off, and from Rugby I was alone. We reached London after ten o'clock; and I took a cab for St. James's Place, No. 32, where I found Mr. B. expecting me. He had secured a bedroom for me at this lodging-house, and I am to be free of his drawing-room during my stay. We breakfasted at nine, and then walked down to his counting-room, in Old Broad Street, in the City. It being a dim, dingy morning, London looked very dull, the more so as it was Good Friday, and therefore the streets were comparatively thin of people and vehicles, and had on their Sunday aspect. If it were not for the human life and bustle of London, it would be a very stupid place, with a heavy and dreary monotony of unpicturesque streets. We went up Bolt Court, where Dr. Johnson used to live; and this was the only interesting site we saw. After spending some time in the counting-room, while Mr. ——— read his letters, we went to London Bridge, and took the steamer for Waterloo Bridge, with partly an intent to go to Richmond, but the day was so damp and dusky that we concluded otherwise. So we came home, visiting, on our way, the site of Covent Garden Theatre, lately burnt down. The exterior walls still remain perfect, and look quite solid enough to admit of the interior being renewed, but I believe it is determined to take them down.

After a slight lunch and a glass of wine, we walked out, along Piccadilly, and to Hyde Park, which already looks very green, and where there were a good many people walking and driving, and rosy-faced children at play. Somehow or other the shine and charm are gone from London since my last visit; and I did not ve⸺

much admire, nor feel much interested in anything. We returned (and I, for my part, was much wearied) in time for dinner at five. The evening was spent at home in various talk, and I find Mr. —— a very agreeable companion, and a young man of thought and information, with a self-respecting character, and I think him a safe person to live with.

This St. James's Place is in close vicinity to St. James's Palace, the gateway and not very splendid front of which we can see from the corner. The club-houses and the best life of the town are near at hand. Addison, before his marriage, used to live in St. James's Place, and the house where Mr. Rogers recently died is up the court,—not that this latter residence excites much interest in my mind. I remember nothing else very noteworthy in this first day's experience, except that on Sir Watkins Williams Wynn's door, not far from this house, I saw a gold knocker, which is said to be unscrewed every night lest it should be stolen. I don't know whether it be really gold; for it did not look so bright as the generality of brass ones. I received a very good letter from J. this morning. He was to go to Mr. Bright's at Sandheys yesterday, and remain till Monday.

After writing the above, I walked along the Strand, Fleet Street, Ludgate Hill, and Cheapside to Wood Street,—a very narrow street, insomuch that one has to press close against the wall to escape being grazed when a cart is passing. At No. 77 I found the place of business of Mr. B——h, who came to see me at Rock Ferry with Mr. Jerdan, not long after my arrival in England. I found him in his office; but he did not at first recognise me, so much stouter have I grown during my residence in England,—a new man, as he says.

Mr. B――h is a kindly, frank, very good man, and was bounteous in his plans for making my time pass pleasantly. We talked of ――, from whom he has just received a letter, and who says he will fight for England in case of a war. I let B――h know that I, at least, should take the other side.

After arranging to go to Greenwich Fair, and afterwards to dine with B――h, I left him and went to Mr. ――'s office, and afterwards strayed forth again, and crossed London Bridge. Thence I rambled rather drearily along through several shabby and uninteresting streets on the other side of the Thames; and the dull streets in London are really the dullest and most disheartening in the world. By-and-by I found my way to Southwark Bridge, and so crossed to Upper Thames Street, which was likewise very stupid, though I believe Clenman's paternal house in "Little Dorrit" stands thereabouts. . . . . Next, I got into Ludgate Hill, near St. Paul's, and being quite foot-weary, I took a Paddington omnibus, and rode up into Regent Street, whence I came home.

March 24th.—Yesterday being a clear day for England, we determined upon an expedition to Hampton Court; so walked out betimes towards the Waterloo Station; but first crossed the Thames by Westminster Bridge, and went to Lambeth Palace. It stands immediately on the bank of the river, not far above the bridge. We merely walked round it, and saw only an old stone tower or two, partially renewed with brick, and a high connecting wall, within which appeared gables and other portions of the palace, all of an ancient plan and venerable aspect, though evidently much patched up and restored in the course of the many ages since its foundation. There is likewise a church, part of which looks old, connected with the palace. The streets surrounding it have many gabled houses, and a general look of antiquity, more than some other parts of London.

We then walked to the Waterloo Station, on the same side of the river; and at twenty minutes past one took the rail for Hampton Court, distant some twelve or fifteen miles. On arriving at the terminus, we beheld Hampton Palace, on the other side of the Thames,—an extensive structure, with a front of red brick, long and comparatively low, with the great Hall which Wolsey built rising high above the rest. We crossed the river, (which is here but a narrow stream) by a stone bridge. The entrance to the palace is about half a quarter of a mile from the railway, through arched gates, which give a long perspective into the several quadrangles. These quadrangles, one beyond another, are paved with stone, and surrounded by the brick walls of the palace, the many windows of which look in upon them. Soldiers were standing sentinels at the exterior gateways, and at the various doors of the palace; but they admitted everybody without question and without fee. Policemen, or other attendants, were in most of the rooms, but interfered with no one; so that, in this respect, it was one of the pleasantest places to visit that I have found in England. A good many people, of all classes, were strolling through the apartments.

We first went into Wolsey's great Hall, up a most spacious staircase, the walls and ceiling of which were covered with an allegorical fresco by Verrio, wonderfully bright and well preserved; and without caring about the design or execution, I greatly liked the brilliancy of the colours. The great Hall is a most noble and beautiful room, above a hundred feet long and sixty high and broad. Most of the windows are of stained or painted glass, with elaborate designs, whether modern or ancient I know not, but certainly brilliant in effect. The walls, from the floor to perhaps half their height, are covered with antique tapestry, which, though a good deal faded, still retains colour enough to be a very effective adornment, and to give an idea of how rich a mode of decking a noble apartment this must have been. The subjects represented were from Scripture, and the figures seemed colossal. On looking closely at this tapestry, you could see that it was thickly interwoven with threads of gold, still glistening. The windows, except one or two that are long, do not descend below the top of this tapestry, and are therefore twenty or thirty feet above the floor; and this manner of lighting a great room seems to add much to the impressiveness of the enclosed space. The roof is very magnificent, of carved oak, intricately and elaborately arched, and still as perfect to all appearance as when it was first made. There are banners, so fresh in their hues, and so untattered, that I think they must be modern, suspended along beneath the cornice of the hall, and exhibiting Wolsey's arms and badges. On the whole, this is a perfect sight in its way.

Next to the hall there is a withdrawing-room, more than seventy feet long, and twenty-five feet high. The walls of this apartment, too, are covered with ancient tapestry, of allegorical design, but more faded than that of the hall. There is also a stained-glass window; and a marble statue of Venus on a couch, very lean and not very beautiful; and some cartoons of Carlo Cignani, which have left no impression on my memory;

likewise, a large model of a splendid palace of some East Indian nabob.

I am not sure, after all, that Verrio's frescoed grand staircase was not in another part of the palace; for I remember that we went from it through an immensely long suite of apartments, beginning with the Guard-chamber. All these rooms are wainscoted with oak, which looks new, being, I believe, of the date of King William's reign. Over many of the doorways, or around the panels, there are carvings in wood by Gibbons, representing wreaths of flowers, fruit, and foliage, the most perfectly beautiful that can be conceived; and the wood being of a light hue (lime-wood, I believe), it has a fine effect on the dark oak panelling. The apartments open one beyond another, in long, long, long succession,—rooms of state, and kings' and queens' bedchambers, and royal closets bigger than ordinary drawing-rooms, so that the whole suite must be half a mile, or it may be a mile, in extent. From the windows you get views of the palace-grounds, broad and stately walks, and groves of trees, and lawns, and fountains, and the Thames and adjacent country beyond. The walls of all these rooms are absolutely covered with pictures, including works of all the great masters, which would require long study before a new eye could enjoy them; and, seeing so many of them at once, and having such a nothing of time to look at them all, I did not even try to see any merit in them. Vandyke's picture of Charles I., on a white horse beneath an arched gateway, made more impression on me than any other, and as I recall it now, it seems as if I could see the king's noble, melancholy face, and armed form, remembered not in picture, but in reality. All Sir Peter Lely's lewd women, and Kneller's too, were in these rooms; and the jolly old stupidity of George III. and his family, many times repeated; and pictures by Titian, Rubens, and other famous hands, intermixed with many by West, which provokingly drew the eye away from their betters. It seems to me that a picture, of all other things, should be by itself; whereas people always congregate them in galleries. To endeavour really to see them, so arranged, is like trying to read a hundred poems at once,—a most absurd attempt. Of all these pictures, I hardly recollect any so well as a ridiculous old travesty of the Resurrection and Last Judgment, where the dead people are represented as coming to life at the sound of the trumpet,—the flesh re-establishing itself on the bones,—one man picking up his skull and putting it on his shoulders,—and all appearing greatly startled, only half-awake, and at a loss what to do next. Some devils are dragging away the damned by the heels and on sledges, and above sits the Redeemer and some angelic and sainted people, looking complacently down upon the scene!

We saw, in one of the rooms, the funeral canopy beneath which the Duke of Wellington lay in state, —very gorgeous, of black velvet embroidered with silver and adorned with escutcheons; also, the state bed of Queen Anne, broad, and of comfortable appearance, though it was a queen's,—the materials of the curtains, quilt, and furniture, red velvet, still brilliant in hue; also King William's bed and his Queen Mary's, with enormously tall posts, and a good deal the worse for time and wear.

The last apartment we entered was the gallery containing Raphael's cartoons, which I shall not pretend to admire nor to understand. I can conceive, indeed, that there is a great deal of expression in them, and

very probably they may, in every respect, deserve all
their fame; but on this point I can give no testimony.
To my perception they were a series of very much
faded pictures, dimly seen (for this part of the palace
was now in shadow), and representing figures neither
graceful nor beautiful, nor, as far as I could discern,
particularly grand. But I came to them with a wearied
mind and eye; and also I had a previous distaste to
them through the medium of engravings.

But what a noble palace, nobly enriched, is this
Hampton Court! The English government does well
to keep it up, and to admit the people freely into it,
for it is impossible for even a Republican not to feel
something like awe—at least, a profound respect—for
all this state, and for the institutions which are here
represented, the sovereigns whose moral magnificence
demands such a residence; and its permanence, too,
enduring from age to age, and each royal generation
adding new splendours to those accumulated by their
predecessors. If one views the matter in another way,
to be sure, we may feel indignant that such dolt-heads,
rowdies, and every way mean people, as many of the
English sovereigns have been, should inhabit these
stately halls, contrasting its splendours with their little-
ness; but, on the whole, I readily consented within
myself to be impressed for a moment with the feeling
that royalty has its glorious side. By no possibility
can we ever have such a place in America.

Leaving Hampton Court at about four o'clock, we
walked through Bushy Park, — a beautiful tract of
ground, well wooded with fine old trees, green with
moss, all up their twisted trunks,—through several villages, Twickenham among the rest, to Richmond. Before entering Twickenham, we passed a lath-and-plaster

castellated edifice, much time-worn, and with the plaster peeling off from the laths, which I fancied might be Horace Walpole's toy-castle. Not that it really could have been; but it was like the image, wretchedly mean and shabby, which one forms of such a place, in its decay. From Hampton Court to the Star and Garter, on Richmond Hill, is about six miles. After glancing cursorily at the prospect, which is famous, and doubtless very extensive and beautiful, if the English mistiness would only let it be seen, we took a good dinner in the large and handsome coffee-room of the hotel, and then wended our way to the rail station, and reached home between eight and nine o'clock. We must have walked not far from fifteen miles in the course of the day.

March 25th.—Yesterday, at one o'clock, I called by appointment on Mr. B———h, and lunched with him and his partners and clerks. This lunch seems to be a legitimate continuation of the old London custom of the master living at the same table with his apprentices. The meal was a dinner for the latter class. The table was set in an upper room of the establishment; and the dinner was a large joint of roast mutton, to which ten people sat down, including a German silk-merchant as a guest, besides myself. Mr. B———h was at the head of the table, and one of his partners at the foot. For the apprentices there was porter to drink, and for the partners and guests some sparkling Moselle, and we had a sufficient dinner with agreeable conversation. B———h said that G. G. used to be very fond of these lunches while in England.

After lunch, Mr. B———h took me round the establishment, which is quite extensive, occupying, I think two or three adjacent houses, and requiring more. He showed me innumerable packages of silk manufactures, and all sorts of silks, from the raw thread to the finest fabrics. He then offered to show us some of the curiosities of old London, and took me first to Barber-Surgeons' Hall, in Monkwell Street. It was at this place that the first anatomical studies were instituted in England. At the time of its foundation, the Barbers and Surgeons were one company; but the former, I believe, are now the exclusive possessors of the Hall. The edifice was built by Inigo Jones, and the principal room is a fine one, with finely carved wood-work on the ceiling and walls. There is a skylight in the roof, letting down a sufficient radiance on the long table beneath, where, no doubt, dead people have been dissected, and where, for many generations, it has been the custom of the society to hold its stated feasts. In this room hangs the most valuable picture by Holbein now in existence, representing the company of Barber-Surgeons kneeling before Henry VIII., and receiving their charter from his hands. The picture is about six feet square. The king is dressed in scarlet, and quite fulfils one's idea of his aspect. The Barber-Surgeons, all portraits, are an assemblage of grave-looking personages, in dark costumes. The Company has refused five thousand pounds for this unique picture; and the keeper of the Hall told me that Sir Robert Peel had offered a thousand pounds for liberty to take out only one of the heads, that of a person named Pen, he conditioning to have a perfect fac-simile painted in. I did not see any merit in this head over the others.

Beside this great picture, hung a most exquisite portrait by Vandyke; an elderly, bearded man, of

noble and refined countenance, in a rich, grave dress.*
There are many other pictures of distinguished men of
the Company, in long past times, and of some of the
kings and great people of England, all darkened with
age, and producing a rich and sombre effect, in this
stately old hall. Nothing is more curious in London
than these ancient localities and customs of the City
Companies,—each trade and profession having its own
hall, and its own institutions. The keeper next showed
us the plate which is used at the banquets. I
should like to be present at one of these feasts. I saw
also an old vellum manuscript, in black letter, which
appeared to be a record of the proceedings of the Company; and at the end there were many pages ruled for
further entries, but none had been made in the volume
for the last three or four hundred years.

I think it was in the neighbourhood of Barber-Surgeons' Hall, which stands amid an intricacy of old
streets, where I should never have thought of going,
that I saw a row of ancient almshouses, of Elizabethan
structure. They looked woefully dilapidated. In front
of one of them was an inscription, setting forth that
some worthy alderman had founded this establishment
for the support of six poor men; and these six, or their
successors, are still supported, but no larger number,
although the value of the property left for that purpose would now suffice for a much larger number.

Then Mr. B——h took me to Cripplegate, and,
entering the door of a house, which proved to be a
sexton's residence, we passed by a side entrance into
the church-porch of St. Giles, of which the sexton's
house seems to be an indivisible contiguity. This is a

* Inigo Jones.

very ancient church, that escaped the great fire of London. The galleries are supported by arches, the pillars of which are cased high upwards with oak; but all this oaken work and the oaken pews are comparatively modern, though so solid and dark that they agree well enough with the general effect of the church. Proceeding to the high altar, we found it surrounded with many very curious old monuments and memorials, some in carved oak, some in marble; grim old worthies, mostly in the costume of Queen Elizabeth's time. Here was the bust of Speed, the historian; here was the monument of Fox, author of "The Book of Martyrs." High up on the wall, beside the altar, there was a black wooden coffin, and a lady sitting upright within it, with her hands clasped in prayer, it being her awakening moment at the resurrection. Thence we passed down the centre aisle, and about midway we stopped before a marble bust, fixed against one of the pillars. And this was the bust of Milton! Yes, and Milton's bones lay beneath our feet; for he was buried under the pew over the door of which I was leaning. The bust, I believe, is the original of the one in Westminster Abbey.

Treading over the tombstones of the old citizens of London, both in the aisles and the porch, and within doors and without, we went into the churchyard, one side of which is fenced in by a portion of London Wall, very solid, and still high, though the accumulation of human dust has covered much of its base. This is the most considerable portion now remaining of the ancient wall of London. The sexton now asked us to go into the tower of the church, that he might show us the oldest part of the structure, and we did so, and, looking down from the organ gallery, I saw a woman sitting alone, waiting for the rector, whose ghostly consolation, I suppose, she needed.

This old church tower was formerly lighted by three large windows,—one of them of very great size; but the thrifty churchwardens of a generation or two ago had built them up with brick, to the great disfigurement of the church. The sexton called my attention to the organ-pipe, which is of sufficient size, I believe, to admit three men.

From Cripplegate we went to Milton Street (as it is now called), through which we walked for a very excellent reason; for this is the veritable Grub Street, where my literary kindred of former times used to congregate. It is still a shabby-looking street, with old-fashioned houses, and inhabited chiefly by people of the poorer classes, though not by authors. Next we went to Old Broad Street, and, being joined by Mr. B., we set off for London Bridge, turning out of our direct course to see London Stone in Watling Street. This famous stone appears now to be built into the wall of St. Swithin's church, and is so encased that you can only see and touch the top of it through a circular hole. There are one or two long cuts or indentations in the top, which are said to have been made by Jack Cade's sword when he struck it against the stone. If so, his sword was of a redoubtable temper. Judging by what I saw, London Stone was a rudely shaped and unhewn post.

At the London Bridge station, we took the rail for Greenwich, and, it being only about five miles off, we were not long in reaching the town. It was Easter Monday; and during the first three days of Easter, from time immemorial, a fair has been held at Greenwich, and this was what we had come to see.

[This fair is described in "Our Old Home," in "A London Suburb."]

* * * * *

Reaching Mr. B———h's house, we found it a pretty and comfortable one, and adorned with many works of art; for he seems to be a patron of art and literature, and a warm-hearted man, of active benevolence and vivid sympathies in many directions. His face shows this. I have never seen eyes of a warmer glow than his. On the walls of one room there were a good many sketches by Haydon, and several artists' proofs of fine engravings, presented by persons to whom he had been kind. In the drawing-room there was a marble bust of Mrs. B———h, and one, I think, of himself, and one of the Queen, by Durham, which Mr. B———h said was very good, and it is unlike any other I have seen. It is a copy of one presented by a number of subscribers to Jenny Lind Goldschmidt. Likewise a crayon sketch of ———, looking rather morbid and unwholesome, as the poor lady really is. Also, a small picture of Mr. B———h in a military dress, as a Commissioner of the Lieutenancy of London. By-and-by came in a young gentleman, son of Haydon, the painter of high art, and one or two ladies staying in the house, and anon Mrs. ———. And so we went in to dinner.

B———h is an admirable host, and warms his guests like a household fire by the influence of his kindly face and glowing eyes, and by such hospitable demeanour as best suits this aspect. After the cloth was removed, came in Mr. Newton Crosland, a young man who once called on me in Liverpool,—the husband of a literary lady, formerly Camilla Toulmin. The lady herself was coming to spend the evening. The husband (and I presume the wife) is a decided believer in spiritual manifestations. We talked of politics and spiritualism and literature; and before we rose from table, Mr. B———h drank the health of the ladies, and especially of Mrs. H., in terms very kind towards her and me. I responded in her behalf as well as I could, and left it to Mr. Bowman, as a bachelor, to respond for the ladies generally,—which he did briefly, toasting Mrs. B.

We had heard the sound of the piano in the drawing-room for some time, and now adjourning thither, I had the pleasure to be introduced to Mrs. Newton Crosland,—a rather tall, thin, pale, and lady-like person, looking, I thought, of a sensitive character. She expressed in a low tone and quiet way great delight at seeing my distinguished self! for she is a vast admirer of "The Scarlet Letter," and especially of the character of Hester; indeed, I remember seeing a most favourable criticism of the book from her pen, in one of the London magazines. . . . .

At eleven o'clock Mrs. Crosland entered the tiniest pony carriage, and set forth for her own residence, with a lad walking at the pony's head, and carrying a lantern. . . . .

March 26*th*.—Yesterday was not a very eventful day. After writing in my journal I went out at twelve, and visited for the first time the National Gallery. It is of no use for me to criticise pictures, or to try to describe them, but I have an idea that I might acquire a taste, with a little attention to the subject, for I find I already begin to prefer some pictures to others. This is encouraging. Of those that I saw yesterday, I think I liked several by Murillo best. There were a great many people in the gallery, almost entirely of the middle, with a few of the lower classes; and I should think that the effect of the exhibition must at least tend towards refinement. Nevertheless, the only emotion that I saw displayed was in broad grins on the faces of a man and two women, at sight of a small picture of Venus, with a Satyr peeping at her with an expression of gross animal delight and merriment. Without being aware of it, this man and the two women were of that same Satyr breed.

If I lived in London, I would endeavour to educate myself in this and other galleries of art; but as the case stands, it would be of no use. I saw two of Turner's landscapes; but did not see so much beauty in them as in some of Claude's. A view of the grand canal in Venice, by Canaletto, seemed to me wonderful,— absolutely perfect,—a better reality, for I could see the water of the canal moving and dimpling; and the palaces and buildings on each side were quite as good in their way.

Leaving the gallery, I walked down into the City, and passed through Smithfield, where I glanced at St. Bartholomew's Hospital. . . . . Then I went into St. Paul's, and walked all round the great Cathedral, looking, I believe, at every monument on the floor. There is certainly nothing very wonderful in any of them, and I do wish it would not so generally happen that English warriors go into battle almost nude; at least, we must suppose so, from their invariably receiving their death-wounds in that condition. I will not believe that a sculptor or a painter is a man of genius unless he can make the nobleness of his subject illuminate and transfigure any given pattern of coat and breeches. Nevertheless, I never go into St. Paul's without being impressed anew with the grandeur of the edifice, and the general effect of these same groups of statuary ranged in their niches and at the bases of the pillars as adornments of the Cathedral.

Coming homeward, I went into the enclosure of the Temple, and near the entrance saw "Dr. Johnson's staircase" printed over a doorway; so I not only looked in, but went up the first flight of some broad, well-worn stairs, passing my hand over a heavy, ancient, broken balustrade, on which, no doubt, Johnson's hand has often rested. It was here that Boswell used to visit him, in their early acquaintance. Before my lunch, I had gone into Bolt Court, where he died.

* * * * *

This morning there have been letters from Mr. Wilding, enclosing an invitation to me to be one of the stewards of the anniversary dinner of the Literary Fund.

No, I thank you, gentlemen!

March 27th.—Yesterday I went out at about twelve, and visited the British Museum; an exceedingly tiresome affair. It quite crushes a person to see so much at once, and I wandered from hall to hall with a weary and heavy heart, wishing (Heaven forgive me!) that the Elgin marbles and the frieze of the Parthenon were all burnt into lime, and that the granite Egyptian statues were hewn and squared into building-stones, and that the mummies had all turned to dust two thousand years ago; and, in fine, that all the material relics of so many successive ages had disappeared with the generations that produced them. The present is burdened too much with the past. We have not time in our earthly existence to appreciate what is warm with life, and immediately around us; yet we heap up these old shells, out of which human life has long emerged, casting them off for ever. I do not see how future ages are to stagger onward under all this dead weight, with the additions that will be continually made to it.

After leaving the Museum, I went to see B——h, and arrange with him an expedition of to-day; and he read me a letter from Tupper, very earnestly inviting me to come and spend a night or two with him. Then I wandered about the City, and was lost in the vicinity of Holborn; so that for a long while I was under a spell of bewilderment, and kept returning, in the strangest way, to the same point in Lincoln's Inn Fields. . . . .

Mr. Bowman and I went to the Princess's Theatre in the evening. Charles Kean performed in Louis XI. very well indeed,—a thoughtful and highly skilled actor,—much improved since I saw him, many years ago, in America.

ALDERSHOTT CAMP.

April 1st.—After my last date, on Thursday, I visited the National Gallery. At three o'clock, having packed a travelling-bag, I went to B——h's office, and lunched with him; and at about five we took the rail from the Waterloo Station for Aldershott Camp. At Farnborough we were cordially received by Lieutenant Shaw,[*] of the North Cork Rifles, and were escorted by him, in a fly, to his quarters. The camp is a large city, composed of numberless wooden barracks, arranged in regular streets, on a wide, bleak heath, with an extensive and dreary prospect on all sides. Lieutenant Shaw assigned me one room in his hut, and B——h another, and made us as comfortable as kind hospitality could; but the huts are very small, and the rooms have no size at all; neither are they air-tight, and the sharp wind whistles in at the crevices; and, on

[*] Now Captain Shaw, of the London Fire Brigade.

the whole, of all discomfortable places, I am inclined to reckon Aldershott Camp the most so. I suppose the government has placed the camp on that windy heath, and built such wretched huts, for the very purpose of rendering life as little desirable as may be to the soldiers, so that they should throw it away the more willingly.

At seven o'clock we dined at the regimental mess, with the officers of the North Cork. The mess-room is by far the most desirable place to be found in camp. The hut is large, and the mess-room is capable of receiving between thirty and forty guests, besides the officers of the regiment, when a great dinner-party is given. As I saw it, the whole space was divided into a dining-room and two ante-rooms by red curtains drawn across; and the second ante-room seems to be a general rendezvous for the officers, where they meet at all times, and talk, or look over the newspapers and the army-register, which constitute the chief of their reading. The Colonel and Lieutenant-Colonel of the regiment received B——h and me with great cordiality, as did all the other officers, and we sat down to a splendid dinner.

All the officers of the regiment are Irishmen, and all of them, I believe, men of fortune; and they do what they can towards alleviating their hardships in camp by eating and drinking of the best that can be obtained of all good things. The table service and plate were as fine as those in any nobleman's establishment; the dishes numerous and admirably got up; and the wines delectable and genuine,—as they had need to be; for there is a great consumption of them. I liked these Irish officers exceedingly; they were really gentlemen, living on the best terms with one another,—courteous, kind, most hospitable, with a ric'

Irish humour, softened down by social refinements,—not too refined either, but a most happy sort of behaviour, as natural as that of children, and with a safe freedom that made me feel entirely at my ease. I think well of the Irish gentlemen; many of them may have been capable of much more intellectual intercourse than that of the mess-table; but I suppose it would not have been in keeping with their camp life, nor suggested by it. Several of the elder officers were men who had been long in the army; and the Colonel —a bluff, hearty old soldier, with a profile like an eagle's head and beak—was a veteran of the Peninsula, and had a medal on his breast with clasps for three famous battles besides that of Waterloo.

The regimental band played during dinner, and the Lieutenant-Colonel apologized to me for its not playing "Hail, Columbia," the tune not coming within their musical accomplishments. It was no great matter, however; for I should not have distinguished it from any other tune; but, to do me what honour was possible, in the way of national airs, the band was ordered to play a series of negro melodies, and I was entirely satisfied. It is really funny that the "wood-notes wild" of those poor black slaves should have been played in a foreign land as an honourable compliment to one of their white countrymen.

After dinner we played whist, and then had some broiled bones for supper, and finally went home to our respective huts not much earlier than four o'clock. But I don't wonder these gentlemen sit up as long as they can keep their eyes open; for never was there anything so utterly comfortless as their camp-beds. They are really worse than the bed of honour,—no wider, no softer, no warmer, and affording not nearly so sound sleep. Indeed, I got hardly any sleep at all, and almost as soon as I did close my eyes, the bugles sounded, and the drums beat reveillé, and from that moment the camp was all astir; so I pretty soon uprose, and went to the mess-room for my breakfast, feeling wonderfully fresh and well, considering what my night had been.

Long before this, however, this whole regiment, and all the other regiments, marched off to take part in a general review, and B——h and I followed, as soon as we had eaten a few mutton-chops. It was a bright, sunshiny day; but with a strong east wind, as piercing and pitiless as ever blew; and this wide, undulating plain of Aldershott seemed just the place where the east wind was at home. Still, it acted, on the whole, like an invigorating cordial; and whereas in pleasanter circumstances I should have lain down, and gone to sleep, I now felt as if I could do without sleep for a month.

In due time we found out the place of the North Cork Regiment in the general battle-array, and were greeted as old comrades by the Colonel and other officers. Soon the soldiers (who, when we first reached them, were strolling about or standing at ease) were called into order; and anon we saw a group of mounted officers riding along the lines, and among them a gentleman in a civilian's round hat, and plain frock and trousers, riding on a white horse. This group of riders turned the front of the regiment, and then passed along the rear, coming close to where we stood; and as the plainly-dressed gentleman rode by, he bent towards me, and I tried to raise my hat, but did not succeed very well, because the fierce wind had compelled me to jam it tightly upon my head. The Duke of C bridge (for this was he) is a comely-looking, gentlemanly man, of bluff English face, with a great deal of brown beard about it. Though a pretty tall man, he appears, on horseback, broad and round in proportion to his height. I looked at him with a certain sort of interest, and a feeling of kindness; for one does feel kindly to whatever human being is anywise marked out from the rest, unless it be by his disagreeable qualities.

The troops, from twelve to fifteen thousand, now fell into marching order, and went to attack a wood, where we were to suppose the enemy to be stationed. The sham fight seemed to me rather clumsily managed, and without any striking incident or result. The officers had prophesied the night before, that General K., commanding the camp, would make a muddle of it; and probably he did. After the review, the Duke of Cambridge with his attendant officers took their station, and all the regiments marched in front of him, saluting as they passed. As each colonel rode by, and as the banner of each regiment was lowered, the Duke lifted his hat.

. . . . .

The most splendid effect of this parade was the gleam of the sun upon the long line of bayonets,—the sheen of all that steel appearing like a wavering fringe of light upon the dark masses of troops below. It was very fine. But I was glad when all was done, and I could go back to the mess-room, whither I carried an excellent appetite for luncheon. After this we walked about the camp,—looked at some model tents, inspected the arrangements and modes of living in the huts of the privates; and thus gained more and more adequate ideas of the vile uncomfortableness of a military life. Finally, I went to the ante-room and turned over the regimental literature,—a Peerage and Baronetage,—an

Army and Militia Register, a number of the *Sporting Magazine*, and one of the *United Service*, while B———h took another walk. Before dinner we both tried to catch a little nap by way of compensation for last night's deficiencies; but, for my part, the attempt was fruitless.

The dinner was as splendid and as agreeable as that of the evening before; and I believe it was nearly two o'clock when B———h and I bade farewell to our kind entertainers. For my part I fraternized with these military gentlemen in a way that augurs the very best things for the future peace of the two countries. They all expressed the warmest sympathies towards America, and it was easy to judge from their conversation that there is no real friendliness on the part of the military towards the French. The old antipathy is just as strong as ever,—stronger than ever, perhaps, on account of the comparatively more brilliant success of the French in this Russian war. So, with most Christian sentiments of peace and brotherly love, we returned to our hut, and lay down, each in his narrow bed.

Early in the morning the drums and bugles began the usual bedevilment; and shortly after six I dressed, and we had breakfast at the mess-room, shook hands with Lieutenant Shaw (our more especial host), and drove off to the railway station at Ash.

I know not whether I have mentioned that the villages neighbouring to the camp have suffered terribly as regards morality from the vicinity of the soldiers. Quiet old English towns, that till within a little time ago had kept their antique simplicity and innocence, have now no such thing as female virtue in them, so far as the lower classes are concerned. This is expressing the matter too strongly, no doubt; but there is too much truth in it nevertheless; and one of the officers remarked that even ladies of respectability had grown much more free in manners and conversation than at first. I have heard observations similar to this from a Nova-Scotian, in reference to the moral influence of soldiers when stationed in the provinces.

. . . . .

WOOTON.

Wooton stands in a hollow, near the summit of one of the long swells that here undulate over the face of the country. There is a good deal of wood behind it, as should be the case with the residence of the author of the "Sylva;" but I believe few, if any, of these trees are known to have been planted by John Evelyn, or even to have been coeval with his time. The house is of brick, partly ancient, and consists of a front and two projecting wings, with a porch and entrance in the centre. It has a desolate, meagre aspect, and needs something to give it life and stir, and jollity. The present proprietor is of the old Evelyn family, and is now one of the two members of Parliament for Surrey; but he is a very shy and retiring man, unmarried, sees little company, and seems either not to know how to make himself comfortable or not to care about it. A servant told us that Mr. Evelyn had just gone out, but T——r, who is apparently on intimate terms with him, thought it best that we should go into the house, while he went in search of the master. So the servant ushered us through a hall,—where were many family pictures by Lely, and, for aught I know, by Vandyke, and by Kneller, and other famous painters,—up a grand staircase and into the library, the inner room of which contained the ponderous volumes which John Evelyn

used to read. Nevertheless, it was a room of most
barren aspect, without a carpet on the floor, with pine
bookcases, with a common whitewashed ceiling, with
no luxurious study-chairs, and without a fire. There
was an open folio on the table, and a sheet of manuscript that appeared to have been recently written.
I took down a book from the shelves (a volume of
annals connected with English history), and T——r afterwards told us that this one single volume, for its rarity,
was worth either two or three hundred pounds. Against
one of the windows of this library there grows a magnolia
tree, with a very large stem, and at least fifty years old.
 Mrs. T——r and I waited a good while, and then
B——h and T——r came back, without having found
Mr. E. T——r wished very much to show the Prayer-
Book used by King Charles at his execution, and some
curious old manuscript volumes; but the servant said
that his master always kept these treasures locked up,
and trusted the key to nobody. We therefore had to
take our leave without seeing them; and I have not
often entered a house that one feels to be more forlorn
than Wooton,—although we did have a glimpse of a
dining-room, with a table laid for three or four guests,
and looking quite brilliant with plate and glass and
snowy napery. There was a fire, too, in this one
room. Mr. E. is making extensive alterations in the
house, or has recently done so, and this is perhaps one
reason of its ungenial meagreness and lack of finish.
 Before our departure from Wooton, T——r had
asked me to leave my card for Mr. E.; but I had no
mind to overstep any limit of formal courtesy in dealing with an Englishman, and therefore declined.
T——r, however, on his own responsibility, wrote his
name, B——h's, and mine, on a piece of paper, and

told the servant to show them to Mr. E. We soon had experience of the good effect of this; for we had scarcely got back before somebody drove up to T——r's door, and one of the girls, looking out, exclaimed that there was Mr. E. himself, and another gentleman. He had set out, the instant he heard of our call, to bring the three precious volumes for me to see. This surely was most kind; a kindness which I should never have dreamed of expecting from a shy, retiring man like Mr. E.

So he and his friend were ushered into the dining-room, and introduced. Mr. E. is a young-looking man, dark, with a moustache, rather small, and though he has the manners of a man who has seen the world, it evidently requires an effort in him to speak to anybody; and I could see his whole person slightly writhing itself, as it were, while he addressed me. This is strange in a man of his public position, member for the county, necessarily mixed up with life in many forms, the possessor of sixteen thousand pounds a year, and the representative of an ancient name. Nevertheless, I liked him, and felt as if I could become intimately acquainted with him, if circumstances were favourable; but, at a brief interview like this, it was hopeless to break through two great reserves; so I talked more with his companion—a pleasant young man, fresh from college, I should imagine—than with Mr. E. himself.

The three books were really of very great interest. One was an octavo volume of manuscript in John Evelyn's own hand, the beginning of his published diary, written as distinctly as print, in a small, clear character. It can be read just as easily as any printed book. Another was a Church of England Prayer-Book, which King Charles used on the scaffold, and which was stained with his sacred blood, and underneath are

two or three lines in John Evelyn's hand, certifying
this to be the very book. It is an octavo, or small
folio, and seems to have been very little used, scarcely
opened, except in one spot; its leaves elsewhere retaining their original freshness and elasticity. It opens
most readily at the commencement of the common
service; and there, on the left-hand page, is a dis-
coloration, of a yellowish or brownish hue, about two-
thirds of an inch large, which, two hundred years ago
and a little more, was doubtless red. For on that
page had fallen a drop of King Charles's blood.

The other volume was large, and contained a great
many original letters, written by the king during his
troubles. I had not time to examine them with any
minuteness, and remember only one document, which
Mr. E. pointed out, and which had a strange pathos
and pitifulness in it. It was a sort of due-bill, promising to pay a small sum for beer, which had been
supplied to his Majesty, so soon as God should enable
him, or the distracted circumstances of his kingdom
make it possible,—or some touching and helpless expression of that kind. Prince Hal seemed to consider
it an unworthy matter, that a great prince should think
of "that poor creature, small beer," at all; but that a
great prince should not be able to pay for it is far worse.

Mr. E. expressed his regret that I was not staying
longer in this part of the country, as he would gladly
have seen me at Wooton, and he succeeded in saying
something about my books; and I hope I partly succeeded in showing him that I was very sensible of his
kindness in letting me see those relics. I cannot say
whether or no I expressed it sufficiently. It is better
with such a man, or, indeed, with any man, to say too

little than too much; and, in fact, it would have been indecorous in me to take too much of his kindness to my own share, B——h being likewise in question.

We had a cup of coffee, and then took our leave; T——r accompanying us part way down the village street, and bidding us an affectionate farewell.

BATTLE ABBEY.

B——h and I recommenced our travels, and, changing from one railway to another, reached Tunbridge Wells at nine or ten in the evening. .... The next day was spent at Tunbridge Wells, which is famous for a chalybeate spring, and is a watering-place of note, most healthily situated on a high, breezy hill, with many pleasant walks in the neighbourhood..... From Tunbridge Wells we transported ourselves to Battle,—the village in which is Battle Abbey. It is a large village, with many antique houses and some new ones, and in its principal street, on one side, with a wide, green space before it, you see the grey, embattled, outer wall, and great, square, battlemented entrance tower (with a turret at each corner), of the ancient Abbey. It is the perfect reality of a Gothic battlement and gateway, just as solid and massive as when it was first built, though hoary and venerable with the many intervening centuries. There are only two days in the week on which visitors are allowed entrance, and this was not one of them. Nevertheless, B——h was determined to get in, and he wished me to send Lady Webster my card with his own; but this I utterly refused, for the honour of America and for my own honour; because I will not do anything to increase the reputation we already have as a very forward people. B——h, however, called at a book-shop on the other side of the street, near the gateway of the castle, and making friends, as he has a marvellous tact in doing, with the bookseller, the latter offered to take in his card to the housekeeper, and see if Lady Webster would not relax her rule in our favour. Meanwhile, we went into the old church of Battle, which was built in Norman times, though subsequently to the Abbey. As we entered the church door, the bell rang for joy at the news of peace, which had just been announced by the London papers.

The church has been whitewashed in modern times, and does not look so venerable as it ought, with its arches and pillared aisles. In the chancel stands a marble tomb, heavy, rich, and elaborate, on the top of which lie the broken-nosed statues of Sir Anthony Browne and his lady, who were the Lord and Lady of Battle Abbey in Henry VIII.'s time. The knight is in armour, and the lady in stately garb, and (save for their broken noses) they are in excellent preservation. The pavement of the chancel and aisles is all laid with tombstones, and on two or three of these there were engraved brasses, representing knights in armour, and churchmen, with inscriptions in Latin. Some of them are very old. On the walls, too, there are various monuments, principally of dignitaries connected with the Abbey. Two hatchments, in honour of persons recently dead, were likewise suspended in the chancel. The best pew of the church is, of course, that of the Webster family. It is curtained round, carpeted, furnished with chairs and footstools, and more resembles a parlour than a pew; especially as there is a fireplace in one of the pointed archways, which I suppose has been bricked up in order to form it. On the opposite side of the aisle is the pew of some other magnate, containing a stove. The rest of the parishioners have to keep themselves warm with the fervour of their own piety. I have forgotten what else was interesting, except that we were shown a stone coffin, recently dug up, in which was hollowed a place for the head of the corpse.

Returning to the bookshop, we found that Lady Webster had sent her compliments, and would be very happy to have us see the Abbey. How thoroughly kind these English people can be when they like, and how often they like to be so!

We lost no time in ringing the bell at the arched entrance, under the great tower, and were admitted by an old woman who lives, I believe, in the thickness of the wall. She told us her room used to be the prison of the Abbey, and under the great arch she pointed to a projecting beam, where she said criminals used to be hanged. At two of the intersecting points of the arches, which form the roof of the gateway, were carved faces of stone, said to represent King Harold and William the Conqueror. The exterior wall, of which this tower is the gateway, extends far along the village street, and encloses a very large space, within which stands the mansion, quite secluded from unauthorised visitors, or even from the sight of those without, unless it be at very distant eyeshot.

We rang at the principal door of the edifice (it is under a deep arch, in the Norman style, but of modern date), and a footman let us in, and then delivered us over to a respectable old lady in black. She was a Frenchwoman by birth, but had been very long in the service of the family, and spoke English almost without an accent; her French blood being indicated only by her thin and withered aspect, and a greater

gentility of manner than would have been seen in an
Englishwoman of similar station. She ushered us first
into a grand and noble hall, the arched and carved
oaken roof of which ascended into the gable. It was
nearly sixty feet long, and its height equal to its
length,—as stately a hall, I should imagine, as is anywhere to be found in a private mansion. It was
lighted, at one end, by a great window, beneath which,
occupying the whole breadth of the hall, hung a vast
picture of the Battle of Hastings; and whether a good
picture or no, it was a rich adornment of the hall.
The walls were wainscoted high upwards with oak:
they were almost covered with noble pictures of
ancestry, and of kings and great men, and beautiful
women; there were trophies of armour hung aloft; and
two armed figures, one in brass mail, the other in
bright steel, stood on a raised dais, underneath the
great picture. At the end of the hall, opposite the
picture, a third of the way up towards the roof, was a
gallery. All these things that I have enumerated
were in perfect condition, without rust, untouched by
decay or injury of any kind; but yet they seemed to
belong to a past age, and were mellowed, softened in
their splendour, a little dimmed with time,—toned
down into a venerable magnificence. Of all domestic
things that I have seen in England, it satisfied me
most.

Then the Frenchwoman showed us into various
rooms and offices, most of which were contrived out
of the old abbey-cloisters, and the vaulted cells and
apartments in which the monks used to live. If any
house be haunted, I should suppose this might be.
If any church-property bring a curse with it, as people
say, I do not see how the owners of Battle Abbey can

escape it, taking possession of and dwelling in these holy precincts, as they have done, and laying their kitchen hearth with the stones of overthrown altars. The Abbey was first granted, I believe, to Sir Anthony Browne, whom I saw asleep with his lady in the church. It was his first wife. I wish it had been his second; for she was Surrey's Geraldine. The posterity of Sir Anthony kept the place till 1719, and then sold it to the Websters, a family of Baronets, who are still the owners and occupants. The present proprietor is Sir Augustus Webster, whose mother is the lady that so kindly let us into the Abbey.

Mr. B——h gave the nice old French lady half a crown, and we next went round among the ruined portions of the Abbey, under the gardener's guidance. We saw two ivied towers, insulated from all other ruins; and an old refectory, open to the sky, and a vaulted crypt, supported by pillars; and we saw, too, the foundation and scanty remains of a chapel, which had been long buried out of sight of man, and only dug up within present memory,—about forty years ago. There had always been a tradition that this was the spot where Harold had planted his standard, and where his body was found after the battle; and the discovery of the ruined chapel confirmed the tradition.

I might have seen a great deal more, had there been time; and I have forgotten much of what I did see; but it is an exceedingly interesting place. There is an avenue of old yew-trees, which meet above like a cloistered arch; and this is called the Monk's Walk. I rather think they were ivy, though growing unsupported.

As we were retiring, the gardener suddenly stopped, as if he were alarmed, and motioned us to do the same, saying, "I believe it is my lady!" And so it was,—a tall and stately lady in black, trimming shrubs in the garden. She bowed to us very graciously,— we raised our hats, and thus we met and parted without more ado. As we went through the arch of the entrance tower, B——h gave the old female warder a shilling, and the gardener followed us to get half a crown.

HASTINGS.

We took a fly and driver from the principal hotel of Battle, and drove off for Hastings, about seven miles distant. Hastings is now a famous watering and sea-bathing place, and seems to be well sheltered from the winds, though open to the sea, which here stretches off towards France. We climbed a high and steep hill, terraced round its base with streets of modern lodging-houses, and crowned on its summit with the ruins of a castle, the foundation of which was anterior to the Conquest. This castle has no wall towards the sea, the precipice being too high and sheer to admit of attack on that side. I have quite exhausted my descriptive faculty for the present, so shall say nothing of this old castle, which indeed (the remains being somewhat scanty and scraggling) is chiefly picturesque and interesting from its bold position on such a headlong hill.

Clambering down on another side from that of our ascent, we entered the town of Hastings, which seems entirely modern, and made up of lodging-houses, shops, hotels, parades, and all such makings up of watering-places generally. We took a delightful warm bath, washing off all weariness and naughtiness, and coming out new men. Then we walked to St. Leonard's,—a part of Hastings, I believe, but a mile or two from the castle,—and there called at the lodgings of two friends of B——h.

These were Mr. Theodore Martin, the author of Bon Gualtier's ballads, and his wife, the celebrated actress, Helen Faucit. Mr. Martin is a barrister, a gentleman whose face and manners suited me at once; a simple, refined, sincere, not too demonstrative person. His wife, too, I liked; a tall, dark, fine, and ladylike woman, with the simplest manners, that give no trouble at all, and so must be perfect. With these two persons I felt myself, almost in a moment, on friendly terms, and in true accord, and so I talked, I think, more than I have at any time since coming to London.

We took a pleasant lunch at their house; and then they walked with us to the railway station, and there they took leave of B——h affectionately and of me hardly less so; for, in truth, we had grown to be almost friends in this very little while. And as we rattled away, I said to B——h earnestly, "What good people they are!"—and B——h smiled, as if he had known perfectly well that I should think and say so. And thus we rushed onward to London; and I reached St. James's Place between nine and ten o'clock, after a very interesting tour, the record of which I wish I could have kept as we went along, writing each day's history before another day's adventures began.

www.ingramcontent.com/pod-product-compliance
Lightning Source LLC
Chambersburg PA
CBHW051745300426
44115CB00007B/694